PRODUCTION

日常生活
英语口语900句

入门篇 | 李因 李俊青 主编

U0107926

中国纺织出版社

图书在版编目（CIP）数据

日常生活英语口语900句. 入门篇／李因，李俊青主编. -- 北京：中国纺织出版社，2018.11（2023.4重印）

IISBN 978-7-5180-4605-8

Ⅰ.①日… Ⅱ.①李… ②李… Ⅲ.①英语—口语—自学参考资料 Ⅳ.① H319.9

中国版本图书馆 CIP 数据核字（2018）第 014762 号

策划编辑：武洋洋　　责任编辑：武洋洋
责任设计：晏子茹　　责任印制：储志伟

中国纺织出版社出版发行
地址：北京市朝阳区百子湾东里 A407 号楼　邮政编码：100124
销售电话：010-67004422　传真：010-87155801
http://www.c-textilep.com
E-mail:faxing@e-textilep.com
中国纺织出版社天猫旗舰店
官方微博 http://www.weibo.com/2119887771
永清县晔盛亚胶印有限公司印刷　各地新华书店经销
2018年11月第1版　2023年4月第3次印刷
开本：710×1000　1/16　印张：17.5
字数：300千字　定价：65.00元

前言

　　有人说金字塔的魅力就在于它完美的建筑结构，有坚实深厚的基础，才造就了塔尖的辉煌。学好英文也是同样的道理，坚实的语言基础很多时候来源于大量的输入，量变达到质变，这种语言便能脱口而出，"语感"则应运而生。

　　本套丛书分为《日常生活英语900句·入门篇》《日常生活英语900句·基础篇》和《日常生活英语900句·提高篇》。通过循序渐进的学习，让你练就纯熟地道的美语。

　　本书为《日常生活英语900句·入门篇》，围绕与现代生活息息相关的话题，分为"衣"、"食"、"住"、"行"四章，每章又分为若干个谈话主题，每个主题由日常用语一点通、经典句型、疯狂表达、疯狂对话、经典影像观摩、词句荟萃和疯狂链接几部分组成。其中日常用语一点通是一些与话题相关的经典表达，比较生活化，不乏幽默、风趣、实用；经典句型在疯狂对话中会得到再次操练；疯狂表达则教会读者举一反三，习得多种表达方法，便于在恰当的场合脱口而出；疯狂对话部分是情节生动、内容实用的情景会话，学习者可以在此了解语言的表达习惯，把所学的知识灵活地运用到具体的情境中。

　　本书为避免内容枯燥、形式陈旧，特配有电影片段，融入了生活气息和时代感，以激发读者的学习兴趣和提高学习效率。笔者查阅了一些口语书籍，有些书也纳入了一些电影片段，但是既包含与话题相关的内容，又易于模仿和应用的却不多见。本书的每一个章节中的若干话题都编排了与其相关的电影片段，让读者在生活情境中体会、模仿，达到学习英语口语的目的。也可以使读者了解更多的西方文化背景。这就是经典影像观摩部分。

　　词句荟萃的部分，可供读者学习一些有用的词汇和短语及有用的表达。每章的最后部分是疯狂链接，是所涉及话题的词汇、句子表达的拓展。

　　本书是一本实用、有趣的英语口语用书。适用于英语学习者自学，或是查阅相关话题的表达，也可以作为教学机构的英语口语参考用书。相信读者通过对本书的学习，能够达到举一反三、脱口而出、随心所欲说英语的水平。

编者

2018年6月

本书选取与日常生活紧密相关的话题，下设"衣"、"食"、"住"、"行"四个章节，每个章节下设句子、对话、词汇、电影片段等，层层深入，反复操练，全面攻克英语口语！

日常用语一点通：
涵盖了本章几乎所有话题，让你对全章内容有一个全面的了解。

经典句型

Section 1 询问建议

A： 王师傅，您看我的身材适不适合穿旗袍？
Mr. Wang, do you think I have the figure for a cheongsam?

Section 2 款式风格

A： 但是现在的样式稍微改变了一点。
But now, styles have changed a little.

经典句型：
抽取了本章每节有代表性的句子，让你提前预览本章精彩内容。

疯狂表达：
对话题进行细分，通过举一反三的方法，你能学到更多表达，达到学以致用的目的。

疯狂表达 Expressions

询问颜色 Asking about Color

你要什么颜色的？
What color do you want?
举一反三
Does this color go with my complexion?　这个颜色适合我的肤色吗？
OK, I will try on that green one. Now, how do I look?
好吧，我试试那件绿的。我现在看起来呢？

Dialogue 1 在裁缝店 At the Tailor's

You have a tall and slim figure, perfect for a cheongsam.

Mr. Wang, do you think I have the figure for a cheongsam?

疯狂对话:

句子最终还是服务于对话,疯狂对话将零散的句子整合成完整的对话,选取贴近生活的场景,配合多彩的图片,让读者有身临其境的感觉,最终达到熟练应用的程度。

经典影像观摩:

精心选取与本节内容相关的经典影视片段,让你学到最地道的表达,同时在辛苦的学习之余也能重温那些经典的声音,达到放松心情、寓学于乐的目的。

Dialogue 3 经典影像观摩 The

对生活充满信心的玛丽亚初涉尘俗来到校进行了第一次对话。谈话内容涉及到玛丽亚

Maria is a girl full of confidence in life, to the house of the Captain to be a governe Captain. It's about her dress.

Captain: In the future, you're kind o

词句荟萃:

摘取本节重点词汇和重要句型,如能熟练掌握,必将为你的口语增添一抹亮丽的色彩。

词句荟萃 Words and Sentences Gathering

fabric ['fæbrɪk] *n.* 布料; 织物; 质地
cut [kʌt] *n.* 剪裁
cheongsam ['tʃɔːŋ'sæm] *n.* 旗袍
slim [slɪm] *adj.* 苗条的

疯狂链接:

全面搜罗本章相关词汇,有了坚实的词汇基础,你就能 "show" 出丰富多变的句子了,从而成为众人瞩目的焦点。通过句子、对话、词汇全方位的强化学习和重复记忆,从而达到熟练掌握本章话题的目的。

疯狂链接 Interlinkage

衣服、服装 clothes
衣柜 wardrobe
服装 clothing

Contents 目录

Chapter 1 衣 Clothes

Chapter 2 食 Food

Chapter 3 住 House

Chapter 4 行 Transportation

900句

入门篇

chapter 1

服饰用语一点通

你真有眼光。
You have a very good taste.

这个颜色很流行。
The color is very popular.

我小时候总是穿别人的旧衣服。
I always wore hand-me-downs when I was young.

你穿这件衣服既合身又好看!
It looks very becoming.

这些夹克是男女通用的。
These jackets are unisex.

牛仔裤上的补丁秀很别致。
The patches on the jeans are fantastic.

我喜欢穿百分百棉的裤子。
I'd like to wear hundred percent cotton pants.

　　服装是人们日常生活中的主要内容，无论是在休闲娱乐中，还是在职场办公中，人们都需要着装得体。关于服装的话题则是你生活中必不可少的一项重要内容，下面的表达定会在着装交际方面助你一臂之力！

这种蓝色和衣服上的淡蓝色小点很配。
This blue color goes well with the light blue dots on the dress.

我想在这儿洗几件衣服。得花多少钱？
I want to do some laundry here. How much does it cost?

试衣间

这件衣服我等着穿，能不能快点洗好？
I really need this shirt urgently. Do you have a rush service?

打扮自己，向老板看齐。
Dress up, manage up.

这件衣服很漂亮，现在短裙很流行。
It looks very smart and short skirts are in fashion now.

这件衣服太棒了！
It's terrific!

要什么牌子的？
Any particular brand?

最好看的衣服永远是女人穿的。
The most beautiful clothes are always for women.

经典句型

Section 1 询问建议

A: 王师傅，您看我的身材适不适合穿旗袍？
Mr. Wang, do you think I have the figure for a cheongsam?

B: 您身材高挑，穿旗袍最合适不过了。
You have a tall and slim figure; perfect for a cheongsam.

Section 2 款式风格

A: 但是现在的样式稍微改变了一点。
But now, styles have changed a little.

B: 或许现在比较保守。
Maybe they are more conservative now.

Section 3 质地、材料（丝绸、亚麻等）

A: 它介绍了一种被称为竹纤维的新材质。
It talked about a new material called bamboo fiber.

B: 竹纤维？新名词。是由竹子制成的吗？
Bamboo fiber? That's a new word. Is it made of bamboo?

Section 4 品牌

A: 哇，这里什么都有啊，国际名牌齐全。雪莉阿姨，你最喜欢的牌子是哪个？
Wow! They've got everything here. All the world's famous brands. Aunt Shirley, what is your favorite brand?

B: 我爱所有时尚的东西。不过，我最喜欢的牌子是香奈尔。
I love all the fashionable things. But my favorite brand is Chanel.

Section 5 搭配

A: 我喜欢那条牛仔裤，不过，你需要一件能搭配那件上衣的衣服。这条有点太普通了。
I like the jeans, but you need something to go with the top. It's too plain on its own.

B: 那这条围巾，这些耳环和这条脚链怎样?
How about this scarf, these earrings, and an anklet?

Section 6 洗涤方式

A: 我有一套西服、一件羊毛衫和一件白色衬衣要洗。
I've got a suit, a woolen sweater and a white shirt to wash.

B: 好的，我看看。白色衬衣可以用水手洗，但这西服和羊毛衫得干洗。
OK, let me see. This white shirt can be washed in water by hand, but this suit and the woolen sweater need to be dry-cleaned.

Section 7 打扮

A: 哇，你今天看起来真漂亮!
Wow, you look so beautiful today!

B: 谢谢。我也很喜欢这条铅笔裤。
Thank you. I also like these pencil pants very much!

Section 8 时装秀

A: 啊，这场时装秀真棒!
Well, it was quite a show!

B: 完全同意。我从来没看过这么精彩的时装秀。
I'll say. I've never seen one as good as that.

> You have a tall and slim figure; perfect for a cheongsam.

■ 询问建议
Asking for Suggestions

> Mr. Wang, do you think I have the figure for a cheongsam?

疯狂表达 Expressions

询问颜色 Asking about Color

你要什么颜色的?

What color do you want?

举一反三

Does this color go with my complexion?　这个颜色适合我的肤色吗?

OK, I will try on that green one. Now, how do I look?

好吧，我试试那件绿的。我现在看起来呢?

颜色建议 Suggestions on Color

棕色。Brown.

举一反三

Try some other colors.　我建议你试一试别的颜色。

You have a very good taste. This color will look very pretty on you.

您很有眼力。这个颜色您穿上一定非常漂亮。

询问质地 Asking about Material

亲爱的，你觉得什么料子的裙子好啊?

Darling, what material do you think is good for dress?

举一反三

How about pure cotton?　纯棉的衣服怎么样？

How about silk?　丝绸怎么样？

质地建议 Suggestions on Material

这大衣的料子很好。

The material of this coat is good.

举一反三

Clothing made of silk is elegant.　丝绸质地的衣服很高贵。

You will be comfortable in cotton T-shirts.　棉质的T恤穿起来很舒服。

询问款式 Inquiry about Style

这件夹克怎么样？

How is this jacket?

举一反三

What about this one?　那这件呢？

Do you like this dress?　你喜欢这件衣服吗？

Do you want a tight-fitting or loose-fitting sweater?　你想买紧身的、还是宽松的毛衣？

Are you looking for a casual shirt or something formal?
你想要件休闲点的衬衫还是正式点的？

款式适合 Good Style

很好看。

It's beautiful.

举一反三

You look good in this new style of woolen sweater.
你穿这件新款的毛衫很好看。

I really like this red skirt. I think the style is unique.
我很喜欢这件红裙，我觉得款式很特别。

The yellow shirt with a V-neck looks pretty.　这件V领的黄色衬衫看起来很漂亮。

款式不适合 Poor Style

这件衣服不适合我。

It doesn't look good on me.

举一反三

The cut does not look good.　剪裁不太好看。

I like the color very much. It's a lovely dress, but it's too fashionable for me.
我很喜欢这种颜色，这件衣服很好看，但对我来说太时尚了。

Dialogue 1 · 在裁缝店 At the Tailor's

> You have a tall and slim figure, perfect for a cheongsam.

> Mr. Wang, do you think I have the figure for a cheongsam?

　　苏珊想要定做一件旗袍，她来到了一家裁缝店。她向王裁缝询问了自己是否适合穿旗袍以及关于选料子的问题。

　　Susan wants to have a cheongsam made so she goes to a tailor's. She asks Tailor Wang if she has the figure for a cheongsam and how to choose the material.

Susan:	Mr. Wang, do you think I have the figure for a cheongsam?
Tailor Wang:	You have a tall and slim figure, perfect for a cheongsam.
Susan:	Thanks! How is the material I chose?
Tailor Wang:	You have a very good taste. This color will look very pretty on you.
Susan:	Great, I think my friends will envy my cheongsam.
Tailor Wang:	Let me take your measurements first. You can come to try it on in three days.
Susan:	OK.

苏珊：	王师傅，您看我的身材适不适合穿旗袍？
王裁缝：	您的身材高挑，穿旗袍最合适不过了。
苏珊：	谢谢！我这料子选得怎么样？
王裁缝：	您很有眼力，这个颜色您穿上一定非常漂亮。
苏珊：	太好了，我的那些朋友一定会羡慕死我的。
王裁缝：	我先给你量一下尺寸，三天以后来试穿。
苏珊：	好的。

Dialogue 2 · 定制西服 Customizing a Suit

> **How about this one?**

> **I think that will do. Let's go talk to the tailor about getting it made.**

　　杰克要去参加一个朋友婚礼，需要一套新西服，正在向朋友露西询问一些建议，包括衣服的料子、颜色、款式等。

　　Jack is going to attend one of his friends' wedding ceremony and needs a new suit. He is asking his friend, Lucy, for some suggestions about the material, color, style, etc.

Jack: 　Can you help me pick out some fabric for a suit? I'm going to get one made for a friend's wedding.

Lucy: 　Sure. What kind of material do you want the suit to be made of?

Jack: 　It depends on the price, but I was thinking of getting a wool and cashmere blend.

Lucy: 　That will probably be very expensive, but the more you pay for the fabric, the longer it'll last and the better it'll look. What color do you want the suit to be?

Jack: 　I was thinking of a brown pin-striped suit.

Lucy: 　Brown, huh? Isn't that a bit dull?

Jack: 　Haven't you heard? Brown is the new black.

Lucy: 　Why don't you just get black? Black suits are always fashionable and can be worn for anything—a funeral, a wedding, a job interview—anything!

Jack: 　That may be true, but black is so boring. Anyway, I already have three black suits. I might as well get a suit that stands out from the rest.

Lucy: 　Here are two different shades of brown. Which one do you prefer?

Jack: 　I like the one on the left, but I don't like the pattern on it. It's too much. I want a pattern that's a bit more subtle.

Lucy: 　How about this one?

Jack: 　I think that will do. Let's go talk to the tailor about getting it made.

Lucy: 　OK, let's go.

杰克：　你能帮我挑块布料做套装吗？我要做身衣服去参加一个朋友的婚礼。

露西：　当然可以。你想要什么料子的？

杰克：　这取决于价格，但是我希望是羊毛和羊绒混纺的。

露西：　那会非常贵，但是你用的料子越贵，衣服就越经穿，而且还非常漂亮。你想做什么颜色的？

杰克：　我正在考虑棕色有细线纹的。

露西：　棕色的，啊？会不会有点暗了？

杰克：　你没听说过吗？棕色是一种新兴的黑色。

露西：　那你干嘛不做件黑色的？黑色西服一直都很时尚，而且适用于任何场合——葬礼、婚礼、面试——什么场合都行！

杰克：　是这样没错，但是黑色有点单调了。不管怎么说，我已经有三件黑西服了。我还是希望能跟其他人不一样。

露西：　这儿有两种暗纹的棕色布料。你比较喜欢哪一个？

杰克：　我喜欢左边那个，但是我不喜欢它上面的图案。图案太复杂了。我喜欢简单含蓄一点的。

露西：　那这个怎么样？

杰克：　这个还不错，咱们去找裁缝做吧。

露西：　好的，走吧。

Dialogue 3　经典影像观摩 The Emulation of Classical Movies

　　对生活充满信心的玛丽亚初涉尘俗来到特拉普上校家里做家庭教师，在那里她和特拉普上校进行了第一次对话。谈话内容涉及玛丽亚的衣着。

　　Maria is a girl full of confidence in life, experiences real life for the first time by coming to the house of the Captain to be a governess. There she has her first conversation with the Captain. It's about her dress.

Captain:　In the future, you're kind of remember there are certain rooms in this house are not to be disturbed.

Maria:　Yes, Captain, sir.

Captain:　Why do you stare at me that way?

Maria:　Well, you don't look at all like a sea captain, sir.

Captain:　I'm afraid you don't look very much like a governess. Turn around, please.

Maria:　What?

Captain:　Turn. Hat off. It's the dress. Put on another one before you meet the children.

Maria:　But I don't have another one. When we enter the abbey, our worldly clothes are given to the poor.

Captain:　What about this one?

Maria:　The poor didn't want this one.

Captain: Hmm.

Maria: Well, I would have made myself a new dress but there wasn't time, I can make my own clothes.

Captain: Well, I'll see you get some material. Today, if possible. Now, Fraulein... er...

Maria: Maria.

上校：　　以后请你记住，这房子里有些房间是不能乱闯的。

玛丽亚：　是，上校，先生。

上校：　　为什么这样盯着我？

玛丽亚：　先生，您看起来一点都不像海军上校。

上校：　　恐怕你也不怎么像家庭教师。请转过身去。

玛丽亚：　什么？

上校：　　转身、脱帽，是衣服不对劲。在和孩子们见面之前，你得换套衣服。

玛丽亚：　但是，我没有其他衣服。当我们进修道院时，就把平时穿的衣服都送给穷人了。

上校：　　那这一件呢？

玛丽亚：　穷人不要这一套。

上校：　　嗯。

玛丽亚：　噢，如果有时间的话，我就自己做一套新衣服。我会给自己做衣服。

上校：　　那么我来给你弄些布料。可能的话，今天就给你。现在，小姐……呃……

玛丽亚：　叫我玛丽亚。

词句荟萃 Words and Sentences Gathering

fabric ['fæbrɪk] *n.* 布料；织物；质地

cut [kʌt] *n.* 剪裁

cheongsam ['tʃɔːŋ'sæm] *n.* 旗袍

slim [slɪm] *adj.* 苗条的

tight-fitting ['taɪt'fɪtɪŋ] *adj.* 紧身的

loose-fitting ['luːs'fɪtɪŋ] *adj.* 宽松的

casual ['kæʒʊəl] *adj.* 休闲的

formal ['fɔːml] *adj.* 正式的

flowery ['flaʊərɪ] *adj.* 有花朵的

striped [straɪpt] *adj.* 有条纹的

complexion [kəm'plekʃən] *n.* 肤色

outgrow ['aʊtgrəʊ] *v.* 超过；长大……已不能穿……

cashmere ['kæʃmɪə] *n.* 开司米；羊绒；羊毛

blend [blend] *n.* 混合；调配

pin-striped ['pɪn'straɪpt] *adj.* 有细条纹的

funeral ['fjuːnərəl] *n.* 葬礼

subtle ['sʌtl] *adj.* 敏感的；细微的；含蓄的

customize ['kʌstəmaɪz] *v.* 定做；定制

worldly ['wɜːdlɪ] *adj.* 世俗的

How is...? ……怎么样?

Do you think…? 你认为……怎么样?

Which pattern do you prefer? 你喜欢哪个图案?

What is …made of…? ……由什么制成的?

疯狂链接 Interlinkage

衣服、服装 clothes

衣柜 wardrobe

服装 clothing

衬衫 shirt

T恤 T-shirt

毛衣 sweater

夹克 jacket

外套、大衣、上衣 coat

连衣裙 dress

短裙 skirt

围巾 scarf

披肩 shawl

斗篷 cloak

鸭舌帽 cap

带沿的帽子 hat

手套 glove

毛皮大衣 fur topcoat

夹大衣 topcoat

背心 vest

套装、西装 suit

比基尼 bikini

睡衣 pajamas

Section 2

Maybe they are more conservative now.

■ 款式风格
Style

But now, styles have changed a little.

疯狂表达 Expressions

挑选款式 Choosing a Style

你想要什么样的款式？

What style do you want?

举一反三

I like things that are loose-fitting.　我喜欢宽松的。

I like formal clothes.　我喜欢正式的。

I like casual clothes.　我喜欢休闲的。

个人风格 Personal Style

好了，说说看，你觉得怎么样。

Alright, tell me what you think.

举一反三

I love the way it looks.　我喜欢它的风格。

I absolutely adore simple styles.　我比较喜欢简约的款式。

That skirt is not really my cup of tea.　那条裙子实在不合我的口味！

地域风格 Regional Style

这里穿得比较随便。

It's even more casual here.

那里服装的样式比较正式。

Clothing styles used to be more formal there.

举一反三

You would see most people dressed very well. Not only university students, but also working people. Many working people in China spend a lot of money on clothes.

你会看到大部分的人都穿得很漂亮，不止大学生，上班族也是。中国很多上班族都花很多钱在服装上。

But sometimes I think the Chinese are too concerned with their clothes. They spend too much money, especially women.

但是有时我觉得中国人过分地关心穿着了。他们花费太多钱，特别是女人。

时代风格 Period Style

是呀！改革开放这40多年来，人们对服装的美感改变了很多！

Yes. During the four decades of reform and opening-up, people's feelings toward style have changed a lot.

举一反三

Oh, then what style did people have forty years ago? 哦，那么40年前人们穿什么样式的衣服呢？

People at that time usually dressed in darker colors, and the styles of clothes were limited. 那时候人们还主要穿深暗色的衣服，衣服的款式也很有限。

But now we have more styles to choose from, and there are lots of rules for dressing. And girls wear less and less clothes over the years!

现在服装款式很多，里面的讲究也很多。而且女孩们的衣服越穿越少了！

风格与场合 Style and Situation

我要参加舞会，这件衣服怎么样？

I am going to a ball, how is this dress?

举一反三

Don't you think it's a bit too gaudy? 你不觉得有点太艳了吗？

Yeah, maybe you're right. How about this outfit?

是的，也许你是对的。这套装怎么样？

What do you think about this? It's casual, yet sophisticated.

你觉得这件怎么样？很休闲，还有点成熟的风情。

风格与身份 Style and Identity

我是学生，穿什么风格的衣服合适？

I'm a student; what style is good for me?

举一反三

That dress looks lovely on you, but it's not very appropriate for a student, is it?

裙子穿在你身上很漂亮。但是好像有点不适合学生，对吧？

As a teacher, you should dress to look graceful and proper.

作为老师，你应该穿得稳重、得体。

Dialogue 1 · 服装变化 Changes of Dress

> Girls wear very beautiful clothes, and every year's fashion trend is different.

> Yes. During the four decades of reform and opening-up, people's feelings toward style have changed a lot.

服装专家正在和朋友们谈论中国的服装变化，让我们也来听听吧。

The fashion professional is talking with his friends about the changes of style in China. Let's listen together!

Professional:	Girls wear very beautiful clothes, and every year's fashion trend is different.
Xiaohuang:	Yes. During the four decades of reform and opening-up, people's feelings toward style have changed a lot.
Xiaoyang:	Oh, then what style did people have forty years ago?
Professional:	People at that time usually dressed in darker colors, and the styles of clothes were limited.
Xiaohuang:	But now we have more styles to choose from, and there are lots of rules for dressing. And girls wear less and less clothes over the years!
Professional:	Right, this shows China is becoming more open. But summer is over, girls will have to wear more clothes; they can't always wear something charming rather than something warm!

服装专家:	女孩子们穿的衣服很漂亮，每年时尚趋势也都不一样！
小黄:	是呀！改革开放这40多年来，人们对服装的美感改变了很多！
小杨:	哦，那么40年前人们穿什么样式的衣服呢？
服装专家:	那时候人们还主要穿深暗色的衣服，衣服的款式也很有限。
小黄:	现在服装款式很多，里面的讲究也很多。而且女孩们的衣服越穿越少了！
服装专家:	对，这也说明中国变得更加开放了。但是夏天过去了，女孩们应该穿点厚衣服啦，不能总"要风度不要温度"啦！

Dialogue 2 · 服装样式 Clothing Style

So, do university students in China dress like the students you see here?

Yes, similarly. But I'm still surprised.

　　简来自于中国，现在在美国的一所大学读书，认识了一位美国朋友艾伦。两人正在谈论着美国和中国的服装样式。

　　Jane is from China. Now she is studying in an American university. There she makes an American friend, Allen. They are talking about style in America and in China.

Allen:	So, do university students in China dress like the students you see here?
Jane:	Yes, similarly. But I'm still surprised.
Allen:	Why?
Jane:	It's even more casual here. In China, styles seem to be more formal.
Allen:	I've been in Madison for almost ten years now. Actually, now, people dress a little better than before. But now, styles have changed a little.
Jane:	Maybe they are more conservative now.
Allen:	I don't know if conservative is the right word. They are just different.

Jane: If you go to China, you would be surprised, I think.

Allen: Why?

Jane: You would see most people dressed very well. Not only university students, but also working people. Many working people in China spend a lot of money on clothes.

艾伦：　中国的大学生穿得和这里的学生一样吗？

简：　　差不多，但是我还是有些惊讶。

艾伦：　为什么？

简：　　这里穿得比较随便，中国服装的样式比较正式。

艾伦：　我在麦迪逊快十年了。事实上，现在，大家穿得比以前好一点。但是现在的样式稍微改变了一点。

简：　　或许现在人们比较保守。

艾伦：　我不知道是不是保守，但它们就是不一样。

简：　　如果你到中国来，一定会很惊讶。

艾伦：　为什么？

简：　·　你会看到大部分的人都穿得很漂亮，不止大学生，上班族也是。中国很多上班族花很多钱在服装上。

Dialogue 3 经典影像观摩 The Emulation of Classical Movies

马琳达正在进行挑选会，也就是为杂志拍摄图片挑选合适的服装。她对衣服的款式和风格提出了自己独特的看法。

Miranda is doing a run-through, that is choosing a suitable dress for the magazine's photo shoot. She gives her unique opinions about the style of the dresses.

Miranda: No. And I've seen all this before.

Clerk: Theyskens is trying to reinvent the drop waist, so actually it's…

Miranda: Where are all the other dresses?

Clerk: We have some right here.

Nigel: Stand, watch and listen.

Clerk: And I think it can be very interesting.

Miranda: No. No, I just, it's just baffling to me. Why is it so impossible to put together a decent run-through? You people have had hours and hours to prepare. It's just so confusing to me. Where are the advertisers?

Clerk: We have some pieces from Banana Republic.

Miranda: We need more, don't we? Oh. This is, this might be. What do you think of?

Nigel: Yeah, well, you know me. Give me a full ballerina skirt and a hint of saloon and I'm on board.

马琳达:	不行，都过时了。
职员:	西斯肯斯正准备重造一下下摆，所以事实上……
马琳达:	其他裙子呢？
职员:	这里还有一些。
奈杰尔:	站着，边看边听。
职员:	我认为这样很时髦。
马琳达:	不，不，我真搞不懂。为什么做个顺利的挑选会这么难？你们有这么多的时间准备，真让我搞不懂。广告部的人呢？
职员:	我们从巴纳纳拿来这些。
马琳达:	我们还需要更多，不是吗？哦，这个，这个可以……你们觉得呢？
奈杰尔:	是啊。你知道我这个人，一条芭蕾舞裙加一点造型，我绝对赞成。

词句荟萃 Words and Sentences Gathering

adore [ə'dɔ:] v. 喜爱

conservative [kən'sɜːvətɪv] adj. 保守的

outfit ['aʊtfɪt] n. 套装

reform and opening-up 改革开放

sophisticated [sə'fɪstɪkeɪtɪd] adj. 成熟的，复杂的，老练的

gracefully ['greɪsfʊlɪ] adv. 优美地；典雅地

properly ['prɒpəlɪ] adv. 合适地，得体地

trend [trend] n. 趋势

charming ['tʃɑːmɪŋ] adj. 迷人的

drop [drɒp] v.&n. 下降，落下

waist [weɪst] n. 腰

baffling ['bæflɪŋ] adj. 阻碍的；不可理解的

decent ['diːsənt] adj. 体面的

run-through n. 挑选会

advertiser ['ædvətaɪzə] n. 广告人

ballerina [ˌbælə'riːnə] n. 芭蕾舞女演员

saloon [sə'luːn] n. 餐车；酒吧

I'm on board. 我绝对赞成。

服装常见词语

成衣 ready-made clothes, ready-to-wear clothes
服装 garments
外衣 town clothes
双排扣外衣 double-breasted suit
男外衣 suit
女式西服 tailored suit
便服 everyday clothes
三件套 three-piece suit
嫁妆 trousseau
婴儿的全套服装 layette
制服 uniform
工装裤 overalls
连背心的背带裤 rompers
礼服 formal dress
大礼服，晨礼服 tailcoat, morning coat
晚礼服 evening dress
燕尾服，礼服 dress coat, tails
男式晚礼服 nightshirt
无尾礼服 dinner jacket (美作:tuxedo)
礼服制服 full dress uniform
双排扣长礼服 frock coat
长袍 gown, robe
短上衣 tunic
夹大衣 topcoat
皮大衣 fur coat
中长大衣 three-quarter coat
风衣 dust coat
斗篷，雨披 poncho
羊皮夹克 sheepskin jacket
皮上衣 pelisse
带兜帽的夹克，带风帽的粗呢大衣 anorak, duffel coat

Section 3

> Bamboo fiber? That's a new word. Is it made of bamboo?

■ 质地、材料（丝绸、亚麻等）
Material

> It talked about a new material called bamboo fiber.

疯狂表达 Expressions

询问材料 Inquiry about Material

这条裙子是由什么制成的?

What is the skirt made of?

举一反三

Is it 100% cotton? 是100%棉的吗?

How is the material I chose? 我这料子选得怎么样?

Have you decided which material you would like the suit to be made of?

你想好了用什么面料做衣服了吗?

应答 Responses

它是由真丝制成的。

It's made of silk.

举一反三

It's made of linen. 它是由亚麻制成的。

It's made of wool. 它是由羊毛制成的。

It's made of cotton. 它是棉质的。

质地与款式 Material and Style

我想做旗袍，选什么材料啊?

I want to make a cheongsam; what material should I choose?

举一反三

You should definitely use Chinese silk and satin to make a cheongsam.
做旗袍当然要用中国绸缎了。

You'd better use wool to make a suit. 做西服最好用羊毛料子。

质地与用途 Material and Usage

哪有适合做晚礼服的布料?

Where can I find the material for an evening gown?

举一反三

How about this cloth for trousers? 这块布料做裤子怎么样?

There is the satin suitable for making cushion covers there.
那里有适宜做垫套的缎子。

质地与季节 Material and Seasons

夏季选择轻薄的布料。

Choose lightweight fabrics in the summer.

举一反三

Choose thick fabrics in the spring and autumn. And it's quite durable.
春秋要用稍厚的布料，会很耐穿。

Wool and cashmere are the best choices for clothes in the winter.
冬季服装最好选羊毛或羊绒的料子。

质地与洗涤 Material and Cleaning

你只能在温水中洗。

You can only wash it in lukewarm water.

举一反三

You don't want to wash them out, do you? 你不想洗坏它们，是吗?

You should hand-wash it. 你要手洗这件衣服。

Remember, hand-wash it in cold water. 记住，冷水手洗。

Dialogue 1 · 质地的变迁 Change in Material

> It talked about a new material called bamboo fiber.

> Bamboo fiber? That's a new word. Is it made of bamboo?

小王昨天看了一场时尚发布会，知道了一种新的服装材料——竹纤维。

Xiao Wang watched a fashion show yesterday and learned about a new material for clothes called bamboo fiber.

Xiao Wang:	Yesterday I watched a fashion show.
Xiao Yang:	Really? About what?
Xiao Wang:	It talked about a new material called bamboo fiber.
Xiao Yang:	Bamboo fiber? That's a new word. Is it made of bamboo?
Xiao Wang:	Yes, it is a natural and safe new material which is smoother and softer than cotton, and has a regulative fiber with a "warm in winter and cool in summer" capability.
Xiao Yang:	Things change a lot. 50 years ago people were wearing Dacron.

小王：昨天我看了一场时尚发布会。
小杨：真的吗？关于什么的？
小王：它介绍了一种被叫做竹纤维的新材质。
小杨：竹纤维？是个新名词。是由竹子制成的吗？
小王：是的，这是种自然安全的新材料，比棉更滑更软，还冬暖夏凉。
小杨：生活变化真大。50年前人们还穿着涤纶。

辛迪和丽丽去逛时装店。辛迪觉得买衣服要考虑衣服的材料、质量和价格，可是当她看到自己喜欢的衣服时，似乎立场就没有那么坚定了!

Cindy and Lily go shopping in a clothing mall. Cindy thinks when buying clothes, people must consider the material, quality and price. But when she finds her favorite dress, she doesn't seem so certain.

Cindy: Oh, Lily, the clothes here are expensive! No wonder there are only a few people here.

Lily: Beauty has a price, my friend. Oh, look at this pink skirt, how cute!

Cindy: Believe it or not, they look cute, but they're not very practical.

Lily: Come on, Cindy, don't talk like my Mom.

Cindy: When you buy clothes, you must consider the material, quality and price.

Lily: But fashion changes!

Cindy: Make sure the clothes can be worn for various occasions.

Lily: All right, Cindy. Hey, look, I'm sure this is the same skirt that the Spice Girls wear.

Cindy: Definitely! Oh, I love the Spice Girls! I would get that skirt!

辛迪: 哦，丽丽，这儿的衣服真贵! 难怪这儿没什么人。

丽丽: 美是有代价的啊，朋友。噢，看看这条粉红色的裙子，好可爱啊!

辛迪: 不管你信不信，它们看起来漂亮，可是不怎么实用。

丽丽: 行啦，辛迪，别说话像我妈一样。

辛迪: 买衣服时，你得考虑它们的材料、质量和价格。

丽丽: 但流行都在变啊!

辛迪: 你要确保衣服可以在多种不同的场合下穿着。

丽丽: 好吧，辛迪。嘿，看，我肯定这是辣妹组合其中的一人穿过的。

辛迪: 真的耶! 哦，我爱死辣妹组合了! 我一定要把这裙子买下来!

安德里亚的化纤衣服遭到了同事奈杰尔的嘲讽，安德里亚是怎么回答的呢？

Andrea's polyester clothes were criticized by Nigel, one of her colleagues. So how did Andrea respond?

Andrea: Well, I'm a six.

Nigel: Which is the new 14?

Andrea: Oh. Shoot.

Nigel: Oh, never mind. I'm sure you have plenty more polyblend where that came from.

Andrea: Okay. You think my clothes are hideous. I get it. But, you know, I'm not going to be in fashion forever. So I don't see the point of changing everything about myself just because I have this job.

Nigel: Yes, that's true. That's really what this multibillion dollar industry is all about anyway, isn't it? Inner beauty.

安德里亚： 我是6号。
奈杰尔： 就要变成14号了。
安德里亚： 哦，该死。
奈杰尔： 哦，没关系。你一定还有很多其他化纤衣服。
安德里亚： 你觉得我的衣服难看，我知道了。但是，你知道我不会一直留在时尚界。我不会为了这个工作而改变自己。
奈杰尔： 那也对。这个值好几亿的产业就只关心一件事，对不对？内在美。

词句荟萃 Words and Sentences Gathering

silk [sɪlk] *n.* 丝

linen ['lɪnɪn] *n.* 亚麻

cheongsam ['tʃiːɑːŋ'sɑːm] *n.* 旗袍

satin ['sætɪn] *n.* 缎子

suit [sjuːt] *n.* 套装

gown [gaʊn] *n.* 长袍

fabric ['fæbrɪk] *n.* 织物；结构

durable ['djuəbl] *adj.* 耐用的

cushion ['kʊʃən] *n.* 坐垫

healthy ['helθɪ] *adj.* 有益健康的

fiber ['faɪbə] *n.* 纤维

dacron ['deɪkrən] *n.* 涤纶织物
wonder ['wʌndə] *n.* 惊奇
practical ['præktɪkl] *adj.* 实用的
quality ['kwɒlɪtɪ] *n.* 质量

疯狂链接 Interlinkage

关于衣服质地的词汇

灯芯绒 cord
棉 cotton
羊羔毛 lambs wool
莱卡 lycra
尼龙 nylon
兔毛 rabbit hair
真丝 silk
羊毛 wool
腈纶 acrylic
羊绒 cashmere
黄麻 jute

亚麻 linen
马海毛 mohair
桑蚕丝 mulberry silk
涤纶 polyester
牦牛毛 yak hair
天然纤维 natural fabric
混合纤维 synthetic fabric
压克力 acryl
呢料 worsted

Section 4

I love all the fashionable things. But my favorite brand is Chanel.

■ 品牌
Brands

Wow! They've got everything here. All the world's famous brands. Aunt Shirley, what is your favorite brand?

疯狂表达 Expressions

个人喜好 Personal Preference

你喜欢什么牌子?

What brand do you like?

举一反三

My favorite brand is Chanel.　我最喜欢的牌子是香奈尔。

All my bags are LV.　我的包都是LV的。

有品牌意识 Brand Consciousness

我喜欢买名牌衣服。

I prefer famous brand clothes.

举一反三

I buy famous brands because I want to keep up with fashion.
我买名牌是因为我要跟上潮流。

I love all the fashionable things.　我爱所有时尚的东西。

没有品牌意识 Brand Unconsciousness

牌子对我来说不重要。

Brand doesn't matter to me.

举一反三
The quality really matters for clothes.　衣服重要的是质量。

I don't like buying clothes with big-name brands.　我不喜欢买品牌衣服。

品牌与品味 Brand and Taste

品牌意味着品味。

Brands mean taste.

举一反三

Yeah, very tasteful.　很有品位啊。

You know my taste by my brand.　看我衣服的牌子就知道我的品位了。

品牌与时尚 Brand and Fashion

有了它们，你看起来更加时尚了。

And with them, you look even more fashionable.

举一反三

Brands always go with fashion.　品牌总是和时尚连在一起啊。

Come on. Fashion is not only for women. Men have an equal right to chase fashion.
拜托。时尚可不是女士的专利啊。男士也有追求时尚的权利啊。

Oh, really, that's really something new. I'm afraid not everyone can accept that.
哦，真的，这可真是新鲜事哦。恐怕不是每个人都可以接受。

品牌与消费 Brand and Consuming

这倒是。对了，时尚显然不是一件廉价的事情。所以，你把你所有的钱都花在这里了吗？

That's true. Well, it's obvious that fashion is not cheap. So, do you spend all your money on it?

没有啊。时尚只是我生活的一部分，它提升了生活的品质。不过，我还擅长理财呢。我有信用卡，但是我从来都不透支。

No. Fashion is just part of my life, which improves its quality. But also, I'm good at finance. I have a credit card, but I never go into overdraft.

举一反三

How can you be my mum's sister? You two are so different. She always shops for bargains and spends more than she earns. You do so much better than her.
你怎么会是我妈妈的妹妹呢？你们俩太不一样了。她总是买便宜货而且入不敷出。你做得比她好多了。

I have to say that's just the result of differences in our shopping habits.
我只能说这是消费习惯的不同而导致的结果吧。

Dialogue 1 · 名牌与潮流 Name-Brand and Fashion

> Thanks. This bag is LV.
> Do you know LV?

> You have a beautiful bag.
> What brand is it?

记者正在路上采访人们对品牌与时尚的理解，我们也来看看大家对品牌与潮流的看法吧。

A reporter is interviewing people about their understanding of brands and fashion. Let's have a look at what they're saying.

Reporter:	Miss, could I ask you a question?
Passer-by:	Yes, of course.
Reporter:	You have a beautiful bag. What brand is it?
Passer-by:	Thanks. This bag is LV. Do you know LV?
Reporter:	Yes, of course, it's a famous international brand. Could you tell me how much it cost?
Passer-by:	My bag cost almost 4000 yuan. I bought it online.
Reporter:	Do you mind me asking about your salary?
Passer-by:	No, I am a secretary in a company and my salary is 3500 yuan per month.
Reporter:	Why did you spend more money than your salary buying a bag?
Passer-by:	I buy famous brands because I want to keep up with fashion.

记者： 小姐，能问你一个问题吗？
路人： 当然可以。
记者： 你的包包很漂亮，是什么牌子的？
路人： 谢谢，这包是LV的包，你知道LV吗？

记者：　当然，知名的国际品牌。你能告诉我这个包多少钱吗？
路人：　我的包大约是4000块钱，我是在网上买的。
记者：　你不介意我问一下你的工资吧？
路人：　不介意，我是一家公司的秘书，薪水是一个月3500元。
记者：　那你为什么花比你工资还多的钱去买一个包呢？
路人：　我买名牌是因为我想跟上潮流。

Dialogue 2 · 时尚消费 Fashion Consumer

Come on. Fashion is not only for women. Men also have an equal right to chase fashion. It's the new fashion for men to wear perfume, which is called cologne.

Oh, really, that's really something new. I'm afraid not everyone can accept that.

丽莎的阿姨雪莉是典型的时尚一族，她热衷于时尚消费。今天她带着丽莎去逛大商场并大谈时尚消费。我们一起来感受一下时尚吧。

Lisa's aunt, Shirley, is one of typical of fashion group members and is keen on fashion consumer. Today, she takes Lisa to go shopping and talks a lot about fashion consumer. Let's sense the fashion together.

Lisa:　　Wow! They've got everything here. All the world's famous brands. Aunt Shirley, what is your favorite brand?

Shirley:　I love all the fashionable things. But my favorite brand is Chanel.

Lisa:　　Oh, that's a very expensive brand, but with good reason.

Shirley:　Yeah. Each style is specially designed by the world's top designers. So they can always make you look amazing.

Lisa: I see. Come here. The high heels here are really attractive. But I wonder whether any of them are comfortable.

Shirley: Not really, especially in the beginning, if you wear high heels all day long, your feet would hurt. But, no big deal. Women always get used to that.

Lisa: It's not easy being beautiful.

Shirley: Sure. But everyone loves to be beautiful. Hey, do you think this pair of sunglasses matches this handbag?

Lisa: Yeah, very tasteful. And with them, you look even more fashionable. Oh, there are so many French perfumes. Oops, cologne for guys? So strange!

Shirley: Come on. Fashion is not only for women. Men also have an equal right to chase fashion. It's the new fashion for men to wear perfume, which is called cologne.

Lisa: Oh, really, that's really something new. I'm afraid not everyone can accept that.

丽莎：   哇，这里什么都有啊，国际名牌齐全。雪莉阿姨，你最喜欢的牌子是哪个？

雪莉：   我爱所有时尚的东西。不过，我最喜欢的牌子是香奈尔。

丽莎：   哦，那个牌子很贵，不过确实值得。

雪莉：   是啊，每一款都是由世界顶级设计师专门设计的。所以它们总是能让你惊喜。

丽莎：   明白。来这边。这些高跟鞋看起来好漂亮啊。但是我怀疑它们穿起来是否舒适。

雪莉：   不会很舒适。尤其是刚开始穿的时候，如果一整天都穿着高跟鞋，脚会很疼。但是，也没什么大不了。女人都会适应那个的。

丽莎：   想变漂亮也不容易啊。

雪莉：   那当然。不过每个人都爱美啊。嗳，你觉得这副太阳镜和这个手提包搭配起来怎样？

丽莎：   很有品位啊。有了它们，你看起来更加时尚了。哦，这里有好多法国香水啊。哦，男士香水？好奇怪啊！

雪莉：   拜托。时尚可不是女士的专利啊。男士也有追求时尚的同等权利啊。男士用香水是一种新时尚，这些香水叫古龙水。

丽莎：   哦，真的，这可真是新鲜事哦。恐怕不是每个人都可以接受。

安德里亚要奈杰尔帮忙把自己打扮成个漂亮而又时尚的女孩，奈杰尔给安德里亚推荐了流行的品牌衣服和鞋子。

Andrea asks Nigel to help make her a beautiful and fashionable girl and Nigel recommends popular name-brand dresses and shoes.

Andrea:	Okay. So I'm screwing it up.
Nigel:	Hmm?
Andrea:	I don't want to. I just wish that I knew what I could do to... Nigel?
Andrea:	Nigel. Nigel.
Nigel:	No. I don't know what you expect me to do. There's nothing in this whole closet that'll fit a size six. I can guarantee you. These are all sample sizes, two and four. All right, we're doing this for you, and…
Andrea:	A poncho?
Nigel:	You'll take what I give you and you'll like it. We're doing this Dolce for you. And shoes. Jimmy Choo's. Hmm. Manolo Blahnik. Nancy Gonzales. Okay, Narciso Rodriguez. This we love. It might fit. It might.
Andrea:	What?
Nigel:	Okay, now, Chanel. You're in desperate need of Chanel. Darling, shall we? We have to get to the beauty department, and God knows how long that's going to take!

安德里亚：	好吧，我搞砸了。
奈杰尔：	嗯？
安德里亚：	我不想的，我只希望自己知道该怎么做。奈杰尔？
安德里亚：	奈杰尔，奈杰尔。
奈杰尔：	不行。我不知道你要我做什么。这衣橱里根本没有6号的衣服，我向你保证。这里都是样品尺寸，2号和4号。好吧，这个给你，还有……
安德里亚：	披风？
奈杰尔：	你穿我给你的，你会喜欢的。穿这件杜嘉吧，还有鞋子。吉米·周，嗯。马诺洛·布拉尼克。哇，南希·冈萨雷斯，我喜欢。纳西索·罗德里格斯，我们要这个。或许合身。
安德里亚：	什么？
奈杰尔：	好了，香奈尔，现在你非常需要香奈尔。亲爱的，走吧。我们还要去美容部，天知道美容要做多久？

tasteful ['teɪstfl] *adj.* 雅致的；有鉴赏力的
fashionable ['fæʃənəbl] *adj.* 时尚的；流行的
perfume [pə'fjuːm] *n.* 香水
chase [tʃeɪs] *v.* 追求
cologne [kə'ləʊn] *n.* 古龙水
financing [faɪ'nænsɪŋ] *n.* 理财
overdraft ['əʊvə'drɑːft] *vi.* 透支
bargain ['bɑːgɪn] *n.* 便宜货

疯狂链接 Interlinkage

国际品牌名称

香奈尔 Chanel
阿尔玛 ALMA
柏帛丽 Burberry
巴黎世家 BALENCIAGA
贝纳通 Benetton
克罗埃 Chloé
瑟琳 Celine
克里斯汀•迪奥 Christian Dior 简称CD
卡文•克莱 Calvin Klein
杜嘉班纳 Dolce&Gabbana
埃斯卡达 Escada
芬迪 FENDI

娇兰 Guerlain
詹妮 Genny
古孜 GUCCI
范思哲 Gianni Versace
高田贤三 Kenzo
兰蔻 LANCOME
路易•威登 Louis Vuitton
朗万 Lanvin
普拉达 Prada
皮尔•巴尔曼 Pierre Balmain
瓦伦蒂诺（亦称华伦天奴）Valentino
维多利亚的秘密 Victoria's Secret

Section 5

I like the jeans, but you need something to go with the top. It's too plain on its own.

■ 搭配
Matching

How about this scarf, these earrings, and an anklet?

疯狂表达 Expressions

服饰搭配 Matching Clothes

这条裤子配你的夹克正合适。

The pants match your jacket very well.

举一反三

Do the earrings go with my blouse?　这耳环跟我的上衣配吗？

Really well.　很配啊。

Just one more thing—you need some high heels to go with those jeans.

只再需要一件东西——你需要一些高跟鞋来搭配这些牛仔服。

服饰不搭配 Clothes that Don't Match

我喜欢那条牛仔裤，不过，你需要一件能搭配那件上衣的衣服。这条有点太普通了。

I like the jeans, but you need something to go with the top. It's too plain on its own.

举一反三

How about this scarf, these earrings, and an anklet?

那这条围巾、这些耳环和这条脚链怎么样?

That might be going a bit overboard. How about just that scarf with a bracelet?

好像有点累赘了。要是只有围巾配手链怎么样?

颜色搭配 Matching Colors

这套衣服的颜色很协调。

There is a harmony to the color of the suit.

举一反三

It definitely does. Trust me, red is the global fashion now.

当然配啦。相信我吧,红色是现在全球流行的颜色。

All right, I will try on the red one. ...Now, what do you think?

好吧,我就试试那件红色的。现在你觉得呢?

Terrific!　棒极了!

颜色不搭配 Colors That Don't Match

但是红色跟我的绿毛衣不配啊。

But red doesn't go with my green sweater.

举一反三

No, you look ridiculous. I suggest you try some other colors.

你看上去真滑稽。我建议你试一试别的颜色。

OK, I will try on that green one. Now, how do I look?

好吧,我试试那件绿的。我现在看起来呢?

You look like a Christmas tree. Why not try on the red one?

你看上去像棵圣诞树。干嘛不试试那件红色的?

Dialogue 1 服饰与时尚 *Clothes and Fashion*

> Yep. Here it is. What do you think?

> That looks great. Just one more thing—you need some high heels with those jeans. Do you want a pair with a plain pattern or ones with a leopard print on them?

　　杰瑞和罗斯一起去逛时装店，两个人从搭配的角度来挑选衣服，这样会使服饰看起来更时尚。

　　Jerry and Rose go shopping in a boutique together. The two choose clothes by matching. That way they can make the clothes look more fashionable.

Jerry: I like the jeans, but you need something to go with the top. It's too plain on its own.

Rose: How about this scarf, these earrings, and an anklet?

Jerry: That might be going a bit overboard. How about just that scarf with a bracelet?

Rose: That's a good idea. You have a good sense of fashion.

Jerry: Thanks. You'd be OK on your own. There are loads of fashion victims out there, and you are not one of them. Have you tried it on yet?

Rose: Yep. Here it is. What do you think?

Jerry: That looks great. Just one more thing—you need some high heels with those jeans. Do you want a pair with a plain pattern or ones with a leopard print on them?

Rose: The leopard print sounds fabulous. Are they a name-brand?

Jerry: No, they're a Prada knock-off for 1/10 of the price of the real thing.

Rose: That's even better than the real thing.

Jerry: If I were you, I'd buy that now while it's on sale. If you spend $100, you get a $50 voucher for more clothes.

Rose: It's too bad I did all that shopping yesterday!

杰瑞： 我喜欢那条牛仔裤，不过，你需要一件能搭配那件上衣的衣服。这条有点太普通了。

罗斯： 那这条围巾、这些耳环和这条脚链怎么样？

杰瑞： 好像有点累赘了。要是只有围巾配手链怎么样？

罗斯： 好主意，你的时尚品位很不错。

杰瑞： 谢谢。你自己也行。现在有很多被时尚所累的人，还好你不是他们中的一员。你试过这件了吗？

罗斯： 嗯，这就是。你觉得如何？

杰瑞： 看起来太棒了！只再需要一件东西——你需要一双高跟鞋来搭配这些牛仔服。你喜欢普通款式还是有豹纹的？

罗斯： 这种豹纹看起来很漂亮。这个是名牌吗？

杰瑞： 这是普拉达的仿制品，大约是正品价格的十分之一。

罗斯： 这可比正品都好。

杰瑞： 如果我是你，我现在就买，正好有打折活动。如果你买东西超过100美元，就能得到50美元的礼券买更多的衣服。

罗斯： 糟了，我昨天逛街的时候已经买过了。

Dialogue 2 · 颜色搭配 *Matching Colors*

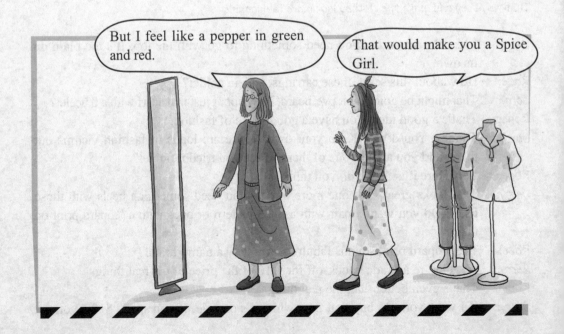

But I feel like a pepper in green and red.

That would make you a Spice Girl.

买衣服的学问还真不少，颜色搭配就很不简单，这下安妮和琳达要好好"研究"一下了。

There's a lot to konw in buying clothes. Matching colors is not simple. Anne and Linda will make a great case study.

Anne:	I'd like to try this on, please. Where is the fitting room?
Salesclerk:	This way, please.
Anne:	How do I look in this skirt, Linda? Am I Spice Girl, or what?
Linda:	No, you look ridiculous. I suggest you try some other colors.
Anne:	OK, I will try on that green one. …Now, how do I look?
Linda:	You look like a Christmas tree. Why not try on the red one?
Anne:	But red doesn't go with my green sweater.
Linda:	It definitely does. Trust me, red is the global fashion now.
Anne:	All right, I will try on the red one. …Now, what do you think?
Linda:	Terrific!
Anne:	But I feel like a pepper in green and red.
Linda:	That would make you a Spice Girl.
Anne:	Don't kid! Anyway I will take this one.
Salesclerk:	Thank you. I will wrap it up for you. You can pay at the front counter. It's 500 yuan.

安妮：	我想试试这件。试衣间在哪儿？
售货员：	请这边走。
安妮：	我看起来怎么样，琳达？像不像辣妹啊？
琳达：	不像，你看上去真滑稽。我建议你试一试别的颜色。
安妮：	好吧，我试试那件绿的。我现在看起来呢？
琳达：	你看上去像棵圣诞树。干嘛不试试那件红色的？
安妮：	但是红色跟我的绿毛衣不配啊。
琳达：	当然配啦。相信我吧，红色是现在全球流行的颜色。
安妮：	好吧，我就试试那件红色的。现在你觉得呢？
琳达：	棒极了！
安妮：	但我感觉穿得又红又绿像个辣椒。
琳达：	那样你才是辣妹啊。
安妮：	别开玩笑了！不过，这件我买了。
售货员：	谢谢。我帮您包好。您可以到前台去付款。一共500元。

瑞贝卡又被商店里的一条绿丝巾吸引住了，不过想到自己的账单，她又望而却步。这时佩戴着绿丝巾的模特却开口和瑞贝卡说话了，瑞贝卡又一次经不住诱惑了。

Rebecca is drawn to a green scarf in the store again. However, thinking about her bills, she stops. The model wearing the green scarf opens her mouth and speaks to Rebecca. Rebecca is trapped again.

Rebecca: Rebecca, you just got a credit card bill of $900. You do not need a scarf.

Model: Then…again…who needs a scarf? Wrap some old jeans around your neck, that'll keep you warm. That's what your mother would do.

Rebecca: You're right, she would.

Model: The point about this scarf is that it would become part of a definition of your…of your psyche. Do you see what I mean?

Rebecca: No, I do. Keep talking.

Model: It would make your eyes look bigger.

Rebecca: Mmm…It would make my haircut look more expensive.

Model: You'd wear it with everything.

Rebecca: It would be an investment.

Model: You would walk into that interview confident.

Rebecca: Confident.

Model: And poised.

Rebecca: Poised.

Model: The girl in the green scarf.

瑞贝卡： 瑞贝卡，你刚刚收到900美元的账单，你不需要丝巾。

模特：   那么再仔细想想……谁需要丝巾呢？随便找一块破布围在脖子上，就能保暖。你妈妈就会这样。

瑞贝卡： 你说得没错，她会那么做。

模特：   这条丝巾的诱人之处在于它能成为你……你灵魂象征的一部分，你明白我的意思吗？

瑞贝卡： 我明白，接着说。

模特：   它会让你的眼睛看起来更大。

瑞贝卡： 嗯……可以使我的发型更显高贵。

模特：   你可以用它搭配自己所有的衣服。

瑞贝卡： 值得的投资。

模特：   你可以信心十足地去参加面试。

瑞贝卡： 满怀自信。

模特：   泰然自若。

瑞贝卡： 泰然自若。

模特：   绿丝巾女郎。

boutique [buːˈtiːk] *n.* 时装店，精品店
shawl [ʃɔːl] *n.* 披肩
earring [ˈɪərɪŋ] *n.* 耳环
ridiculous [rɪˈdɪkjʊləs] *adj.* 荒谬的
tights [taɪts] *n.* 长筒袜
bracelet [ˈbreɪslɪt] *n.* 手链
high heels 高跟鞋
cuff links 袖扣
go with something 搭配
consumption ability 消费能力
by a long way 非常地

疯狂链接 Interlinkage

服饰商品名称

风帽 hood

围巾 scarf, muffler

大披巾 shawl

头巾，编织的头巾 knitted shawl

毛皮长围巾 fur stole

皮手筒 muff

晨衣 housecoat, dressing gown (美作:duster)

短晨衣 short dressing gown

浴衣 bathrobe

女睡衣 nightgown, nightdress

睡衣裤 pyjamas (美作:pajamas)

衣袋 pocket

(上衣)翻领 lapel

假领，活领 detachable collar

硬翻领，上浆翻领 wing collar

V型领 V-neck

袖子 sleeve

袖口 cuff
纽扣孔 buttonhole
衬衫 shirt
紧身女衫 blouse
短袖圆领衫，T恤衫 T-shirt
汗衫 vest (美作:undershirt)
球衣 polo shirt
水手衫 middy blouse
运动衫，毛衣 sweater
短袖运动衫 short-sleeved sweater
高翻领运动衫 roll-neck sweater
圆领运动衫 round-neck sweater
套服 suit, outfit, ensemble
两件套，运动衫裤 twinset
猎装 jerkin
和服 kimono
一种长而宽松的外套 ulster
带风帽的外衣 jellaba, djellaba, jelab
开襟毛衣 cardigan
橡胶雨衣 mackintosh, raincoat
裤子 trousers
牛仔裤 jeans
短裤 short trousers
儿童灯笼短裤 knickers
灯笼裤 knickerbockers
高尔夫球裤，半长裤 plus fours
裤子背带 braces (美作:suspenders)
裤角折边，挽脚 turnup
马裤 breeches
裤带 belt
裙子 skirt

裙裤 divided skirt, split skirt
内衣，衬裙 underskirt
内衣 underwear, underclothes
内裤 underpants, pants
(美作:shorts)
短内裤，三角裤 briefs
女短内裤 panties
乳罩 brassiere, bra
紧身胸衣 corselet
束腰，胸衣 stays, corset
背心 waistcoat
衬裙 slip, petticoat
腰带 girdle
长袜 stockings
袜带 suspenders (美作:garters)
吊袜腰带 suspender belt (美作:garter belt)
短袜 socks
紧身衣裤 tights, leotard
手帕 handkerchief
游泳裤 bathing trunks
游泳衣 swimsuit, bathing suit
比基尼泳衣 bikini
围裙 apron
(带护胸)围裙 pinafore

Section 6

OK, let me see. This white shirt can be washed in water by hand, but this suit and the woolen sweater need to be dry-cleaned.

■ 洗涤方式
Washing Methods

I've got a suit, a woolen sweater and a white shirt to wash.

疯狂表达 Expressions

洗涤方式 Washing Methods

最好手洗。

It's better to wash it by hand.

举一反三

You can wash it in the machine.　可以机洗。

It's better to take it to a dry cleaner's.　最好交给干洗店。

洗涤要求 Washing Requirements

哦，谢谢。你看，我对此了解很少，请告诉我一些洗衣服时需要注意的事项吧。

Oh, thanks. You know, I know little about this, so please tell me anything that I should pay more attention to when I do the washing.

很简单。把衣服按颜色分类，在冷水中洗。如果上面有特殊的污渍，像糖渍、咖啡或是其他东西，干洗时要说明。

It's very simple. Divide the clothes by color, and wash them in cold water. If you've got stains on them from sugar, coffee or something else, please let the dry cleaner know.

Can I wash it in the machine?　可以用洗衣机洗吗?

Yes, but it's better to turn it inside out when you wash it, to keep the surface from piling.　可以，但洗的时候最好反面洗涤，这样可以避免起球。

What do you suggest to keep it from shrinking?　你说我要怎样才能防止它缩水?

It's better to dry it in the shade.　最好在阴凉处晾干。

How do you prevent discoloration?　要如何防止褪色?

It's better to wash it in cold water.　最好冷水洗涤。

Can I wash it with other clothes?　我可以将它和其他衣服一起洗吗?

Yes, but it's better to button the buttons when washing it, to keep it from losing its shape.　可以，但洗的时候最好扣上扣子，这样可以防止变形。

干洗 Dry-Cleaning

你应该干洗一下那件外套。

You ought to have that coat dry-cleaned.

举一反三

I really need the shirt back quickly. Do you have a rush service?

这衣服我等着穿，能不能快一点儿洗好?

Usually we need one day. But we can do it faster for special requests. Why don't you come back in an hour?

一般都要一天的时间。但如果有特殊需要，我们可以赶一赶。你一个小时之后来取吧。

Thank you so much. You're doing me a big favor.　太谢谢你了，你可帮了我的大忙。

It's what we do. We always try to please our customers.

应该的。我们会全力使客户满意!

询问价钱 Asking about Cost

我想在这儿洗几件衣服。得花多少钱?

I want to do some laundry here. How much does it cost?

嗯，这得看您要洗几缸衣服了。通常洗一缸我们收400块钱。

Well, it depends on how many loads you want to do. We usually charge 400 yuan per load.

The cost for a dry-cleaning is three times of that for ordinary laundering. But suits and sweaters, can only be dry-cleaned.

干洗的价钱是普通洗衣的三倍，但是西服和羊毛衫你只能干洗。

Do I need to bring my own detergent?　我需要自带洗涤剂吗？

No, you don't need to. If you prefer, you can use our detergent. However, there is a small fee.　不需要。您愿意的话，也可以用我们的洗涤剂，但需要付点儿钱。

改动 Making Alternations

你好，我想把这套西装改一下。

Hi. I'd like to have this suit tailored.

好的。哪儿不合适？

Sure. What's wrong with it?

袖子有点儿短。能加长点儿吗？

The arms are a little short, can they be lengthened?

举一反三

Well, let's have you try it on first and see.　那您先穿上让我看看。

OK. Do you have a fitting room?　好的。你们这儿有试衣间吗？

Yes, right this way. When you're finished, just come on out.

有，就在这边。您穿好了就出来吧。

OK, thanks.　好的，谢谢。

取衣服 Picking up Clothes

好吧，我什么时候来取呢？

Now, when shall I pick them up?

一般洗衣需要三天，请星期五来取吧。

Usually it takes three days to have laundry done. Please pick them up on Friday.

举一反三

I'm here to pick up my coat.　我来取大衣。

OK, could I see your receipt, please?　好的，给我看一下您的收条好吗？

Dialogue 1 ● 湿洗和干洗 *Ordinary Washing and Dry-cleaning*

Did it ever shrink or fade? Generally speaking, the dark-colored clothes always fade away gradually.

I see. The woolen sweater shrunk in the wash.

妈妈不在家时，爸爸的西服、衬衫、羊毛衫要洗，可遇到麻烦了，只能拿到干洗店里洗。看看爸爸是怎样和别人沟通干洗和湿洗的吧。

When mum isn't around, it's a problem to clean dad's suit, shirts and woolen sweaters. He has to take them to dry-cleaners'. Let's have a look at how dad communicates with others about ordinary washing and dry-cleaning.

Laundrywoman: What can I do for you?

Thomas: I've got a suit, a woolen sweater and a white shirt to wash.

Laundrywoman: OK, let me see. This white shirt can be washed in water by hand, but this suit and the woolen sweater need to be dry-cleaned.

Thomas: That's fine. But that must be expensive.

Laundrywoman: Yes, the cost for dry-cleaning is three times of that for ordinary laundering. But for suits and sweaters, can only be taken to the dry cleaners'.

Thomas: Oh, my wife just threw them into the washer.

Laundrywoman: Did it ever shrink or fade? Generally speaking, the dark-colored clothes always fade away gradually.

Thomas: I see. The woolen sweater shrunk in the wash.

Laundrywoman: Never mind. You can leave them to me.

Thomas: Oh, thanks. You know, I know little about this, so please tell me anything that I should pay more attention to when I do the washing.

Laundrywoman: It's very simple. Divide the clothes by color, and wash them in cold water. If you've got stains on them from sugar, coffee or something else, please let the dry cleaner know.

Thomas: I'll keep that in mind. And how much is it altogether?

Laundrywoman: That will be 200 Yuan altogether. Here is your invoice.

Thomas: It's a bit too expensive.

Laundrywoman: It's worth every cent.

Thomas: Alright then. Now, when shall I pick them up?

Laundrywoman: Usually it takes three days to have laundry done. Please pick them up on Friday.

Thomas: OK, thanks.

洗衣工：有什么需要帮忙的吗？

托马斯：我有一套西服、一件羊毛衫和一件白色衬衣要洗。

洗衣工：好的，我看看。白色衬衣可以用水手洗，但西服和羊毛衫得干洗。

托马斯：好的，但是那肯定很贵。

洗衣工：是的，干洗的价钱是普通洗衣的三倍，但是西服和羊毛衫你只能干洗。

托马斯：噢，我妻子就只是把它们放洗衣机里洗。

洗衣工：那缩水或退色了吗？一般来说，深色衣服是会慢慢褪色的。

托马斯：哦。羊毛衫洗后缩水了。

洗衣工：不用担心。交给我就行了。

托马斯：哦，谢谢。你看，我对此了解很少，请告诉我一些洗衣服时需要注意的事项吧。

洗衣工：很简单。把衣服按颜色分类，在冷水中洗。如果上面有特殊的污渍，像糖渍、咖啡或是其他东西，干洗时要说明。

托马斯：我会记住的。一共多少钱呢？

洗衣工：一共200元。这是发票。

托马斯：有点贵了。

洗衣工：很值得的。

托马斯：好吧，我什么时候来取呢？

洗衣工：一般洗衣需要三天，请星期五来取吧。

托马斯：好的，谢谢了。

It doesn't seem so. Sorry, sir, we've tried everything, but we were not able to get it out of the shirt. It was a sugar stain, I think.

Well, oh my God, there is another problem, I'm afraid. There is still a stain on the shirt.

约定的取衣时间到了，托马斯递交发票取衣。在检查的时候却发现衣服掉了扣子，接着又发现了另一个问题，到底是什么问题呢？

The appointed time to pick up the clothes is approaching. Thomas shows his invoice to get his clothes. He finds a button missing when checking the clothes. Then there is another problem. What is it indeed?

Thomas:	Hi, I've come to pick up my laundry. Here is the invoice.
Laundrywoman:	OK, wait a minute. I'll get them for you.
(A short while)	
Laundrywoman:	Here you are. We've ironed them for you already. Please check and see if there is any damage.
Thomas:	I'm afraid that a button is missing.
Laundrywoman:	I'm terribly sorry. You know we are so busy today and we forgot to sew the button back on. Please wait a moment. It will be ready soon.
Thomas:	OK.
Laundrywoman:	Would you like to have a look? Is it to your satisfaction?
Thomas:	Well, oh my God, there is another problem, I'm afraid. There is still a stain on the shirt.

Laundrywoman: It doesn't seem so. Sorry, sir, we've tried everything, but we were not able to get it out of the shirt. It was a sugar stain, I think.

Thomas: It's been several days now, I am not sure.

Laundrywoman: It was, the sugar was burnt during the dry-cleaning process. And there you go.

Thomas: Oh, that's too bad. I know little about that. Is there a remedy for it?

Laundrywoman: No, I am awfully sorry. Please tell us about the stains before the dry-cleaning next time.

Thomas: OK, I will.

Laundrywoman: Here is a membership card. You can get a 20 percent discount next time.

Thomas: Thanks a lot.

Laundrywoman: Hope to see you again. We will provide you the best service.

托马斯：你好，我来取我的衣服，这是发票。

洗衣工：好的，稍等。我给您取去。

（过了一会儿）

洗衣工：这些是您的。我们已经熨过了。请检查一下看是否有损坏。

托马斯：恐怕这里掉了颗扣子。

洗衣工：非常抱歉。您看我们今天太忙了，忘记给您缝上去了。您稍等一下，马上就好。

托马斯：好的。

洗衣工：您看一下吧，满意吗？

托马斯：噢，天哪，恐怕又有一个问题。衬衣上还有个污点呢。

洗衣工：好像不是那样的。抱歉，先生，我们试了所有的方法，但是都不能从衬衣上去除那个污点。我想那应该是糖渍。

托马斯：已经过了很多天了，我不确定。

洗衣工：是的，在干洗的过程中，糖糊掉了。然后就是这样了。

托马斯：噢，那太糟了。我不知道会这样，有什么可以补救吗？

洗衣工：没办法了，非常抱歉。请下次干洗前告诉我们都有什么污点。

托马斯：好的，我会的。

洗衣工：这是一张会员卡。下次来能打八折。

托马斯：非常感谢。

洗衣工：下次再来，我们将提供最好的服务。

威廉在伦敦的诺丁山经营着一家书店，这天大明星安娜·斯科特来光顾他的书店了。所以他心情很好。现在他正在帮自己的店员买橙汁，可是不幸又幸运地，他把橙汁洒到了安娜的衣服上。他们是怎么解决这件事情的呢？

William runs a book store in Notting Hill in London. One day, the super star, Anna Scott comes to his store, so he is in good mood. Now he is buying a cup of juice for his assistant. But unfortunately and fortunately, he pours some juice on Anna's clothes. How do they solve this matter?

Anna:　　　Oh!

William:　　Oh! Shit!

Anna:　　　Oh, my God! Bugger!

William:　　I'm so sorry. I'm so sorry. Here. Let me…

Anna:　　　Get your hands off!

William:　　I'm really sorry. I…I live just over the street. I have, um, water and soap. You can get cleaned up.

Anna:　　　No, thank you. I just need to get my car back.

William:　　I also have a phone. I'm confident that in five minutes, we could have you spick-and-span and back on the street again. In the non-prostitute sense, obviously.

Anna:　　　All right. Well, what do you mean, "Just over the street"? Give it to me in yards.

William:　　Uh, 18 yards. That's my house there with the blue front door.

安娜：　哦。

威廉：　哦，该死！

安娜：　哦，老天，该死！

威廉：　对不起，我非常抱歉。来，让我……

安娜：　把手拿开！

威廉：　我真的很抱歉，我……我就住在街对面，那有水和肥皂，可以让你弄干净。

安娜：　不，谢谢，我只想找到我的车。

威廉：　我那有电话，我想只要五分钟，就能让你弄干净回到街上了，绝对没有不尊重你的意思。

安娜：　好吧，你说"就在街对面"是多远？具体是多少？

威廉：　大概18码。那扇蓝色的门就是我的家。

shrink [ʃrɪŋk] *vi.* 缩水
fade [feɪd] *vi.* 褪色
stain [steɪn] *n.* 污点
iron ['aɪən] *vt.* 熨烫
sew [səʊ] *vt.* 缝
remedy ['remɪdɪ] *n.* 补救
awfully ['ɔːflɪ] *adv.* 很，非常

疯狂链接 Interlinkage

洗衣标识 LAUNDRY SIGNS

干洗 dry-clean
不可干洗 do not dry-clean
可用各种干洗剂干洗 compatible with any dry-cleaning methods
熨烫 iron
低温熨烫 (100℃) iron on low heat
中温熨烫 (150℃) iron on medium heat
高温熨烫 (200℃) iron on high heat
不可熨烫 do not iron
可漂白 bleach
不可漂白 do not bleach
干衣 dry
无温转笼干燥 tumble dry with no heat
低温转笼干燥 tumble dry with low heat
中温转笼干燥 tumble dry with medium heat

高温转笼干燥 tumble dry with high heat
不可转笼干燥 do not tumble dry
悬挂晾干 line dry
随洗随干 hang dry
平放晾干 dry flat
冷水机洗 wash with cold water
温水机洗 wash with warm water
热水机洗 wash with hot water
只能手洗 hand wash only
不可洗涤 do not wash

Section 7

Thank you. I also like this pencil pants very much!

■ 打扮
Dressing

Wow, you look so beautiful today!

疯狂表达 Expressions

赞扬 Compliment

你看起来又漂亮又时髦。

You look beautiful and stylish.

你这样打扮真好看。

You look good in that dress.

你的衣服很配。

Your clothes match well.

举一反三

How cool you are with this blue silk scarf!　你戴着这条蓝色丝质围巾太酷了!

The colorful tie looked fashionable.　这条花领带看起来很时尚。

You look so handsome with the jacket.　你穿上它显得更帅气了。

The patches on the jeans are fantastic.　牛仔裤上的补丁绣很别致。

批评 Criticism

你这样打扮有点老气。

You look a little bland in that dress.

你的衣服不太适合你。

Your clothes don't suit you.

举一反三

Your sweater is too fancy.　你这件毛衣太花了。

Daniel's trainers are out of fashion.　丹尼尔的运动鞋过时了。

Your hat is strange.　你的帽子很奇怪。

妒忌 Jealousy

我要是穿上那件衣服更漂亮。

If I wear it, I'll be prettier.

举一反三

That coat would look better on me!　那件外套穿在我身上会更合适!

When she went to buy that skirt, it was the last one. She was so lucky!

她去买那件裙子的时候，只有一件了，她真幸运!

羡慕 Envy

要是我有双普拉达的鞋子多好啊!

If only I had Prada shoes!

举一反三

Mum, I'm also very fond of Jane's dress.　妈妈，我也很喜欢简那件连衣裙。

Kate is like a proud princess in that dress.　凯特穿那件衣服真像高傲的公主啊。

讽刺 Sarcasm and Making Fun

他穿上那件衣服像小丑一样!

He looks like a clown in it!

举一反三

You're really pretty in it, just like a nun!　你穿这件衣服太好看了，像修女!

Your hat is special, did you get it from the Middle Ages?　你的帽子真别致，从中世纪买来的吧?

嘲笑 Mocking

你穿得太正式，难道是去参加婚礼吗?

You dress is very formal, are you attending a wedding?

举一反三

You should learn to match. You are so tan, why do you wear white?

要学会搭配，你皮肤很黑，怎么穿白色衣服啊?

It's very fashionable, last year that is!　这件衣服很流行啊，不过是在去年。

Dialogue 1 时髦的铅笔裤 *Fashionable Pencil Pants*

青青今天穿了一条漂亮的铅笔裤，看起来非常时髦。
Qingqing wears a pair of beautiful pencil pants and looks very fashionable.

Li Ming:	Wow, you look so beautiful today!
Qingqing:	Thank you. I also like these pencil pants very much!
Li Ming:	Pencil pants. Are they a kind of skinny jeans?
Qingqing:	Yes, they're also called drainpipe jeans and cigarette pants.
Li Ming:	Very nice!
Qingqing:	The slender cut of this trendy style makes the legs appear longer—an effect which can be emphasized with high heels.

李明：	哇，你今天看起来真漂亮！
青青：	谢谢。我也很喜欢这条铅笔裤。
李明：	铅笔裤？是紧身裤的一种吗？
青青：	是的，它也常被称为烟管裤、吸烟裤。
李明：	非常棒！
青青：	这一时尚风格的剪裁使腿看起来更长，这个效果可以用高跟鞋来加强。

That makes people feel formal, right?

Yes, you're right.

苏珊参加了一个关于职业素养的讲座，学到了不少东西。原来工作当中的衣着也很重要，来看看吧。

Susan attends a lecture about profession. She knows that appearance in the work place is very important. Let's have a look.

Jack: Hi, Susan, how are things going with you recently?

Susan: Not bad. I only have a few classes each day. I just attended a lecture about uniforms this morning. I really learned a lot from the lecture. I didn't know how important uniforms are for a company.

Jack: Can you tell me more about that?

Susan: Sure, Uniform is representative of a company. Different professions will choose different colors for their uniforms.

Jack: Doctors wear white, firefighters wear red, and the police wear blue.

Susan: Right. The professions you mentioned are all in public sectors. They can't change their uniforms. For private companies, they have more choices.

Jack: Why do most people wear uniforms when they are at work?

Susan: So they are always aware that they are representative for their organization. What they do and what they say all represent the company. Most companies require their employees to wear uniforms at work.

Jack: That makes people feel more formal, right?

Susan: Yes, you're right.

杰克： 嗨，苏珊。最近怎么样？

苏珊： 还不错，我们每天的课不多。今天早上我听了一场关于着装的讲座。我在讲座中学到了不少东西。我原来不知道着装对于一个公司的重要性。

杰克： 你能多说点那方面的东西吗？

苏珊： 好啊，制服代表的是公司的形象。不同的行业会选择不同的制服。

杰克： 医生穿白色，消防队员穿红的，警察穿蓝的。

苏珊： 嗯，你所说的都是公关服务单位，他们的制服是不能变的。但对于私企来说，他们会有更多的选择。

杰克： 为什么大家在工作的时候要穿制服啊？

苏珊： 这样可以使他们意识到自己是属于一个团队。他们一言一行都代表了公司的形象。大部分公司都会要求员工穿统一的制服。

杰克： 那样显得比较正式，对吧？

苏珊： 是的，很对。

Dialogue 3 经典影像观摩 The Emulation of Classical Movies

爱德华要带维维安去参加一个晚会，所以他要维维安打扮得体并且要高贵。

Edward is taking Vivian to a party, so he needs her to dress decently and elegantly.

Edward: Vivian, Vivian. Is that a yes?

Vivian: Yes. Yes.

Edward: I'll be gone most of the day. I want you to buy some clothes.

Vivian: You really should think about traveler's check.

Edward: We may be going out evenings, You'll need something to wear.

Vivian: Like what?

Edward: Nothing too flashy or too sexy. Conservative, you understand?

Vivian: Boring!

Edward: Elegant! Any questions?

Vivian: Can I call you "Eddie"?

Edward: Not if you expect me to answer.

Vivian: I would have stayed for two thousand.

Edward: I would have paid four, I'll see you tonight.

Vivian: Baby, I'm going to treat you so nice; you're never gonna wanna let me go!

Edward: Three thousand six days and Vivian, I will let you go.

Vivian: But I'm here now. Ha —ha — three thousand dollars!!

爱德华： 维维安，维维安，同意了吗？

维维安： 好，好。

爱德华: 白天我基本不在，我要你去买些衣服。

维维安: 你应该准备点旅行支票。

爱德华: 我们晚上要出去，你需要些穿的。

维维安: 什么样的?

爱德华: 不要太花哨，太性感。保守点的，知道吗?

维维安: 老气的!

爱德华: 高贵的! 还有问题吗?

维维安: 我可以叫你"爱迪"吗?

爱德华: 想让我理你就别这么叫。

维维安: 我可能只要你2000美元。

爱德华: 我可能会付你4000美元，今晚见。

维维安: 亲爱的，我会好好伺候你的，让你永远也不想让我走!

爱德华: 3000美元六天，维维安，到时我会让你走的。

维维安: 但我已经在这里了。哈—哈— 3000美元!

词句荟萃 Words and Sentences Gathering

pants [pænts] *n.* 裤子

skinny ['skɪnɪ] *adj.* 瘦的；皮包骨的

drainpipe ['dreɪnpaɪp] *n.* 排水管

trendy ['trendɪ] *adj.* 时髦的；流行的

representative [ˌreprɪ'zentətɪv] *n.* 代表

firefighter ['faɪə,faɪtə] *n.* 消防人员

supervisor ['sjuːpəvaɪzə] *n.* 领导，主管

slang [slæŋ] *n.* 俚语

dialect ['daɪəlekt] *n.* 方言

flashy ['flæʃɪ] *adj.* 艳俗的；浮华的

elegant ['elɪgənt] *adj.* 高贵的

鞋帽服饰名称

鞋 shoe

鞋底 sole

鞋后跟 heel

鞋带 lace

鹿皮鞋 moccasin

黑漆皮鞋 patent leather shoes

靴子 boot

便鞋 slippers

凉鞋 sandal

帆布鞋 canvas shoes, rope soled
　　　shoes

木拖鞋 clog

套鞋 galosh, overshoe

手套 glove

领带 tie (美作:necktie)

领结 bow tie

领巾 cravat

便帽 cap

带沿的帽子 hat

圆顶硬礼帽 bowler hat

高顶丝质礼帽 top hat

巴拿马草帽 Panama hat

贝蕾帽 beret

尖顶帽 peaked cap, cap with a visor

宽边草帽 broad-brimmed straw hat

头饰 headdress

Section 8

Well, it was quite a show!

■ 时装秀
Fashion Show

I'll say. I've never seen one as good as that.

疯狂表达 Expressions

秀的风格 Show Style

我觉得主题也很好——有点像30年代的风格。

I thought the theme was good, too—that kind of 30s style.

举一反三

Not very Chinese, though.　但是不怎么像中国的风格。

I think it was supposed to be influenced by Scottish style—you know, the designer was talking about house parties before the war, aristocrats, that sort of decadent sexy style. I'm glad they didn't just do that pre-war Shanghai style, because that's been so common recently.

我觉得它应该受到了苏格兰风格的影响——你知道，设计师在表现战前的社交聚会、贵族那种颓废的性感。我很高兴他们没有做战前旧上海的风格，最近这个风格很泛滥。

秀的场合 Show Occasions

苏格兰人真的是这种打扮吗？看起来很奇怪，尤其是在男士身上。

Do Scottish people really wear that kind of outfit? It looks very strange, especially on the men.

不，他们只在非常正式的场合或者举行历史庆典的时候穿。它像一种礼仪性的旧式服装。像旗袍之类的。

No, they just wear them on very formal occasions or when doing historical things. It's like a ceremonial old-style dress. Like cheongsam or something.

举一反三

Oh, I see. So it's kind of like dressing-up?

哦，明白了。那它就有点盛装打扮的意味了？

Yes, for weddings and balls and so on. Normally we'd wear suits, but Scotsmen can wear kilts on some occasions. Not for business though.

是的，在婚礼、舞会等晚会上穿着的。在某些场合我们通常会穿西装，但是苏格兰男士就能穿苏格兰短裙。但在商业场合就不会。

时尚元素 Fashion Elements

她给我的第一印象很棒，在她的身上总能找到最前沿的时尚元素。

She impressed me so much. I often catch the most fashion forward elements from her.

举一反三

From the picture, we can see her very unique taste in clothes.

看图片可以知道她的着装品味非常与众不同。

Catherine makes bold attempts in makeup, which can not be worn by all women.

凯瑟琳在妆容上有很大胆的尝试，这种化妆并不是所有女性都可以接受的。

Dialogue 1 看一场时装秀 *Enjoying a Fashion Show*

> And the funny things that looked like furry animals.

> Oh, that's why they had the skirts that looked like kilts, and those things half-slung over their shoulders.

乔和林芝一起欣赏了一场很棒的时装秀，两个人都感觉这场秀棒极了。

Joe and Lin Zhi went to a great fashion show. They both thought it was terrific.

Joe: Well, it was quite a show!

Lin Zhi: I'll say. I've never seen one as good as that. That final dress was amazing! I don't even know what the material was.

Joe: Some kind of silk, I think.

Lin Zhi: But the way it was folded—really great. I thought the theme was good, too—that kind of 30s style.

Joe: Not very Chinese, though.

Lin Zhi: I think it was supposed to be influenced by Scottish style—you know, the designer was talking about house parties before the war, aristocrats, that sort of decadent sexy style. I'm glad they didn't just do that pre-war Shanghai style, because that's been so common recently.

Joe: Oh, that's why they had the skirts that looked like kilts, and those things half-slung over their shoulders.

Lin Zhi: And the funny things that looked like furry animals.

Joe: Sporrans!

Lin Zhi: Do Scottish people really wear that kind of outfit? It looks very strange, especially on the men.

Joe: No, they just wear them on very formal occasions or when doing historical things. It's like a ceremonial old-style dress. Like cheongsam or something.

Lin Zhi: Oh, I see. So it's kind of like dressing-up?

Joe: Yes, for weddings and balls and so on. Normally we'd wear suits, but Scotsmen wear kilts on some occasions. Not for business though.

乔：   啊，这场秀真棒！

林芝：   完全同意。我从来没看过这么精彩的秀。压轴的那件衣服真是叫人称奇！我甚至都不知道是什么材料做的。

乔：   我觉得应该是某种丝绸。

林芝：   但是它打褶的方式——真是太棒了。我觉得主题也很好——有点像30年代的风格。

乔：   但是不怎么像中国的风格。

林芝：   我觉得它应该受到了苏格兰风格的影响——你知道，设计师在表现战前的社交聚会、贵族那种颓废的性感。我很高兴他们没有做战前旧上海的风格，最近这个风格很泛滥。

乔：   这就是为什么他们的裙子看起来像苏格兰短裙，肩上还搭着半垂下来的东西。

林芝：   还有那些看起来像皮毛动物的有趣的东西。

乔：   毛皮袋！

林芝：   苏格兰人真的是这种打扮吗？看起来很奇怪，尤其是在男士身上。

乔：   不，他们只在非常正式的场合或者举行历史庆典的时候穿。它像一种礼仪性的旧式服装。像旗袍之类的。

林芝：   哦，明白了。那它就有点盛装打扮的意味？

乔：   是的，在婚礼、舞会等晚会上穿着的。在某些场合我们通常会穿西装，但是苏格兰男士就能穿苏格兰短裙。但是商业场合不会。

Dialogue 2 设计师的影响力 *Power of Stylist*

Do you know Catherine Baba?

I have never heard of her.

杰克和玛丽正在谈论一个著名时装设计师的影响力，让我们一起来看看吧。

Jack and Mary are talking about the power of a famous stylist. Let's read it together.

Jack:　Do you know Catherine Baba?

Mary:　I have never heard of her.

Jack:　She is a famous designer.

Mary:　Really? Very influential?

Jack:　The collections and styles of models are wholly designed by her, isn't she so amazing?

Mary:　In China, there are no designers with very strong influence.

Jack:　She never has fewer than five accessories and she loves furs and colorful overcoats.

Mary:　You can tell that her taste is distinctive from others just by looking at the pictures.

Jack:　Catherine makes bold attempts in makeup, which can not be worn by all women.

Mary:　She impressed me so much. I often catch the most fashion forward elements from her.

杰克：你知道凯瑟琳·芭芭吗？
玛丽：从没听说过这个名字。
杰克：她是一位很出名的设计师。
玛丽：是吗？影响力很大吗？
杰克：整个时装秀的所有搭配和模特造型全部由她设计，难道影响力还不算大吗？
玛丽：在中国，没有造型师能有这样的影响力啊。
杰克：她身上的配饰从来不低于5件。她喜欢皮草和颜色很艳丽的外套。
玛丽：看图片可以知道她的着装品位非常与众不同。
杰克：凯瑟琳在妆容上有很大胆尝试，这种化妆并不是所有女性都可以接受的。
玛丽：她给我的第一印象很棒，在她的身上总能找到最前沿的时尚元素。

安迪和上司马琳达一起去巴黎，刚刚参加了一场漂亮的时装秀。
Andy and her boss, Miranda, just took part in a fashion show in Paris.

Maestro:	How are you? So glad to see you. Thank you for coming. You like the collection?
Miranda:	Absolutely, I think it's the best in years.
Maestro:	This is very important for me. Very, very important.
Miranda:	I'm very happy for you. This is my new Emily.
Maestro:	Hello. How do you do?
Andy:	I'm good. Pleasure. Nice to meet you.
Maestro:	You love the show?

麦斯特：	你好吗？见到你真高兴，谢谢你能过来。你喜欢这场秀吗？
马琳达：	太喜欢了，我觉得这是近年来最好的一场。
麦斯特：	这对我非常重要，非常、非常重要。
马琳达：	我也替你高兴。这是我的新助理。
麦斯特：	哦，你好吗？
安迪：	很好，很荣幸。很高兴见到你。
麦斯特：	喜欢这场秀吗？

词句荟萃 Words and Sentences Gathering

fold [fəʊld] *v.* 折叠

aristocrat ['ærɪstəkræt] *n.* 贵族

decadent ['dekədənt] *adj.* 堕落的，颓败的

kilt [kɪlt] *n.* 苏格兰格呢褶裙

slung [slʌŋ] *v.* （sling的过去式）悬吊

furry ['fɜːrɪ] *adj.* 皮毛的

sporran ['spɒrən] *n.* 苏格兰毛皮皮袋

dressing-up *n.* 盛装

be supposed to 应该，被期望

dress up 穿上特殊服装、打扮、梳理

I'll say.（=I agree.）我同意。

kind of 有点

服装颜色

黑色 black

炭黑 carbon black; charcoal black

暗黑 pitch-black ; pitch-dark

漆黑 dull black

白色 white

象牙白 ivory white

牡蛎白 oyster white

珍珠白 pearl white

玉石白 jade white

银白 silver white

羊毛白 wool white

乳白 milky white

米白 off-white; shell

雪白 snow-white

灰白 greyish white

纯白 pure white

本白 raw white; off white

粉红白 pinkish white

浅紫白 lilac white

灰色 grey

银灰色 silver grey

炭灰色 charcoal grey

烟灰 smoky grey

雾灰 misty grey

黑灰 grey black

金色 gold

银色 silver

青古铜色 bronze; bronzy

驼色 camel; light tan

米色 beige; cream; gray sand

卡其色 khaki

奶油色 cream

豆沙色 cameo brown

水晶色 crystal

荧光色 iridescent

彩虹色 iris; rainbow

棕色 brown

赤褐色 umber; auburn

淡褐色 light brown

咖啡色 coffee

琥珀色 amber

chapter 2

饮食用语一点通

想不想出去吃?
Do you like to eat out?

你想吃点什么?
What would you like?

请给我菜单。
May I have a menu, please?

想要喝点什么?
Can I get you something to drink?

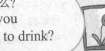

我不喜欢蔬菜煮得太烂，或者浸在汤里。
I don't like overcooked or soggy vegetables.

我最喜欢的食物是比萨。
My favorite food is pizza.

来吧，跟我们一起去喝一杯。
Come on, have a drink with us.

那里有一家熟食店，你喜不喜欢呢?
There is a deli over there, would you like that?

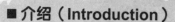

自古以来，饮食就是人类最重要的生活内容之一了。古语云："民以食为天。"可见食物是人类赖以生存的基础。随着生活水平的提高，食品的种类越来越多，吃的讲究也越来越多。那么，关于"吃"的内容、种类、方式以及健康与否的英文表达你知道吗？

Section 1　在家就餐

A： 妈妈，这是你的第三碗米饭了!

　　Mom, it is your third bowl of rice!

B： 我知道，但是我没办法，我的胃总是想要吃更多。

　　I know but I can't help it. My stomach just keeps crying for more and more.

Section 2　外出就餐

A： 你这么解释我就明白了，我只是觉得把剩菜打包会更好。

　　I guess that makes sense. I just think it would make more sense to take the leftovers home.

B： 嗯，如果你愿意，你就打包带回去吧.

　　Well, if you want, you can take the leftovers home.

Section 3　西餐

A： 你的主菜想点什么?

　　What are you going to have for your main course?

B： 我想要一份蔬菜咖喱。

　　I think I might have a dahl.

Section 4　中餐

A： 你吃过中国传统的饺子吗?

　　Have you tried traditional Chinese dumplings yet?

B： 吃过一次了，不过用筷子夹太难了。

　　I tried them once, but they're quite difficult to eat with chopsticks.

Section 5　快餐

A: 您要什么？
　　Can I help you?

B: 3个双层芝士汉堡带走。
　　Three double cheeseburgers to go, please!

Section 6　酒水饮料

A: 先生，要喝点儿什么？
　　What would you like to drink, sir?

B: 喝茶吧。你们这儿都有什么茶？
　　I'd like some tea. What kinds of tea do you have?

Section 7　风味小吃

A: 臭豆腐？是什么东西啊？听起来怪怪的。
　　Stinky tofu? What's that? It sounds strange.

B: 它是一种湖南的小吃，而且它在北京非常流行。你要试试吗？
　　It's a famous Hunan snack. And it's very popular in Beijing. Would you like to try some?

Section 8　饮食偏好

A: 你今晚过来吃晚饭吗？
　　Would you like to come over for dinner tonight?

B: 好啊，但是我得告诉你，我现在开始吃素了，不吃任何肉类食品。
　　Sure, but I have to tell you that I've become a vegetarian. I don't eat any kind of meat.

Section 1

I know but I can't help it. My stomach just keeps crying for more and more.

■ 在家就餐
Dining at Home

Mom, it is your third bowl of rice!

疯狂表达 Expressions

餐前询问 Asking Before Dinner

你吃饭了吗?

Have you eaten yet?

举一反三

What would you like? 你想吃什么?

Would you like ice-cream? 你想吃冰淇淋吗?

It's time for lunch. 该吃午饭了。

Please sit down at the table. 请坐下吃饭吧。

Do you have any plans for dinner tonight? 你想好今天晚饭吃什么了吗?

在家做饭 Making a Meal at Home

你擅长做饭吗?

Are you a good cook?

不太擅长, 不过我是个美食家!

No, but I'm pretty good at eating!

举一反三

Do you like cooking, Julia? 茱莉亚, 你喜欢做饭吗?

I really enjoy it, especially when it ends up tasting good! 我很喜欢, 尤其是做得好吃的时候。

How often do you usually cook? 你一般多久做一次饭?

What kind of dishes do you usually make? 你一般做什么菜？

What's your favorite dish to make? 你最喜欢做什么菜？

I was thinking maybe we could make dinner together tonight. What do you think?
我正在想咱们今晚可以一起做晚饭。你觉得怎么样？

准备原料 Preparing Ingredients

原料都齐全了吗？

Do you have all the ingredients?

我今天早上都买齐了，咱们现在就开始吧！

I bought all the ingredients this morning, so let's get started!

举一反三

What do we need to do first? 第一步先干什么？

First, you need to wash the vegetables and then chop them into little pieces.
首先，先把蔬菜洗干净，切成小块备用。

That needs to be cut into thin strips about 3 centimeters long. 把鸡肉切成三厘米左右的窄条。

Chop the carrots up into small pieces. 把胡萝卜切成小块。

Add the finely chopped onions. 加入切碎的洋葱。

Cut the meat into strips. 把肉切成条。

炒菜 Making Dishes

需要热锅吗？

Should I heat the wok?

行。锅烧热之后，倒一点油，把蔬菜都倒进去翻炒几分钟。

Yes. Once it gets hot, put a little oil in it, add the vegetables and stir-fry them for a few minutes.

举一反三

What about the chicken? 鸡肉怎么办？

It can be stir-fried on its own until it's cooked through. 单独炒熟。

米饭 Rice

米饭呢？

What about the rice?

举一反三

I'll prepare it. Do you prefer white rice or brown rice?
我来弄米饭。你喜欢吃白米还是糙米？

White rice, please! 白米饭吧。

调味品 Seasonings

你准备用什么样的调味品来炒肉呢?

What seasonings are you going to cook the meat with?

举一反三

I am gonna go with salt and sauce!　恩，用盐和酱汁就可以了。

Coconut is a basic ingredient for many curries.　椰子是多种咖喱菜的基本成分。

对菜肴给出好评 Good Evaluation of Dishes

这个菜你觉得怎么样?

What do you think of this dish?

味道好极了。

It's delicious.

举一反三

It's quite good. 这汤很好。

It's just right. 这汤正好。

It's well-seasoned. 调味适当。

It's well-done. 这肉做得很熟。

This beef is just to my taste. 这牛肉正合我的胃口。

对菜肴给出差评 Bad Evaluation of Dishes

这鸡肉做得怎么样?

How do you like the chicken?

这鸡肉做老了。

It's tough.

有点咸了。

It's a little salty.

举一反三

It's soggy.　太烂了。

It's overdone.　做得过老了。

It's underdone.　做得过嫩了。

Fish cooked like this tastes awful. I don't like it.

这样做的鱼真难吃。我不喜欢。

This duck is not quite my taste. I don't care for it.

这鸭肉不合我的胃口，我不爱吃。

疯狂对话 Dialogues

Dialogue 1 ● 烹饪 Cooking

> Really?

> I remember Mom using a lot of pepper for fish.

妈妈不在家，只好由爸爸亲自做饭了，那么很少做饭的爸爸会闹出什么样的笑话呢？

Mum isn't in, so Dad has to cook the meal. And as he seldom cooks, what funny things will Dad do?

Dad: You stay beside me; I'll fry the fish in the oil first.

Jack: Daddy, what seasonings are you going to cook the fish with?

Dad: Er, I am gonna go with salt and sauce!

Jack: What? Are you kidding?

Dad: Is there anything wrong with that?

Jack: I remember Mom using a lot of pepper for fish.

Dad: Really?

Jack: Of course, sure!

Dad: All right, pass me some pepper.

Jack: Oh, Dad, you are burning the fish.

Dad: Oh my god!

Jack: Haha!

爸爸： 我先把鱼炸一下，你站在我旁边。
杰克： 爸爸，你准备用什么样的调味品呢？
爸爸： 恩，用盐和酱汁就可以了。
杰克： 什么？你没有开玩笑吧？
爸爸： 有什么不对吗？
杰克： 我记得妈妈在炸鱼的时候都会放很多的辣椒。
爸爸： 真的吗？
杰克： 当然啦！
爸爸： 好，那就给我一些辣椒吧！
杰克： 噢，爸爸，鱼糊了。
爸爸： 噢，我的天哪！
杰克： 哈哈！

Dialogue 2 健康与节食 Health and Diet

自从妈妈开始健身之后，精神变得特别好，不过胃口似乎也跟着长，这么一来减肥是没希望了，看看杰克给妈妈出了什么好主意？

Since going to the gym, Mum is very cheerful. However, she has a bigger appetite. She has no hope of losing weight. What good ideas does Jack think of?

Jack: Mom, it is your third bowl of rice!

Mom: I know, but I can't help it. My stomach just keeps crying for more and more.

Jack: Why? I've never seen you eat so much before.

Mom: I've been going to the gym these past few days. The exercise makes me hungry all the time.

Jack: So your stomach is the one that actually gets a work-out.

Mom: Don't tease.

Jack: This way you'll probably end up putting on more weight. Will you give up?

Mom: Definitely not. I can feel the results. I'm starting to feel different now.

Jack: Then how are you gonna deal with the problems of gaining extra weight?

Mom: I'm planning on meeting my personal trainer to have the work-out plan fixed.

Jack: Oh, I've got an idea. Why don't you ask Dad to go with you? He really needs to exercise.

Mom: That's a good idea!

杰克：妈妈，这是你的第三碗米饭了！

妈妈：我知道，但是我没办法，我的胃总是想要吃更多。

杰克：为什么？以前我从没见过你吃这么多啊。

妈妈：我最近去健身房。锻炼时我总是觉得很饿。

杰克：你的胃一定做了很多的运动喽！

妈妈：别拿我开心了。

杰克：这样你可能会增肥的。你会放弃吗？

妈妈：当然不了，我觉得非常有效果。现在，我开始感觉到（身体的）变化了。

杰克：那你要怎么处理变胖的问题呢？

妈妈：我在考虑见一下我的私人健身教练，改一下健身计划。

杰克：哦，我有一个主意。干吗不叫爸爸和你一起去呢？他很需要运动。

妈妈：好主意！

朱莉认为做荷包蛋很容易，可事实并非如此。不过，最终朱莉还是成功地做出了荷包蛋，并且在晚饭时吃了她平生第一个鸡蛋。

Julie thought that it was easy to make a poached egg. However, the truth is it's not. Eventually she makes a poached egg successfully. And she eats her first egg of her whole life at dinner.

(In the kitchen)

Julie's friend:　Explain to me why you've never eaten an egg in your whole life.

Julie:　I've had eggs in, like, cakes. Never had an "egg" egg. I was a very willful child. It's simmering.

(The words in Julie's blog: I had this notion, God knows why, that poaching eggs would be simple. But I was deeply wrong.)

Friend:　Immediately and gently push the white over the yolk with a wooden spoon for two to three seconds immediately.

Julie:　Disgusting.

Friend:　Oh, maybe the eggs aren't fresh. Julia says the eggs have to be fresh.

Julie:　They are fresh.

Friend:　Okay. You don't have to bite my head off. I'm just quoting Julia.

(The words in Julie's Blog: It took three of us, crammed into the kitchen over a pot of simmering water. But, eventually, we nailed it.)

Julie:　Hello, welcome.

Julie's husband:　How cute is that?

(The words in Julie's Blog: And I ate my very first egg of my whole life, ever, ever, ever.)
(During the dinner)

Julie:　I thought egg were going to be greasy and slimy, but it tastes like, cheese sauce. Yum. Julia Child, you are so good.

Friend:　Cheers.

Husband:　Cheers. And, may I say, excellent wine?

（在厨房）

朱莉的朋友：　跟我说说，你为啥从来不吃鸡蛋。

朱莉：　我吃含有鸡蛋的食物，比如蛋糕。从没吃过"蛋形的"蛋，我是个很任性的小孩。水开了。

（朱莉的博客：我有个感觉，无来头的，煮荷包蛋会非常简单。但我完全错了。）
朋友：　　　　马上用木勺将蛋白翻面，覆盖在蛋黄上。大概两到三秒，马上。
朱莉：　　　　真恶心。
朋友：　　　　哦，也许是鸡蛋不新鲜，茱莉亚说要新鲜的鸡蛋。
朱莉：　　　　它们很新鲜。
朋友：　　　　好吧，你没必要想揍我，我只是在重复茱莉亚的话。

（朱莉的博客：我们三个挤在厨房里，凑在一锅沸腾的水面前。但是，最终，我们搞定了。）
朱莉：　　　　好啊，欢迎。
朱莉的丈夫：　这个真可爱啊！

（朱莉的博客：我吃了我这辈子的第一个鸡蛋。）
（晚饭期间）
朱莉：　　　　我本以为鸡蛋会又腻又滑，可是它吃起来就像奶酪酱汁美味。朱莉•查尔德，你
　　　　　　　真棒！
朋友：　　　　干杯！
丈夫：　　　　干杯！而且，我得说，美酒啊！

词句荟萃 Words and Sentences Gathering

fry [fraɪ] *vt.* 油煎，油炸

ingredient [ɪn'gri:djənt] *n.* 原料

chop [tʃɒp] *v.* 切块

wok [wɒk] *n.* 炒锅；炒勺

stir-fry ['stɜ:'fraɪ] *v.* 翻炒

coconut ['kəukənʌt] *n.* 椰子

curry ['kʌrɪ] *n.* 咖喱粉；咖喱饭菜

seasoning ['si:zənɪŋ] *n.* 调味品；佐料

sauce [sɔ:s] *n.* 调味品，酱汁

pepper ['pepə] *n.* 辣椒

diet ['daɪət] *n.* 饮食；节食 *v.* 节食

overweight ['əuvəweɪt] *n.* 超重 *adj.* 肥胖的

obese [əu'bi:s] *adj.* 肥胖的，肥大的

poach [pəutʃ] *v.* 水煮

willful ['wɪlfl] *adj.* 任性的，故意的

blog [blɒg] *n.* 博客

notion ['nəuʃn] *n.* 观念，看法

yolk [jəuk] *n.* 蛋黄

disgusting [dɪs'gʌstɪŋ] *adj.* 令人讨厌的

quote [kwəut] *v.* 引用

cram [kræm] *v.* 塞，挤

simmer ['sɪmə] *v.* 慢煮，文火煨

nail [neɪl] *v.* 钉住，用钉子钉

cute [kju:t] *adj.* 可爱的

be good at 擅长

cook through 炒熟

常见调料、炊具及餐具名称

调味品 dressing; flavor; seasoning

盐 salt

酱油 soy sauce

花椒 wild pepper

味精 monosodium glutamate

大蒜 garlic

生姜 ginger

小葱 shallot

青葱 green onion

洋葱 onion

青椒 green pepper

糖 sugar

醋 vinegar

干辣椒 chilli

咖喱 curry

猪油 lard

花生油 peanut oil

番茄酱 tomato ketchup

奶酪 cheese

人造黄油 margarine

蛋黄酱 mayonnaise

黄油 butter

八角，茴香 star anise

芥末 wasabi (注：mustard是芥末的学名，在美国日常口语中只用wasabi)

色拉油 salad oil

煤气灶 gas cooker

烧水壶 kettle

炖锅 sauce pan

炒锅 frying pan

高压锅 pressure cooker

烤箱 oven

碗 bowl

盘子 plate; dish

叉子 fork

勺子 spoon

餐刀 knife

筷子 chopsticks

Section 2

I guess that makes sense. I just think it would make more sense to take the leftovers home.

■ 外出就餐
Eating Out

Well, if you want, you can take the leftovers home.

疯狂表达 Expressions

预定 Making a Reservation

您好，这是公园餐厅。我可以为您服务吗?

Hello, this is the Park Restaurant. May I help you?

我想订餐。今天晚上6点，8个人的位子。

I'd like to make a reservation for eight people at six o'clock tonight.

举一反三

May I book a table? 我想预订张桌子可以吗?

I'd like to reserve a table for eight. 我想订8个人的餐。

What time, sir? 什么时间，先生?

Could we have a table close to the band? 我们能不能要张离乐队近一点儿的桌子?

I'm sorry. They're all booked up tonight. 对不起，今天晚上的都订满了。

I'm sorry. We are quite full tonight. 很抱歉，我们今晚的预约已经满了。

I'm sorry; all the tables are booked tonight. 很抱歉，今晚所有的桌子都已经预订出去了。

What time can we make a reservation? 可以预订几点的?

Till how late are you open? 你们营业到几点?

How many in your group? 请问您几位?

I'm sorry, but I have to cancel my reservation. 对不起, 我想取消订餐。

去哪吃饭 Where to Eat

想不想出去吃呢?

Do you like to go out to eat?

举一反三

Do you have anywhere in mind?　你想好去哪儿吃了吗?

There is a Deli over there, would you like that?　那里有一家 Deli (餐厅), 你喜不喜欢呢?

Is there a Mexican restaurant around here?　这附近有墨西哥餐馆吗?

Where is the closest Mexican restaurant?　最近的墨西哥餐馆在哪儿?

Are there any restaurants still open near here?　这附近有没有还在营业的饭馆?

推荐餐馆 Recommending a Restaurant

您推荐哪家饭馆?

Which restaurant would you recommend?

举一反三

Could you recommend a good restaurant near here?　这附近您能推荐家好吃的饭馆吗?

We could try that new French place.　我们可以去试试那家新开的法国餐厅。

侍者询问 Waiter Asking

想要喝什么?

What would you like to drink?

想现在点菜吗?

Do you want to order now?

举一反三

Can I get you something to drink?　要来点喝的吗?

Are you ready to order or need a minute?　你们准备好了吗? 还是要再等一会?

Just a minute.　请等一下。

Wait a few more minutes.　再等一会。

OK. I'll be back.　好, 那我等下再来。

Would you like something to drink before dinner?　晚餐前想喝些什么吗?

How would you like your steak?　你的牛排要如何烹调?

Well done (medium/rare), please.　全熟(五分熟/一分熟)。

点餐 Ordering Dishes

请给我菜单。

May I have a menu, please?

是否有中文菜单?

Do you have a menu in Chinese?

我可以点餐了吗?

May I order, please?

举一反三

What is the house specialty?　餐厅最特别的菜式是什么?

Do you have today's special?　餐厅有今日特餐吗?

Can I have the same dish as his?　我可以点与他相同的餐吗?

I'd like appetizers and a meat (fish) dish.　我想要一份开胃菜与肉餐(鱼餐)。

特殊要求 Special Requirements

我必须避免含油脂的食物。

I have to avoid fatty food.

举一反三

I have to avoid food with salt.　我必须避免含盐分的食物。

I have to avoid food with sugar.　我必须避免含糖分的食物。

Do you have any vegetarian dishes?　餐厅是否有供应素食餐?

结账 Paying the Bill

这顿饭多少钱?

How much is the dinner?

服务员,买单。

Waiter, give me the bill.

举一反三

Do you accept credit cards?　可以用信用卡吗?

Do you want separate checks?　你们要不要分开付账?

Together.　一起付。

One check.　一起付。

Could we have separate checks?　我们可以分别付款吗?

Could we pay separately?　我们可以各付各的吗?

We'd like to have separate checks.　我们想分别付款。

Dialogue 1 点菜 Order

OK, shrimp rolls. Do you want anything else?

We will have this one first then order something else later.

杰克和汤姆中午放学后到餐馆吃午餐，两个小家伙点了看起来不错的虾球。

After school in the morning, Jack went to a restaurant to have dinner with Tom. The two boys ordered shrimp rolls that looked good.

Jack:	Tom, we are in the restaurant now.
Waitress:	May I take your order?
Jack:	I'd like to see the menu, please.
Waitress:	OK, here you are.
Jack:	Thanks. I am starving. Tom, what are you getting?
Tom:	I have no idea. First time here.
Jack:	Let me see…What's this, shrimp rolls?
Waitress:	They're rice rolls with fried shrimp inside.
Tom:	Twenty-five yuan is a little expensive.
Waitress:	There are twenty rolls in a bowl. You can get another bowl for free if there aren't enough rolls.
Jack:	Sounds nice. We will take this, two bowls of shrimp rolls.
Waitress:	OK, shrimp rolls. Do you want anything else?
Jack:	We will have this one first then order something else later.
Waitress:	OK, wait a moment please.

杰克： 汤姆，我们到了饭馆了。

服务员： 可以点菜了吗?

杰克： 我想看看菜单。

服务员： 好的，给你菜单。

杰克： 谢谢。我快饿死了。汤姆，你吃点什么?

汤姆： 不知道，我是第一次来这儿。

杰克： 让我看看……这是什么，虾球?

服务员： 哦，就是面卷里包着炸虾。

汤姆： 25块钱有点贵了吧。

服务员： 一碗里有20个。如果数量不够的话，还可以免费送一碗。

杰克： 听上去不错。我们就要这个，两碗虾球。

服务员： 好的，虾球。还要点别的什么吗?

杰克： 我们先要这个，一会儿再点别的。

服务员： 好的。请等一下。

Dialogue 2 他们带走剩菜吗?
Do They Take Their Leftovers Home?

弗兰克和苏珊在中国一家餐馆吃饭，弗兰克很疑惑大家是否把剩菜打包回家。如果不，就太浪费了。不过最后他也决定入乡随俗了。

Frank and Susan are dining in a Chinese restaurant. Frank is curious about whether or not Chinese people take leftovers home. If not, it's an awful waste. However, in the end, he decides "When in Rome, do as the Romans do."

Frank: Susan, can I ask you a question?

Susan: Sure, what is it?

Frank: I was just wondering if most Chinese people take their leftover food home from a restaurant.

Susan: In most cities in China, doggie bags are quite uncommon.

Frank: What happened to all the leftover food?

Susan: It usually goes to the dump.

Frank: That seems like an awful waste! Why don't people order fewer dishes so that they don't have to throw so much away at the end of the meal?

Susan: Ordering a lot of food at restaurants is just a tradition in China. You know, in the past, people could not afford to eat out like they can today.

Frank: I guess that makes sense. I just think it would make more sense to take the leftovers home.

Susan: Well, if you want, you can take the leftovers home.

Frank: No, that's OK. You know what they say: when in Rome…

弗兰克: 苏珊，我可以问你一个问题吗？

苏珊: 当然可以，什么事？

弗兰克: 我想知道中国人在饭馆吃完饭之后，会不会把没吃完的东西打包带回家。

苏珊: 中国大多数城市的人都很少打包的。

弗兰克: 那剩饭剩菜怎么处理呢？

苏珊: 一般就倒掉了。

弗兰克: 那可太浪费了！大家为什么不少点一些菜呢，这样就可以避免吃完饭后剩下太多了。

苏珊: 在饭馆吃饭点很多菜是中国人的一个传统习惯。要知道，过去人们可不像现在这样什么都能吃得起。

弗兰克: 你这么解释我就明白了。我只是觉得把剩菜打包会更好。

苏珊: 嗯，如果你愿意，你就打包带回去吧。

弗兰克: 不用，没关系的。你知道俗话说得好：入乡……（随俗）。

今天是杰克和凯特结婚周年纪念日，杰克带凯特去高级餐馆吃饭来庆祝他们的结婚周年纪念日。

Today is the wedding anniversary of Jack and Kate. And Jack takes Kate to dinner at a superior restaurant to celebrate their anniversary.

Kate: Jack, can we afford this place?

Jack: I'm taking my baby out for our anniversary, damn the costs.

Waiter: May I take your order now?

Jack: We'll have the terrine of quail breast with shitake mushrooms, to start. Then the veal medallions in raspberry truffle sauce and the sea scallops with pureed artichoke hearts.

Waiter: Very good, sir. And may I say those are excellent selections?

Jack: You may. Also, we'll have a bottle of Lafitte '82.

Kate: Honey, that's an $800 bottle of wine.

Jack: We'll just have some red wine by the glass.

凯特：杰克，这里不会太贵吧？

杰克：我们庆祝纪念日，管它贵不贵。

侍者：来点什么？

杰克：先来一份砂锅鹌鹑肉煮蘑菇，然后薄片小牛肉淋覆盆子酱汁，然后鲍鱼煮朝鲜蓟花苞。

侍者：很好，先生。您真会点菜。

杰克：过奖，再来一瓶82年的拉非特。

凯特：亲爱的，一瓶要800美元呢。

杰克：那就两杯红葡萄酒吧。

deli ['delɪ] *n.* 熟食店；餐厅

buffet ['bʌfɪt] *n.* 自助餐厅

menu ['menju:] *n.* 菜单

aperitif [ə,perɪ'ti:f] *n.* （餐前）开胃酒

local ['ləʊkl] *adj.* 当地的

specialty ['speʃəltɪ] *n.* 特色菜；特餐

appetizer ['æpɪtaɪzə] *n.* 开胃菜

avoid [ə'vɔɪd] *v.* 避免

steak [steɪk] *n.* 牛排

shrimp [ʃrɪmp] *n.* 虾

leftover ['left,əʊvə] *n.* 剩菜

uncommon [ʌn'kɒmən] *adj.* 不寻常；不平常

dump [dʌmp] *n.* 垃圾堆

doggie bag 打包袋

anniversary [,ænɪ'vɜ:sərɪ] *n.* 周年纪念，周年纪念日

quail [kweɪl] *n.* 鹌鹑

breast [brest] *n.* 胸部，鸡胸肉

mushroom ['mʌʃrʊm] *n.* 蘑菇

veal [vi:l] *n.* 小牛肉

medallion [mɪ'dæljən] *n.* 圆形装饰，圆形浮雕

raspberry ['rɑːzbərɪ] *n.* 悬钩子树，山莓树

truffle ['trʌfl] *n.* 块菌

scallop ['skɒləp] *n.* 扇贝，干贝

puree ['pjʊəreɪ] *n.* 酱，泥 *v.* 煮成浓汤，做成酱

artichoke ['ɑːtɪtʃəʊk] *n.* 朝鲜蓟

make sense　……有意义。

May I...?　我可以……吗?

Could you recommend some ...?　你能为我推荐……吗?

...be impressed with/by/that...　对……印象深刻。

常见菜名翻译

脆皮炸子鸡 fried chicken

红烧石岐项鸽 roast pigeon

豉油皇乳鸽 pigeon with soy sauce

姜葱油淋鸡 green onion chicken

北京片皮鸭 Peking duck

酸甜明炉烧鸭 roast duck

柠檬鸡球 lemon chicken

西芹腰果鸡球 vegetable cashew
     chicken

咖喱鸡 curry chicken

豉汁炒鸡球 chicken with black bean
     sauce

四川炒鸡球 Szechuan chicken

菜远鸡球 chicken with tender green

宫保鸡丁 kungpao chicken

豉汁黄毛鸡 chicken with soy sauce

咕噜鸡 sweet & sour chicken

八珍发菜扒鸭 combination duck

子罗炒鸡片 ginger & pineapple
     chicken

游龙戏凤 chicken, shrimp, squid with
     mixed vegetable

龙凤琵琶豆腐 egg, chicken, shrimp,
     steam tofu

酸甜咕噜肉 sweet & sour pork

菜远炒排骨 sautéed spare ribs with
     green vegetable

豉椒排骨 steamed spareribs

凉瓜排骨 bitter melon spareribs

京都骨 Peking spareribs

椒盐排骨 pepper salt spareribs

豉椒焖排骨 spareribs with black bean,
     pepper

菜远炒牛肉 broccoli beef

凉瓜炒牛肉 bitter melon beef

黑椒牛仔骨 black pepper short rib

椒盐牛仔骨 pepper salt short rib

中式牛柳 Chinese style beef

四川牛肉 Szechuan beef

干煸牛柳丝 string beef

柠檬牛肉 lemon beef

麻婆豆腐 Mar-boh tofu

Section 3

I think I might have a dahl.

■ 西餐
Western Food

What are you going to have for your main course?

疯狂表达 Expressions

招呼顾客 Greeting

先生，女士，晚上好。欢迎来到柏丽餐厅，有什么可以帮到您?

Good evening, Madam and Sir. Welcome to the Parkland restaurant. May I help you?

举一反三

Can we sit here by the window?　我们可以坐到靠窗的位吗?

I'm sorry, Sir. The table has been reserved. There is a sign on it. I'll seat you at another table.　不好意思，先生，这个座位已经被预订了，这里有标志。我给您找另一张桌子吧。

Would you like to sit in the smoking or no-smoking area?　你们喜欢坐吸烟区还是无烟区呢?

Follow me, please. I'll seat you. How about this table?

请跟我来。我给你们找位子。这张桌子可以吗?

询问预订 Asking about Reservation

晚上好，先生们，请问您有预定吗?

Good evening, gentlemen. Have you made a reservation?

没有。

No. I'm afraid we haven't.

没关系，先生，是两位吗? 请这边走。

Never mind, sir. A table for two? This way, please.

Do you have a reservation? 请问您有预订吗?

Yes, I reserved a table for two yesterday afternoon, in the name of Mr. White.
是的，我昨天下午以怀特先生的名义预订了一张两人桌。

Just a moment, please. I'll have a look at our reservation book.
请稍候，我查一下我们的预订记录。

Oh, yes, Mr. White. We're expecting you. We have a window seat reserved for you.
This way, please. Will this table be fine?
哦，是的，怀特先生，我们恭候您的光临。我们给您留了一张靠窗的位子，请这边走。这张桌子
可以吗?

点食物 Ordering Food

我要一个60美元的晚餐包括酒水。

I'd like to have a dinner for sixty dollars including drinks.

我要一份牛排。

I want a steak. / I'd like a steak.

举一反三

How would you like it?

How would you like it done?

How would you like your steak cooked?

How would you like your steak prepared? 牛排要几成熟的?

Well-done, please. 全熟。

Rare. 一成熟。

Medium. 适中的，五成熟。

Can you make it mild? 可以做得清淡些吗?

点饮料 Ordering Drinks

我要红葡萄酒。

I'd like some red wine, please.

您用早餐吗?

Are you having breakfast?

不，只要一杯咖啡。

No, I'll just have a cup of coffee.

举一反三

Would you like some coffee?

Would you care for some coffee? 来杯咖啡怎么样?

That would be great. 那太好了。

Is coffee included with this meal? 套餐里包括咖啡吗?

I'd like a cup of coffee, please. 请给我来一杯咖啡。

早餐 Breakfast

早上好，小姐。您准备好点菜了吗？您要吃早餐自助餐还是散点呢？

Good Morning, Madam. Are you ready to order? Would you have the breakfast buffet or order a la carte?

散点吧。我会从菜单上挑选餐点。

A la carte, please. I'll choose something from the menu.

举一反三

May I take your order now, madam?　现在您要点菜了吗，小姐？

Yes. I'd like to have the continental breakfast. 是的，我要欧式早餐。

I'd like to have a full breakfast.　我想要美式早餐。

Certainly, Madam. Would you like toast, breakfast rolls, croissants or Danish pastries?

好的，小姐。你要吐司、早餐软包、牛角包还是丹麦酥皮饼？

Croissants, please.　牛角包。

Would you like sausage, bacon or ham?　您要香肠、熏肉还是火腿？

How would you like your eggs, Sir?　您喜欢鸡蛋怎么做？

Two fried eggs, fried over.　两个鸡蛋，两面煎。

What kind of fruit juice would you like?　您喜欢哪一种果汁呢？

Pineapple juice.　菠萝汁。

Coffee or tea, madam?　您要咖啡还是茶，小姐？

Black coffee, please.　纯咖啡。

So that's Croissants, pineapple juice and black coffee.　您点的是牛角包、菠萝汁和纯咖啡。

午餐 Lunch

中午好，先生们。欢迎来到皇朝西餐厅。请问总共有几位呢？

Good afternoon, gentlemen. Welcome to Royalty Western Restaurant. How many people are there in your group?

三位。

Three.

我可以点中午套餐吗？

Yes. Can I order a set lunch?

当然可以。

Certainly.

举一反三

How do you want your set lunch of, sir?　先生，您想要什么中午套餐？

I'll have cream of white bean soup, grilled sirloin steak with gravy, a fresh fruit plate, and hot coffee.

我要白豆汤、西冷牛扒配烧汁、鲜水果碟和热咖啡。

Shall I bring your coffee now or later?　您的咖啡要现在上还是饭后上呢？

Later.　稍候再上。

Would you like anything else?　请问您还要其他东西吗？

No. That is all.　不了，就这些。

Your lunch will be ready in 10 minutes.　10分钟后我们会把你点的午餐做好。

Good. Thank you.　非常好。谢谢。

You are welcome. It's our pleasure.　不用谢。能为您服务是我们的荣幸。

晚餐 Supper

先生，女士，晚上好。有什么可以帮到你们？

Good evening, Madam and Sir. May I help you?

是的。

Yes, please.

举一反三

Would you like to have a drink first?　先来点喝的怎么样？

Yes. We'll have two beers.　好的，先来两杯啤酒吧。

Two beers. Certainly, Sir.　好的，两杯啤酒，先生。

Can we have the menu, please?　请拿菜单给我们。

Here's the menu, Sir. I'll be back to take your order in a minute.　菜单在这里，先生。
我稍后再来取您的点菜单。

衣着规定 Dress Code

衣着上有什么规定吗？

What is your dress code?

举一反三

Are we required to wear a jacket and tie?　我们必须得穿礼服吗？

Should I wear a jacket and tie?　我必须穿礼服吗？

疯狂对话 Dialogues

Dialogue 1　点菜的学问 *Knowledge of Ordering*

> **What are you going to have for your main course?**

> **I think I might have a dahl.**

凯特和杰克打算去吃西餐，餐厅里人很多，幸运的是，两个人坐上了最后一张两人桌。

Kate and Jack want to have Western food. It's very crowded in the canteen. Fortunately, they get the last available table for two.

Jack: We were really lucky. We got the last available table for two!

Kate: Yeah, I'm glad that we didn't have to wait long. I'm starving!

Jack: Let's take a look at the menu so that we can order. Do you want to choose an appetizer?

Kate: What would you rather have, samosas or poppadoms?

Jack: I heard that one of their specialties is the samosa.

Kate: Well, let's get a plate of those then.

Jack: Sounds good. What are you going to have for your main course?

Kate: I think I might have a dahl.

Jack: What's in a dahl?

Kate: It's got chickpeas and vegetables in a spicy curry sauce with rice.

Jack: That sounds nice. Do you want to share some kebabs as well?

Kate: OK. How about some lamb kebabs?

Jack: Those are my favourite. Do you want to have some wine or beer?

Kate: I think I'll have a beer.

Jack: OK, shall I flag down the waitress?

Kate: I wouldn't. That might seem a bit rude.

Jack: You're right.

杰克:	咱们真走运。能坐上最后一张两人桌!
凯特:	是啊,不用等那么长时间,我真开心。饿死了。
杰克:	先看看菜单吧,这样才好点菜。你想不想选个开胃菜?
凯特:	你想吃哪个?萨摩萨三角饺还是印式炸面包片?
杰克:	我听说他们的招牌菜是萨摩萨。
凯特:	哦,那咱们点一份好了。
杰克:	听起来不错。你的主菜想点什么?
凯特:	我想要一份蔬菜咖喱。
杰克:	里面都有什么?
凯特:	有用咖喱辣酱煮的鹰嘴豆和一些蔬菜,再配上一份米饭。
杰克:	听起来很好吃。你想不想跟我分一点烤肉串?
凯特:	行。羊肉怎么样?
杰克:	我最爱吃羊肉了。你想不想喝点葡萄酒或者啤酒?
凯特:	我想喝啤酒。
杰克:	好了,咱们可以招手叫服务员过来吗?
凯特:	我觉得不好。那样做看起来有点不礼貌。
杰克:	你说得对。

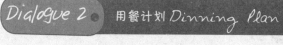

Dialogue 2 · 用餐计划 Dinning Plan

Honey, which hand should I use to hold the fork?

Left for the fork and right for the knife. Just remember that the stronger one is for the knife.

威廉和雪莉今天晚上要去西餐厅吃饭，于是两个人整个下午都在忙着做准备，尤其是威廉认真地学起了西餐的餐桌礼仪，来看看效果怎么样吧。

William and Shirley will have dinner in a Western restaurant this evening, so they are busy making preparations the whole afternoon, especially once William starts to learn Western table manners. Let's have a look at what happens.

William:　Honey, which hand should I use to hold the fork?

Shirley:　Left for the fork and right for the knife. Just remember that the stronger one is for knife.

William:　Got it. It's so troublesome having Western food. I've been learning the table manners for hours but still can't really remember it.

Shirley:　I know. Rather than eating, having Western food is more about western culture.

William:　Yeah. Which restaurant are we going to tonight?

Shirley:　I reserved a table for us at a newly opened Western restaurant downtown. The environment there was really pleasant.

William:　Fine. I trust your taste. Oh, what should I wear?

Shirley:　You should put on the black suit I bought for you last week.

William:　OK. I'm going to the bank to withdraw some money. How much do we need?

Shirley:　There is no need to do that. I think the restaurant accepts credit cards.

William:　I'll take care of the order.

Shirley:　OK then. Well, 50 Yuan for appetizer, 200 Yuan for dinner and 200 Yuan for wine. Anything else?

William:　Don't forget about the dessert.

Shirley:　OK, then 50 Yuan for dessert.

威廉：　亲爱的，应该用哪只手来拿叉子啊？

雪莉：　左手拿叉右手拿刀。只要记住强壮点的那只手拿刀就可以了。

威廉：　知道了。吃西餐可真是麻烦啊。我学习这些餐桌礼仪都用了好几个小时了，可还是没能真正记住。

雪莉：　当然。吃西餐可不只是吃，还包含了很多西方文化呢。

威廉：　是啊。我们今晚去哪家餐厅呢？

雪莉：　我已经在市区新开的一家西餐厅预订好位置了。那里的环境很不错。

威廉：　不错。我相信你的眼光。哦，我该穿什么衣服呢？

雪莉：　你就穿我上周给你买的那套黑色西服吧。

威廉：　好的。我去银行取点钱。我们大概需要多少钱？

雪莉：　没有必要。我想餐厅一定可以刷信用卡的。

威廉：　我来负责点餐。

雪莉：　那好吧。这样，开胃菜50元，200元正餐，还有200元的酒。还有别的吗？

威廉：　别忘了甜点。

雪莉：　行，再加50元的甜点。

泰德的妻子真的离他而去了，第二天早晨，泰德·克莱默和衣而卧睡在床上，儿子比利叫醒了他，他必须自己做早餐了，现在他们正在厨房里。

Ted's wife leaves him. The next morning Ted krammer, still fully dressed, is asleep in the bed. His son Billy wakes him up. He has to make breakfast for himself. They are in the kitchen.

Ted: Come on, now you and I are gonna have some breakfast! Okay? Just you and me. OK. What do you want for breakfast?

Billy: Some French toast.

Ted: French toast. You want French toast, you got it. Put up a little water for Daddy to have some coffee. And we got how many eggs? Two for you and two for me. We got milk. We got butter. We got $5. I got $5. Here, you sit here. Okay, can you be my number one helper? Okay, now Watch this. One hand. Here we go. Did you know that all the best chefs are men? Isn't this terrific? This is terrific. We gotta do this more often.

Billy: You dropped some shell in there.

Ted: That's all right. Makes it crunchier. You like your French toast crunchy, don't you? All right, tell you what, why don't you beat them, and I'll get everything else going. What time will you be going to school?

Billy: 8:30.

Ted: We gotta get the show on the road. I gotta shower, shave and shampoo my hair. And I got people to see. And Daddy's gotta bring home the bacon. I want to bring home the bacon but he's gotta cook it. We're having a good time! Now where does Mommy keep the...?

Billy: In the stove.

Ted: The pan. The stove. Okay. First, we need a nice fire. No, no, you're not doing it right. Come on, come on. You're not doing it right. Look, you gotta do it fast. The wrist, the wrist. So the gucky part gets dissolved. Then you take the bread, and we.... we.... we.... We fold. That's what we do. We fold the French toast.

Billy: I think you forgot the milk.

Ted: I didn't. Milk comes last. When you're having a good time you forget the most important thing. Right? I just wanted to see if you're paying attention. That's fun, isn't it? When's the last time Mommy let you in the kitchen?

Billy: I don't like it in pieces.

Ted: The French toast tastes the same whether it's in pieces or whole. I mean, bread is bread. You know? Besides, what you don't know is that French toast is always folded. You go into best restaurants anywhere in the world, and you see folded French toast. You get more bites that way. Right? And while that's going, Daddy's gonna make a little bit coffee for himself. You're having a good time? All right, we're having a good time. I don't remember the last time I ever had such a good time. Daddy's gonna make himself coffee.

Billy: That's too much coffee!

Ted: No, no, I like it strong. Mommy always makes it too weak.

Billy: Can I have some orange juice?

Ted: Orange juice? Right. One OJ coming up for the kid.

Billy: Daddy, it's burning! It's burning!

Ted: What?

Billy: It's burning!

泰德： 来吧，现在你和我要一起吃早餐，知道吗？就我们两个，你想吃什么？

比利： 法国土司。

泰德： 法国吐司。要法国土司就给你做法国土司，煮点水给爹地泡咖啡，我们要几个鸡蛋？一人两个，我们有牛奶，还有奶油，我们有五块钱，我有五块钱，你坐在这里，好，你可以当我的首席助手吗？好。现在看好，用一只手，就像这样。你知道最出色的大厨都是男的吗？这不是很棒吗？我们要常常这样。

比利： 有一些蛋壳掉进去了。

泰德： 没关系，吃起来脆脆的，你喜欢吃脆的法国土司吧？你把蛋打一下，我来做其他的事。你几点到学校？

比利： 八点半。

泰德： 那我们得快点，我得洗澡、刮胡子、洗头，我要见客户，爹地还要赚钱开饭，我要赚钱开饭还要把饭煮熟。我们很高兴吧！妈咪把平底锅放在……？

比利： 在烤箱里。

泰德： 锅在烤箱里。好的。首先要点火，不对，不对，不是那样，这样不对，你要打得很快，看到没？用腕力，腕力，这样才会打散。然后拿土司，然后……然后我们……折起来，就这样，我们把土司折起来。

比利： 你忘了加牛奶。

泰德： 我没忘，牛奶最后加。高兴的时候就会忘记最重要的事。是吧？我是想看你有没有注意到。很好玩吧？妈咪上次让你进厨房是什么时候？

比利： 我不喜欢吃碎的。

泰德： 碎的和整片吃起来味道一样，面包就是面包，还有，法国土司都是折起来的，你到全世界最好的餐厅去看，法国土司都是折起来的，这样吃起来比较多对吧？同时，爹地要泡一些咖啡。好玩吗？我不记得上回这么高兴是什么时候了。我要泡点咖啡。

比利： 太多了！

泰德： 不会，我喜欢喝浓一点，妈咪泡得太淡。

比利： 我可以喝橙汁吗？

泰德： 橙汁，好，马上来。

比利： 爹地，烧焦了！

泰德：　什么？
比利：　锅烧焦了！

词句荟萃 Words and Sentences Gathering

dessert [dɪ'sɜːt] *n.* 甜品
kebab [kɪ'bæb] *n.* 烤肉串
appetizer ['æpɪtaɪzə] *n.* 开胃菜
troublesome ['trʌbəlsəm] *adj.* 麻烦的
manners ['mænəz] *n.* 礼仪
downtown [ˌdaʊn'taʊn] *adv.* 在市区
crumple ['krʌmpl] *vi.* 弄皱
budget ['bʌdʒɪt] *n.* 预算
table for two　两人桌
main course　主菜

疯狂链接 Interlinkage

关于西方食品词汇

冰淇淋 ice cream
薯条 potato chip
三明治 sandwich
比萨 pizza
热狗 hotdog
巧克力 chocolate
奶酪 cheese
牛排 steak
熏肉 bacon
意大利面 pasta
寿司 sushi
面条 noodle

沙拉 salad
煎饼 pancake
苹果派 apple pie
芝士蛋糕 cheese cake
炸薯条 French fries
汉堡 hamburger
蔬菜沙拉 green salad
通心粉 macaroni
松饼 muffin
洋葱汤 onion soup
牛尾汤 oxtail soup
浓汤 potage

Section 4

I tried them once, but they're quite difficult to eat with chopsticks.

■ 中餐
Chinese Food

Have you tried traditional Chinese dumplings yet?

疯狂表达 Expressions

主食 Staple Food

相对炒饭，我更喜欢白饭。

I prefer white rice to fried rice.

举一反三

I'm a northerner and I like wheat-based food.　我是北方人，爱吃面食。

Do you like eating dumplings?　你喜欢吃饺子吗?

Chinese noodles are great!　中式面条很好吃!

酒水饮料 Drinks and Beverage

想喝什么饮料啊?

Any drinks?

我们带了啤酒，我有它就行了。

We've got beer. That's enough for me.

To drink?　喝点什么啊?

Water will do.　水就可以了。

I want some alcohol.　想喝点酒。

I want some juice.　我想喝果汁。

I'd like some milk.　我要牛奶。

汤 Soup

晚餐做什么汤?

What's the soup for this evening?

酸辣汤。

Hot and Sour.

举一反三

I like egg drop soup.　我喜欢蛋花汤。

I want to have some wonton soup.　我想喝点馄饨汤。

菜 Dishes

我喜欢中国菜。

I like Chinese dishes.

举一反三

I'll have the Almond Chicken.　我要杏仁鸡片。

I'll have the Kung Pao Shrimp.　我吃宫保虾。

What's your favorite Chinese dish?　你最喜欢中餐的哪道菜?

Like most foreigners, I really like Sweet and Sour Pork and Kung Pao Chicken. I eat them almost every day.

和大多数外国人一样，我喜欢吃酸甜咕噜肉和宫保鸡丁。我几乎天天都吃。

传统食物 Traditional Food

你吃过中国传统的饺子吗?

Have you tried traditional Chinese dumplings yet?

吃过一次了，不过用筷子夹太难了。

I tried them once, but they are quite difficult to eat with chopsticks.

举一反三

If you want, I can introduce you to some typical Chinese dishes.　如果你愿意，我可以向你介绍几种经典菜式。

That would be great. I really want to try some authentic Chinese food, not just the food that foreigners like to eat!

那可太好了，我真的想吃正宗的中餐，而不是外国人喜欢吃的那种!

个人口味 Personal Taste

菜里不要放味精，少放辣椒。

No MSG and only a little pepper, please.

太好了。我还要辣的。

Great, I want it spicy.

举一反三

You wanna try the Chinese rice pudding?　你想尝尝八宝粥吗?

Sure. Is it sweet?　当然了。它是甜的吗?

Yes, of course. But I think they can make you a salty one, too.

是啊，当然了。但是我觉得他们也可以给你做一碗咸的。

I want it to be special. And you know that I always like hot food.

我就想要点特别的啊。而且您知道我一直喜欢辣味的食物啊。

Dialogue 1 正宗的中餐 Authentic Chinese Food

I tried them once, but they are quite difficult to eat with chopsticks.

Have you tried traditional Chinese dumplings yet?

约翰刚来到中国，还不习惯吃中餐，朋友小李向他介绍中国食物和文化，并邀请他去品尝正宗的北京烤鸭。

John has just arrived in China and is not accustomed to Chinese food. His friend XiaoLi introduces him to Chinese food and culture and invites him to taste authentic Beijing roast duck.

XiaoLi: Are you a good cook?

John: No, but I'm pretty good at eating!

XiaoLi: Do you prefer Chinese food or Western food?

John: Well, to be honest with you, Chinese food is really different from Western food.

XiaoLi: Are you used to the food here?

John: I'm not really used to it yet.

XiaoLi: What's your favorite Chinese dish?

John: Like most foreigners, I really like Sweet and Sour Pork and Kung Pao Chicken. I eat them almost every day.

XiaoLi: Have you tried traditional Chinese dumplings yet?

John: I tried them once, but they are quite difficult to eat with chopsticks.

XiaoLi: You know, foreigners are not expected to know how to use chopsticks proficiently. If you do, you'll make your Chinese friends to know how quite an impression is.

John: That's good to know. I'd like to try more Chinese food, but since I can't read any of the menus in the restaurants near my home, it's difficult to try new food.

XiaoLi: If you want, I can introduce you some typical Chinese dishes.

John: That would be great. I really want to try some authentic Chinese food, not just the food that foreigners like to eat!

XiaoLi: If you haven't tried Beijing Roast Duck yet, I'd like to treat you to a meal at a famous duck restaurant near Qianmen. It would be a shame if you left Beijing without tasting it!

小李: 你擅长做饭吗?

约翰: 不太擅长，不过我是个美食家!

小李: 你喜欢吃中餐还是西餐?

约翰: 嗯，坦白说，中餐和西餐可是大相径庭。

小李: 你吃得惯这儿的饭菜吗?

约翰: 还没习惯呢。

小李: 你最喜欢中餐的哪道菜?

约翰: 和大多数外国人一样，我喜欢吃咕噜肉和宫保鸡丁。我几乎天天都吃。

小李: 你吃过中国传统的饺子吗?

约翰: 吃过一次了，不过用筷子夹太难了。

小李: 要知道，中国人并不要求老外能对筷子运用自如。但是如果你能用得好，会让人对你印象深刻的。

约翰: 知道这个真是太好了。我很想品尝更多的中餐，可是我家附近餐馆里的菜单我都读不懂，所以想要尝试新的品种就很困难。

小李: 如果你愿意，我可以向你介绍几种经典菜式。

约翰: 那可太好了，我是真的想吃正宗的中餐，而不是外国人喜欢吃的那种!

小李: 如果你还没吃过烤鸭，我请你去前门附近的那家有名的烤鸭店去吃一顿。你要是没吃过烤鸭就离开北京那可太遗憾了!

I'd like to have a hamburger and a bottle of coca-cola.

Hey, kid, that's not right. This is a Chinese restaurant. Let's eat something traditional.

爷爷带着凯特到一家中餐厅吃饭，没有想到凯特一上来就要点汉堡和可口可乐，看来爷爷要教教凯特怎么吃中餐了。

Grandpa took Kate for a meal in a Chinese restaurant. Out of habit Kate ordered a hamburger and a coke. It seems that Grandpa wants to teach Kate about Chinese food.

Kate:	Grandpa, this restaurant looks really old! How long ago was it built?
Grandpa:	I'm not sure when it opened. But I know it's older than me. As a young boy, I ate here a lot.
Kate:	Oh, that's interesting. Dad told me you brought him here when he was young, too. Now, it's my turn.
Grandpa:	Yeah. We are VIP customers here. So, what do you want to eat today?
Kate:	I'd like to have a hamburger and a bottle of coca-cola.
Grandpa:	Hey, kid, that's not right. This is a Chinese restaurant. Let's eat something traditional.
Kate:	Then there is nothing in particular I'd like to eat. Grandpa, what's your favorite here?
Grandpa:	The Chinese rice pudding. Your father loves it, too. You wanna try it?
Kate:	Sure. Is it sweet?
Grandpa:	Yes, of course. But I think they can make you a salty one, too.
Kate:	Great, I want it spicy.
Grandpa:	Come on. Let's not go too far.
Kate:	I want it to be special. And you know that I always like hot food.

Grandpa:	OK then. We shall ask them to put some red chilli on it.
Kate:	I'm sure I'll like it.
Grandpa:	I hope so.

凯特：爷爷，这个餐厅看起来好旧啊。它建成多少年了啊？
爷爷：我不是很确定它是什么时候开张的。但我知道它比我还老呢。我小的时候，就经常来这里吃东西的。
凯特：哦，真有趣。爸爸告诉过我他小的时候您也常常带他来这里。现在，轮到我了。
爷爷：是啊。我们可是这里的会员啊。那么，你今天想吃点什么呢？
凯特：我要一个汉堡包和一瓶可乐。
爷爷：嗨，孩子，别弄错了。这是中餐厅。我们得吃点传统的食品。
凯特：那我就不知道有什么特别想吃的了。爷爷，您最喜欢这里的什么呢？
爷爷：八宝粥。你爸爸也很喜欢的。你想尝尝吗？
凯特：当然了。它是甜的吗？
爷爷：是啊，当然了。但是我觉得他们也可以给你做一碗咸的。
凯特：太好了。我还要辣的。
爷爷：哎呀。别太过了。
凯特：我就想要点特别的啊。而且您知道我一直喜欢辣味的食物啊。
爷爷：那好吧。我们就叫他们给你往上面放点红辣椒。
凯特：我确定我一定会喜欢的。
爷爷：希望如此。

Dialogue 3 经典影像观摩 The Emulation of Classical Movies

　　柯夫人和她的未婚夫莱恩带着孩子们去"旧中国城"餐馆吃饭，未来的继父很想讨安娜高兴，可安娜却似乎不领情。

　　Mrs. Coleman and her fiancé Ryan take her children to have dinner in a restaurant named "Old China Town". The future stepfather wants to make Anna happy, but Anna seems ungrateful.

Owner:	Hello. How are you?
Mrs. Coleman:	Hello, Pei-Pei.
Owner:	Anna, Harry, you're so big now. What happened? Are you happy for your mommy?
Anna:	About what?
Owner:	Oh. She's such a joker. Who's catering? Chinese food good luck.
Mrs. Coleman:	Actually, it's all planned already.
Owner:	Okay, how about me?
Ryan:	I preordered the Peking duck.
Anna:	Joy.
Ryan:	I know that's your favorite.

Anna:	Whatever.
Mrs. Coleman:	The wedding is in two days.
Owner:	Please think about it. Ok?
Mrs. Coleman:	Ok.
Owner:	All right. See you soon. Happy dining!

店主:	柯医生，你好啊。
柯夫人:	你好，佩佩。
店主:	安娜，哈利，你们长得真高啊，发生什么事了？你们为自己的妈妈高兴吗？
安娜:	高兴什么？
店主:	她真爱开玩笑。宴席谁办？中国菜能带来好运。
柯夫人:	全都计划好了。
店主:	找我吧。
莱恩:	我定了一只北京烤鸭。
安娜:	真好。
莱恩:	听说那是你最爱吃的。
安娜:	随便啦。
柯夫人:	婚礼过两天就要举行了。
店主:	考虑一下吧？
柯夫人:	好的。
店主:	好啊，回头见。用餐愉快!

词句荟萃 Words and Sentences Gathering

proficient [prəˈfɪʃənt] *adj.* 熟练的；娴熟的；精通的；训练有素的

menu [ˈmenjuː] *n.* 菜单

VIP (very important person) 贵宾，会员

hamburger [ˈhæmbɜːgə] *n.* 汉堡包

salty [ˈsɔːltɪ] *adj.* 咸的

hot [hɒt] *adj.* 辣的

chilli [ˈtʃɪlɪ] *n.* 辣椒

to ask for/look at the menu 要/看菜单

What's on the menu(= for dinner)tonight? 今晚有什么菜？

关于中国传统菜肴的词汇

家常豆腐 brown bean curd

麻婆豆腐 Mapo tofu / tofu sautéed in hot and spicy sauce

火锅 hot pot

宫保鸡丁 kungpao chicken

香酥鸡 crispy chicken

清蒸桂鱼 steamed mandarin fish

素什锦 sautéed assorted vegetables

鱼香茄子 eggplant sautéed with spicy garlic sauce

什锦炒饭 mixed fried rice

蛋炒饭 fried rice with eggs

西红柿炒鸡蛋 scrambled eggs with tomatoes

糖醋排骨 sweet and sour pork steak

八宝饭 Chinese rice pudding

蛋花汤 egg drop soup

广东菜 Cantonese cuisine

水饺 boiled dumpling

烤乳猪 roast suckling pig

砂锅 casserole

豆豉 fermented black bean

勾芡 sauce thickened with cornstarch

酸甜咕噜肉 sweet & sour pork

紫菜汤 seaweed soup

Section 5

Can I help you?

Three double cheeseburgers to go, please!

■ 快餐
Fast Food

疯狂表达 Expressions

点餐 Ordering Food

要一个汉堡和一杯冰茶。

I'd like a hamburger and an iced tea.

举一反三

May I have two hot dogs, please?　我要两个热狗。

Anything else?　还要别的吗？

With ketchup and mustard, please.　请加番茄酱和芥末。

在这吃还是带走 For Here or to Go

在这儿吃还是带走？

Will that be for here or to go?

举一反三

Will that be to go?

Take-out? 您带走吗？

Will you be eating here? 您是在这儿吃吗？

I'd like it to go, please. 带走。

To go, please. 带走。

For here, please. 在这儿吃。

喜欢快餐 Like It

你喜欢麦当劳吗?

Do you like MacDonald's?

还行。

It's okay.

举一反三

I like junk food.　我就是喜欢垃圾食品。

They are tasty.　它们很好吃。

I've got this intense craving for a Big Mac.　我现在太想吃麦当劳巨无霸了。

为什么喜欢 Why You Like It

我喜欢快餐,因为它好吃。

I like fast food because it's delicious.

举一反三

My son likes to go to the fast food restaurants because they often offer free toys and gifts with kids' meals.　我儿子非常愿意去快餐店,因为那随儿童餐赠送免费的玩具和礼物。

讨厌快餐 Dislike It

说实话,美国快餐让我感到恶心。

To tell you the truth, American fast food makes me sick.

举一反三

I'm sick of McDonald's. Do you know that there are over 14,000 restaurants in the U.S. alone and over 32,000 franchises worldwide? By the year 2030, everyone will eat at McDonald's every day!

我讨厌麦当劳,你知不知道,单在美国就有超14000多家麦当劳,而世界各地有32000多家麦当劳连锁店。到2030年,每人每天的用餐都在麦当劳解决了!

Junk food, pizza, ice cream, hamburger and so on, you know.　比萨、冰激凌、汉堡包等你知道的,都是些垃圾食品。

You know those foods aren't good for you.　你知道那些东西对你没好处。

And no junk food.　不要再吃垃圾食物了。

有害健康 Bad for Your Health

快餐使你变胖,并且有害健康。

Fast food makes you fat and it's bad for your health.

举一反三

Fast food is junk food.　快餐是垃圾食品。

Those foods are full of fat.　那些食物富含脂肪。

Yeah, right. Fat and salt.　对啊,就是脂肪加盐。

Dialogue 1 点快餐 *Order Fast Food*

> Hello, may I help you?

> A Spicy Chicken Combo and two pineapple pies, please.

林涛正在一家肯德基店点餐。
Lin Tao is ordering some fast food in a KFC.

Waitress: Hello, may I help you?
Lin Tao: A Spicy Chicken Combo and two pineapple pies, please.
Waitress: Sorry. We don't have any pineapple pies right now. Would you like to order something else?
Lin Tao: Yeah, two banana pies.
Waitress: OK. That's 50 RMB.
Lin Tao: Here you are.
Waitress: Thank you. Would you like it for here or to go?
Lin Tao: To go.

服务员: 您好，点餐吗？
林涛: 一个香辣鸡腿套餐和两个菠萝派。
服务员: 对不起，菠萝派现在没有了。您能换个别的吗？
林涛: 好，两个香蕉派吧。
服务员: 好的。总共50元。
林涛: 给。
服务员: 谢谢。您是在这儿吃还是带走？
林涛: 带走。

车开在路上，杰克看见了路边的麦当劳店，就想吃汉堡，但是爸爸妈妈会不会给他买呢？

While driving by, Jack sees a McDonald's on the roadside. He wants a hamburger. However, will Mum and Dad buy him one?

Jack:	Dad, how long till we get there?
Dad:	Won't take much longer now.
Jack:	Mommy, can I ask you something?
Mom:	Yes, please!
Jack:	Do you think we have enough food?
Mom:	Yeah?
Jack:	I mean there is a McDonald's right over there.
Mom:	Hold on, I know where this is going.
Jack:	Come on, just some cheeseburgers.

(Dad can't help but drive the car to the McDonald's drive-through.)

Attendant:	Can I help you?
Dad:	3 double cheeseburgers to go, please!
Attendant:	All right. Would you care for a cup of coffee?
Dad:	No, thanks. I've got what I need.

杰克:	爸爸，我们什么时候才能到啊？
爸爸:	用不了多久。
杰克:	妈咪，我能问一个问题吗？

妈妈:	好的，说吧！
杰克:	你认为我们的食物够吗？
妈妈:	呃？
杰克:	我的意思是那边有个麦当劳。
妈妈:	打住，我知道你的最终目的。
杰克:	妈妈，就只买几个芝士汉堡而已。

（爸爸没有办法，只有把车开到了麦当劳餐厅的外卖窗口。）

服务员:	您要什么？
爸爸:	3个双层芝士汉堡带走。
服务员:	好的，您还要一杯咖啡吗？
爸爸:	谢谢，不用了。我已经买了该买的。

Dialogue 3 经典影像观摩 The Emulation of Classical Movies

瑞贝卡为了换零钱买丝巾，来到热狗摊前和老板协商，打算用支票买下所有的热狗，最后发生了什么呢？

Rebecca needs change for scarf. She goes to a hot dog stand and makes a deal with the salesman. She will buy all his hot dogs with a check. What happens in the end?

Rebecca:	Excuse me. It's an emergency.
Others:	Back of the line!
Rebecca:	Excuse me, this is an emergency. this is an emergency, Excuse me! Excuse me! Did you cash back?
Peddler:	What?
Rebecca:	If I give you a check for $23, will you give me one of your delicious hot dogs and $20 cash back, please.
Peddler:	Do I look like a bank?
Rebecca:	No, no. I have an interview in four minutes. They don't hold items. It's a desperately important scarf.
Peddler:	Desperately important scarf.
Rebecca:	You know what? It's for my great-aunt. She's very sick in the hospital actually.
Man:	Can you ask them to turn the heating up?
Peddler:	Want mustard with that?
Rebecca:	Please. I will buy all of your hot dogs.
Peddler:	You'll take 97 hot dogs?
Rebecca:	Done. …who do I make it…

(The man gives $20 to Rebecca and $3 to the peddler.)

Rebecca:	That means you just paid $23 for a hot dog.
Man:	You want your scarf; I want my hot dog. Cost and worth are very different things.
Rebecca:	Thank you! My aunt will really appreciate it.

瑞贝卡:	不好意思，十万火急！
其他人:	往后排队！
瑞贝卡:	对不起，我有急事，请原谅。你这里能返现金吗？
小贩:	什么？
瑞贝卡:	我给你开一张23美元的支票买一只热狗，你给我找零20美元，好吗？
小贩:	我这看起来像银行吗？
瑞贝卡:	我四分钟后有一个面试，店铺不滞留出售品，那是一条极为重要的丝巾。
小贩:	极为重要的丝巾。
瑞贝卡:	你知道吗？是送给我婶祖母的，她住院了，她病得很重。
男士:	你就不会让医院打开暖气吗？
小贩:	要加芥末酱吗？
瑞贝卡:	求你了，我愿买下你所有的热狗。
小贩:	买下97只热狗吗？
瑞贝卡:	成交。为了婶祖母的丝巾……

（男士给了20美元瑞贝卡，给了3美元小贩。）

瑞贝卡:	这意味着你花了23美元买了一只热狗！
男士:	你要买你的丝巾，我要吃我的热狗，只要能得到想要的，成本不用考虑。
瑞贝卡:	谢谢！我代我婶婶表示感谢。

词句荟萃 Words and Sentences Gathering

spicy ['spaɪsɪ] adj. 辣的

combo ['kɒmbəʊ] n. 结合物；社团；套餐

get [get] vi. 到达

enough [ɪ'nʌf] adj. 足够的

mean [miːn] vt. 意味着

cheeseburger ['tʃiːzbɜːgə] n. 芝士汉堡

window ['wɪndəʊ] n. 窗户

coffee ['kɒfɪ] n. 咖啡

疯狂链接 Interlinkage

西式快餐食品名称

薯条 French fries

汉堡包 hamburger

芝士汉堡包 cheeseburger

炸薯饼 hash browns

玉米棒子 corn on the cob (corn-cob)
热狗 hot dog
炸鸡 fried chicken
圈状硬面包 bagel
松饼 muffin
鱼柳包 fish burger
烤马铃薯 baked potato
洋葱圈 onion rings
潜艇三明治 submarine sandwich
椒盐脆饼干 pretzels
羊倌肉饼 shepherd's pie
鸡派 chicken pot pie
沙拉 / 沙拉酱 salad / salad dressing
田园沙拉 garden salad
薯仔沙拉 potato salad
凯撒沙拉 caesar salad
凉拌生菜丝 cole slaw
鸡蛋沙拉 egg salad
青菜沙拉 green salad
厨师沙拉 chef salad
水果沙拉 fruit salad
通心粉沙拉 macaroni salad
蔬菜沙拉 vegetable salad
虾沙拉 shrimp salad
三明治 sandwich
公司三明治 club sandwich
火腿三明治 ham sandwich

火腿鸡蛋三明治 ham and egg sandwich
鸡蛋沙拉三明治 egg salad sandwich
鸡肉三明治 roast chicken sandwich
烤牛肉三明治 roast beef sandwich
吞拿鱼三明治 tuna sandwich
西红柿三明治 tomato sandwich
芝士肉丸三明治 meatball sandwich with cheese
火鸡三明治 turkey sandwich
烟肉，生菜，西红柿三明治 B.L.T. (bacon, lettuce, tomato) sandwich
汤 soup
马铃薯汤 potato soup
西红柿汤 tomato soup
蔬菜汤 vegetable soup
法国洋葱汤 French onion soup
鸡汤 chicken soup
奶油蘑菇汤 cream of mushroom soup
牛尾汤 oxtail soup
奶油西红柿汤 cream of tomato soup
奶油菠菜汤 cream of spinach soup
奶油西兰花汤 cream of broccoli soup
周打蚬汤 clam chowder
意式蔬菜浓汤 minestrone soup
玉米青豆汤 corn and pea soup
蔬菜什豆汤 vegetarian split pea soup

Section 6

> I'd like some tea. What kinds of tea do you have?

■ 酒水饮料
Wines and Drinks

> What would you like to drink, sir?

疯狂表达 Expressions

点酒 Ordering Wines

可否让我看看酒单？
May I see the wine list?

我可以点杯酒吗？
May I order a glass of wine?

举一反三
What kind of drinks do you have for an aperitif? 餐厅有些什么餐前酒？
What kind of wine do you have? 餐厅有哪几类酒？
I'd like to have some local wine. 我想点当地出产的酒。
I'd like to have a French red wine. 我想要喝法国红酒。
Could you recommend some good wine? 是否可建议一些不错的酒？

点饮料 Ordering Drinks

那让我们先点饮料吧。
Let's start with drinks.

举一反三
I'll have a Coke. 我要可乐。
I'll have a Sprite. 我要雪碧。
I'll have the Strawberry Smoothie. 我要草莓果肉汁。

请客 Treating Someone

这次由我请客。

This is my treat.

举一反三

The drinks are on me!　这酒我请客!

The cocktails are on me.　鸡尾酒我付钱。

I'll take this round.　这轮我来付。

Thanks, Jim. I'm the next.　谢谢你，吉姆。下轮我来付。

提议干杯 Proposing a Toast

我提议为格林先生的健康干杯。

May I propose a toast to the health of Mr. Green?

举一反三

Allow me to propose a toast to our professor.　允许我提议为老师干杯。

I propose a toast to our chairman.　我提议为我们主席干杯。

祝酒 Toast

让我们为我们的友谊干杯!

Let's drink to our friendship!

To our friendship!

Our friendship!

举一反三

Let me drink to your health!　让我为你的健康干杯!

Let me drink to your success!　让我为你的成功干杯!

如何说 "喝醉" How to Say "drunk"

他喝醉了。

He's drunk.

举一反三

He's tipsy.　他有点微醺。

He's wasted.　他喝得烂醉。

He's as drunk as a skunk.　他烂醉如泥。

He drank himself under the table.　他喝得不省人事。

He's pickled.　他醉了。

He's plastered.　他醉醺醺的。

He's tanked.　他醉茫茫的。

He's canned.　他醉醺醺的。

He's the worse for drink.　他喝得酩酊大醉。

Dialogue 1　点酒水 Ordering Drinks

> What would you like to drink, sir?

> I'd like some tea. What kinds of tea do you have?

杰克来到中国的一家餐馆，想点一些喝的东西，服务员向他推荐了具有中国特色的绿茶。

Jack is at a Chinese restaurant and wants to order something to drink. The waitress recommends a typical Chinese drink—green tea.

Waitress:　　What would you like to drink, sir?

Jack:　　　 I'd like some tea. What kinds of tea do you have?

Waitress:　　We have black tea, green tea and Oolong tea. Which kind would you like?

Jack:　　　 I don't know. What would you recommend?

Waitress:　　I would suggest a green tea. Green tea has a cooler flavor, good for drinking during the summer.

Jack:　　　 What green tea do you have then?

Waitress:　　Longjing, Biluochun and Huangshan Maofeng.

Jack:　　　 I'd like a pot of Biluochun.

服务员：　　先生，要喝点儿什么？

杰克：　　　喝茶吧。你们这儿都有什么茶？

服务员：　　有红茶、绿茶还有乌龙茶等。您要喝哪种？

杰克：　　　我也不知道，你给我推荐一下吧。

服务员：　　我建议您喝点儿绿茶。绿茶性凉，适合夏天喝。

杰克：　　　那你们绿茶有哪些呢？

服务员：　　有龙井、碧螺春和黄山毛峰。

杰克：　　　那给我来一壶碧螺春吧。

This is my first time being in a bar.

Oh, then I'm honored to be here with you. Do you like this place?

贝蒂在美国认识了一个名叫吉姆的朋友。贝蒂对美国的酒吧文化很感兴趣，于是吉姆就带她去实地感受一下美国的酒吧文化。我们也来一起体验一下吧。

Betty has a friend named Jim in America. Betty is interested in American bar culture. So Jim takes her to a bar to experience American bar culture first-hand. Let's experience it together.

Betty: This is my first time being in a bar.

Jim: Oh, then I'm honored to be here with you. Do you like this place?

Betty: Sure. I love this place, especially the decoration. So tasteful!

Jim: Yeah. But the real attraction is the excellent drinks. Can I have your ticket?

Betty: Here it is. But, what for? We're already in.

Jim: Well, with the ticket, you can get a free drink. What would you like? Orange juice?

Betty: Yes, orange juice will be fine for me. But how do you get the drink? It's so crowded there around the counter. You can barely move.

Jim: I'll show you how. The bar tenders know whose turn it is. And also, I can snap my fingers to catch his attention.

Betty: Cool. Thanks.

(Jim brings Betty a glass of orange juice.)

Betty: Oh, fresh juice, I love it. Well, I heard American people love hanging out in bars. Is that true?

Jim: Not everyone. But a lot of people do, especially young people. It's a fun place to spend an evening with friends or to make some new friends.

Betty: Thank you.

贝蒂：	这是我第一次来酒吧。
吉姆：	哦，那么我很荣幸能陪你来这儿了。你喜欢这个地方吗?
贝蒂：	当然，我很喜欢这个地方，尤其是它的布置，很风雅。
吉姆：	是啊。除了那个，它真正的特点在于酒水特别棒。可以把你的门票给我吗?
贝蒂：	给你。可是，干什么用啊? 我们都已经进来了啊。
吉姆：	用这票，你可以得到一杯免费的饮料。你想要什么? 橙汁吗?
贝蒂：	好的，我喝橙汁就行。可是你怎么能买到饮料呢? 吧台那边太挤了，动都动不了。
吉姆：	我告诉你。酒吧服务员知道该轮到谁了，而且，我可以打响指来吸引他的注意。
贝蒂：	好酷。多谢。

（吉姆给贝蒂拿来了一杯橙汁。）

贝蒂：	哦，鲜榨的橙汁，我喜欢。对了，我听说美国人都很喜欢逛酒吧。是真的吗?
吉姆：	不是每个人，但是很多人都喜欢，尤其是年轻人。这是一个朋友聚会和认识新朋友的好地方。
贝蒂：	谢谢!

Dialogue 3　经典影像观摩 The Emulation of Classical Movies

电影画面外是男主角福克斯的信的独白，画面中是女主角凯莉去咖啡店买咖啡。

You hear the main character Fox's confessions in letters; and you see the heroin, Kelly, go to a coffee shop to buy a cup of coffee.

Confession:	The whole purpose of places like Starbucks is for people with no decision-making ability whatsoever to make six decisions just to buy one cup of coffee. Short, tall, light, dark, caf, decaf, low-fat, nonfat, etc.
Customer:	Mocha frappuccino grande.
Salesman:	Mocha frappuccino grande.
Confession:	So people who don't know what the hell they're doing or who on earth they are can, for only $ 2.95 get not just a cup of coffee but an absolutely defining sense of self.
Salesman:	Big cup of nonfat machiya coffee.
Confession:	Tall! Decaf! Cappuccino!

独白：	之所以有连锁咖啡店，就是让那些三心二意的人做六个选择买一杯咖啡，小杯的，大杯的，淡的，浓的，有咖啡因的，低咖啡因的，低热量的，无热量的，诸如此类。
顾客：	摩卡研磨咖啡。
售货员：	摩卡研磨咖啡。
独白：	只花2.95美元就可以让这些无所适从的人或是没有自信的人，不仅买到咖啡，还能买到自信。
售货员：	大杯的脱脂马奇亚咖啡。
独白：	大杯的，低咖啡因，卡布奇诺!

decoration [ˌdekəˈreɪʃn] *n.* 装饰

tasteful [ˈteɪstfl] *adj.* 风雅的

barely [ˈbeəlɪ] *adv.* 几乎不

packed [ˈpækt] *adj.* 挤满的

fancy [ˈfænsɪ] *n.* 喜好

croissant [krwɑːsɔːŋt] *n.* 牛角面包

medium [ˈmiːdɪəm] *adj.* 适中的

well-done [welˈdʌn] *adj.* 熟透的

bar tender 酒吧招待员

dance floor 舞池

疯狂链接 Interlinkage

关于西方酒水的词汇

白兰地 brandy

鸡尾酒 cocktail

红葡萄酒 red wine

朗姆酒 rum

伏特加 vodka

威士忌 whisky

白葡萄酒 white wine

黄酒 yellow rice wine

百威啤酒 Budweiser

加士伯啤酒 Carlsberg

香槟 champagne

苹果酒 cider

杜松子酒 gin

马提尼 martini

烧酒 samshu

雪利酒 sherry

Section 7

Stinky tofu? What's that? It sounds strange.

■ 风味小吃
Delicacies and Snacks

It's a famous Hunan snack. And it's very popular in Beijing. Would you like to try some?

疯狂表达 Expressions

推荐 Recommending

你能推荐一些一定得尝尝的小吃吗?

Can you recommend something that's a real must-try?

举一反三

How about stinky tofu?　臭豆腐怎么样?

I'll think about it. Anything else?　我考虑一下，那还有些什么呢?

Grilled corn, glutinous rice dumplings, fried peanuts, and bean curd jelly. Good enough?

烤玉米、汤圆、炸花生和豆腐脑。够多了吧?

品尝 Tasting

快尝尝这种小吃吧。

Taste it, please.

Do you want to taste it? 想尝尝这个吗?

Have a taste! 尝一下吧!

What do you think? 味道怎么样?

好吃 Good Taste

真美味!

It's terrific!

It tastes good!

举一反三

That tastes great! 那个好吃极了!

It's unforgettable! 真令人难忘啊!

It's marvelous! 太棒了!

不好吃 Bad Taste

那个太难吃了。

That tastes terrible.

举一反三

That tastes awful! 那个真难吃。

That tastes like nothing. 那个没什么味道。

节日小吃 Festival Snacks

春节一定要吃饺子啊!

For the spring festival you must have dumplings.

中秋节要品尝月饼啊。

You'll get to taste mooncakes on Mid-autumn day.

在元宵节,你当然不可以错过元宵啦。

For the Lantern Festival, you should never miss out on the Yuanxiao.

Oh, I know Tangyuan. It's a sweet snack, good for dessert.

哦，汤圆我知道。它是一种甜的小吃，用来做甜点很好。

Yes. And also, you can get Yuanxiao with both sweet and salty fillings.

是啊。不过我们的元宵有甜的还有咸的呢。

各地小吃 Regional Snacks

鸭脖是一种湖北的小吃，而且它在北京非常流行。你要试试吗？

Duck neck is a famous Hubei snack. And it's very popular in Beijing. Would you like

to try some?

举一反三

Got it. Are there any other regional snacks here?   我知道了。那这儿还有其他地方小吃吗？

Of course. For example, there are some from Sichuan, Fujian, and Guangzhou. Their

snacks are also very famous.

当然有啊。比如说这儿有来自四川、福建、广州的小吃。这些也非常有名。

Are there any Beijing snacks?   那有北京小吃吗？

Of course. Look, it is over there.   当然有啊。看，那边就有一个。

健康与否 Healthy Or Not

我选择炸花生。我非常喜欢吃花生。对了，那卫生吗？

I prefer fried peanuts. I like peanuts very much. By the way, are they healthy?

举一反三

Mom always tells us not to eat out, because they often use the recycled oil.

妈妈经常告诉我们不要在外面吃东西，因为他们经常用地沟油。

Don't think about it too much. You said you were really hungry, so you just eat.

别想太多了，你说你非常饿，那你就别无选择，只能吃了。

Dialogue 1 ● 小吃 Snacks

> Grilled corn, glutinous-rice dumplings, fried peanuts, and bean curd jelly. Good enough?

> I prefer fried peanuts. I like peanuts very much.

　　凯特买完了发夹，杰克说饿了，凯特就给他介绍起夜市上的小吃。那么夜市上究竟有哪些小吃呢？杰克最后都吃了什么呢？

　　After Kate bought hair clips, Jack was hungry. Kate introduced him the snacks at the night fair. What were the snacks at the night fair and what did Jack have?

Jack:　　Girls always like these Japanese-style hair clips.

Kate:　　They are cute, but most importantly, they're very cheap.

Jack:　　Anyway, I need to get myself some supper. I'm starving.

Kate:　　How about stinky tofu?

Jack:　　Stinky tofu? What's that? It sounds strange.

Kate:　　It's a famous Hunan snack. And it's very popular in Beijing. Would you like to try some?

Jack:　　I'll think about it. Anything else?

Kate:　　Grilled corn, glutinous-rice dumplings, fried peanuts, and bean curd jelly. Good enough?

Jack:　　I prefer fried peanuts. I like peanuts very much. By the way, are they healthy? Mom always tells us not to eat out, because they often use recycled oil.

Kate:　　Don't think about it too much. You said you were really hungry, so just eat.

Jack:　　I'd rather not. I'll eat when I get home.

杰克: 女孩子都喜欢这些日本风格的发夹。

凯特: 它们很可爱，最重要的是很便宜。

杰克: 不管怎样，我很饿，我要去吃点夜宵。

凯特: 臭豆腐怎么样？

杰克: 臭豆腐？是什么东西啊？听起来怪怪的。

凯特: 它是一种湖南的小吃，而且它在北京非常流行。你要试试吗？

杰克: 我考虑一下，那还有些什么呢？

凯特: 烤玉米、糯米汤圆、炸花生和豆腐脑。够多了吧？

杰克: 我选择炸花生。我非常喜欢吃花生。对了，那卫生吗？妈妈经常告诉我们不要在外面吃东西，因为他们经常用地沟油。

凯特: 别想太多了，你说你非常饿，那你就别无选择，只能吃了。

杰克: 算了，我还是回家吃吧。

Dialogue 2 ● 美食街 Gourmet Food Street

Actually, they are small dumpling balls made of glutinous rice flour. They are like Tangyuan.

What's that? It gets its name from the festival itself. That's really funny!

元宵节，杰瑞和雪莉来逛庙会，她们到了美食街上。全国各地的小吃令她们目不暇接，都有什么好吃的呢？

It's the Lantern Festival. Jerry and Shirley go to temple fair. They arrive at the gourmet food street. There are so many snacks from throughout the country that they are dazzled. What delicious snacks are there?

Jerry: Can you recommend something that's a real must-try?

Shirley:	OK. Let's go over there. For the Lantern Festival, you should never miss out on the Yuanxiao.
Jerry:	What's that? It gets its name from the festival itself. That's really funny!
Shirley:	Actually, they are small dumpling balls made of glutinous rice flour. They are like Tangyuan.
Jerry:	Oh, I know Tangyuan. It's a sweet snack, good for dessert.
Shirley:	Yes. And also, you can get Yuanxiao with both sweet and salty fillings.
Jerry:	I'd like to try the salty ones. Where is that strange smell coming from?
Shirley:	Oh, the smelly bean curd. My favorite!
Jerry:	What? You love smelly food?
Shirley:	Well, the smell of it may be unpleasant, but it's really delicious.
Jerry:	Really? You've made me curious. I'd like to try it now.
Shirley:	A wise decision! I'm pretty sure that you will be addicted to it as soon as you take a bite.
Jerry:	Are you sure?

杰瑞:	你能推荐一些一定得尝尝的小吃吗？
雪莉:	好的，我们去那边。在元宵节，你当然不可以错过元宵啦。
杰瑞:	元宵是什么呢？它和节日是同一个名字哦。这可真有趣啊！
雪莉:	其实呢，它们是用糯米粉做的小圆球，有点像汤圆。
杰瑞:	哦，汤圆我知道。它是一种甜的小吃，用来做甜点很好。
雪莉:	是啊。不过我们的元宵有甜的还有咸的呢。
杰瑞:	我想尝一下咸的。那奇怪的味道是从哪里来的啊？
雪莉:	哦，臭豆腐。我的最爱！
杰瑞:	什么？你喜欢臭的食物？
雪莉:	这个啊，它的味道可能不好闻，但是它真的很美味。
杰瑞:	真的吗？你勾起我的好奇心了。我现在很想尝一下。
雪莉:	聪明的决定！我敢肯定你只要尝一口就会迷上它的。
杰瑞:	是吗？

Dialogue 3 经典影像观摩 The Emulation of Classical Movies

一位男士走进了燕麦饼干店，可他好像不是普通的顾客，他似乎对开燕麦饼干这种风味小吃店很感兴趣。店里的人展开了一场关于谷物食品的讨论。

A man comes into the Flakes'. However, he is not an ordinary customer. He seems to be interested in opening a snack bar like Flakes. The people have a discussion about cereal.

Neal:	How are you?
Man:	Good. Great. So, uh. This is like a, uh…, like a cereal bar, or…

Neal:	Yeah.
Man:	Cool. Cool idea. Cool. Cool. Cool. Um, what's the most popular?
Neal:	Uh, here, it's anything cocoa. We got a lot of stoners here. I think, nationally, it's Corn Flakes.
A bald man:	Correct, Corn Flakes. The first and still the favorite.
An old man:	Corn Flakes wasn't first, man.
The bald man:	First mass-produced.
The old man:	Oh. Okay, all right. Mass-produced. Uh-huh.
The bald man:	You know that's what I meant.
Man:	So, uh, what was the first? Like, wheaties or something?
The bald man:	Like no. wheaties is 1924.
The old man:	The first cereal was Kellogg brothers. Took a bunch of wheat and mashed it up. Made, like a giant flake which you could break up into little smaller flakes. Cereal was health food then. The whole thing was started by these radical, religions, health-freak nuts up in Battle Creek. Disciples of this, uh. Christian science chick.
The bald man:	Mary Baker Eddy.
The old man:	Yeah. Isn't that a trick, man? Cereal as religion?

尼尔:	你好。
男士:	很好。很好。那么，嗯。这就像，嗯……就像压缩饼干，或者……
尼尔:	是的。
男士:	酷，好主意。好，很好。什么最受欢迎？
尼尔:	呃，在这儿，只要带可可的都不错。我们这有很多可可的忠实消费者。当然，我想玉米片最受欢迎。
秃顶的人:	好啊，玉米片，第一种也仍然会是最受欢迎的。
老人:	玉米片不是第一种，伙计。
秃顶的人:	第一种大规模制造的。
老人:	噢。好的，大规模制造的，呃，哦。
秃顶的人:	你知道我的意思。
男士:	那个，嗯，哪个是第一种？麦片还是别的？
秃顶的人:	没有别的。麦片是在1924年。
老人:	第一种谷类食品是Kellogg兄弟。把一批小麦捣碎，做成一个巨大的薄片。你要把它打成小碎片。谷类食品是那时候的健康食品。这些激进分子开始了整件事的进程。教义上说，热衷健康的怪诞思想是从克里克运动中兴起的。这方面的信众，呃，就好像基督教学派的萌芽。
秃顶的人:	玛丽贝克•艾迪。
老人:	是啊，那不是一场骗局吗？伙计，把谷类食品作为一种信仰？

glutinous ['gluːtɪnəs] *adj.* 黏的；胶质的；糯米的

dumpling ['dʌmplɪŋ] *n.* 饺子；面团；团子

stinky ['stɪŋkɪ] *adj.* 发恶臭的

recycled [ˌriː'saɪkld] *adj.* 循环使用的

grill [ɡrɪl] *v.* 烤；烧烤

lunar ['luːnə] *adj.* 阴历的

sample ['sæmpl] *vt.* 试吃，试做

culinary ['kʌlɪnərɪ] *adj.* 烹饪的

filling ['fɪlɪŋ] *n.* 馅儿

beancurd ['biːnkəd] *n.* 豆腐

unpleasant [ʌn'plezənt] *adj.* 讨厌的

flake [fleɪk] *n.* 薄片

cereal ['sɪərɪəl] *n.* 谷物

radical ['rædɪkl] *adj.* 激进的 *n.* 激进分子

religion [rɪ'lɪdʒən] *n.* 宗教

disciple [dɪ'saɪpl] *n.* 信徒

Christian ['krɪstʃən] *adj.* 基督教的，基督徒的

疯狂链接 Interlinkage

关于各式小吃的词汇

烧饼 clay oven rolls

油条 fried bread stick

韭菜盒 fried leek dumplings

火锅 Chafing dish/hot pot

牛肉面 beef noodles

北京烤鸭 Beijing Roast Duck

奶黄包 custard buns

糖炒栗子 fried chestnut

绿豆糕 green bean cakes

春卷 spring rolls

麻花 twist of dough

腐乳 preserved bean curd

猪脚 pig's knuckle/feet
包子 bun
肉包子 crispy bun
豆沙包 smashed bean bun
小笼包 small steamed buns
馒头 steamed bread
花卷 twist bread
馄饨 wonton
锅贴 fried wontons
水饺 boiled dumpling
蒸虾饺 steamed prawn dumpling
虾饺 shrimp dumpling
烧卖 shao-mai
皮蛋 preserved egg
上汤云吞 wonton soup
打卤面 noodles with sweet bean sauce
粥 porridge
燕窝 bird's nest
叉烧 barbecued pork
豆腐 bean curd
咸鸭蛋 salted duck egg
豆浆 bean milk
豆腐花 bean curd jelly
肠粉 rice noodle roll
葱油饼 green onion pie
油饼 cruller
千层糕 layer cake
马拉糕 Cantonese sponge cake

八宝饭 rice pudding
凉粉 agar-agar jelly
河粉 fried rice noodles
干炒牛河 fried rice noodles with beef
年糕 rice cake
炒面 chow noodles
汤面 noodle soup
阳春面 plain noodles
刀削面 sliced noodles
炸酱面 noodles with soybean paste
芝麻糊 sesame paste
萝卜丝饼 shredded turnip cake
碗糕 salty rice pudding
凤梨酥 pineapple cake
豆沙 sweet bean paste
糯米 sticky rice
血糯米 black sticky rice
白粥 congee

Section 8

Would you like to come over for dinner tonight?

■ 饮食偏好
Preference in Food

Sure, but I have to tell you that I've become a vegetarian. I don't eat any kind of meat.

疯狂表达 Expressions

询问 Asking

你有什么饮食偏好吗？

Do you have a preference in food?

你喜欢比萨饼吗？

Are you keen on pizza?

举一反三

What's your favorite? Sichuan style food or Shanghai style?

你喜欢什么？四川菜还是上海菜？

Would you prefer apple or peach?　你喜欢苹果还是桃子？

The choice is yours, English breakfast or the continental one?

由您来选，英式早餐还是大陆式早餐？

喜欢的口味 Taste

我们喜欢辛辣的食物。

We love hot spicy foods.

举一反三

Generally speaking, I like bland foods.　总体来说，我喜欢清淡的食品。

I prefer a strong buttery flavor.　我喜欢很重的黄油味道。

不喜欢的口味 Dislikes in Flavor

我不吃辣的食物。

I don't eat spicy foods.

举一反三

I don't like oily food. I'm a vegetarian.　我不喜欢太油的东西，我是个素食者。

If they are too salty or too buttery, I won't like them.

如果它们太咸或者太油，我就不喜欢了。

喜欢的食物 Likes in Food

我喜欢新鲜蔬菜，像白菜、芹菜、西红柿。

I love fresh vegetables like cabbage, celery, and tomatoes.

我喜欢鸡肉和鱼，因为它们有营养还能给我提供能量。

I enjoy chicken and fish because they are nutritious and they provide me with energy.

举一反三

I really go for shellfish.　我确实喜欢贝类。

You can't beat beef.　没什么比牛肉更好吃的。

The chicken is delicious. Crispy on the outside and really juicy inside.　鸡肉真好吃，外酥里嫩。

My favorite food is grilled chicken, because it's healthy. It has less oil than other foods.

我最喜欢的食物是烤鸡肉，因为它很健康。它不像其他食物那样油腻。

不喜欢的食物 Dislikes in Food

我不喜欢蔬菜，它们没什么味道。

I dislike vegetables because they taste like nothing.

我不怎么喜欢肉，因为它们会使我发胖。

I don't care for meat because it makes me put on weight.

举一反三

But I have to tell you that I've become a vegetarian. I don't eat any kind of meat.

但是我得告诉你我现在开始吃素了。我不吃任何肉类食品。

My God! I could never put up with vegetarian meals.　天啊，我可受不了素食。

流行食品 Popular Food

最近巧克力火锅特别受年轻女孩子欢迎。

The chocolate fondue is really popular with young girls.

举一反三

No girls can resist this!　没有哪个女孩能抵制它。

It's true that a piece of chocolate can cheer you up!

一块巧克力就能使人高兴起来，说得真没错啊。

That's for sure. Chocolate is to die for!　那当然。为巧克力死都愿意呢!

Dialogue 1 巧克力火锅 *Chocolate Fondue*

May it be a chocolate horse.

Hey, I'm starving. I could eat a horse.

下午3点，乔治和翠西都感到有些饿，翠西是个很时尚很西化的女孩，又爱吃巧克力，于是就建议乔治两人去吃巧克力火锅。巧克力火锅？感觉很诱人哦！

George and Tracy are hungry at 3 o'clock in the afternoon. Tracy is a fashionable, Western girl and is crazy about chocolate, so she suggests that they go to have chocolate fondue. Chocolate fondue? That sounds wonderful!

Tracy:	Hey, I'm starving. I could eat a horse.
George:	May it be a chocolate horse!
Waitress:	Can I take your order now?
George:	What do you recommend?
Waitress:	The chocolate fondue is really popular with young girls. The chocolate fondue—you know the hot pot with chocolate in it and you can throw in cookies or whatever.
Tracy:	Wow, that should be perfect for me!
George:	Okay, that's it.
Waitress:	Anything else?
Tracy:	No, be quick, please!

翠西:	嗨，我饿死了。我能吃下一匹马。
乔治:	希望有一匹巧克力马。
服务生:	点餐吗？
乔治:	你有什么可以推荐的吗？
服务生:	最近巧克力火锅特别受年轻女孩子欢迎。巧克力火锅，就是火锅里面放有巧克力，你可以往里放甜点或者别的任何东西。
翠西:	哇噻，对我来说那太诱人了。
乔治:	好的，我们就点它吧。
服务生:	还要别的吗？
翠西:	不要了，请快一点。

Dialogue 2 · 我现在开始吃素了 I've Become a Vegetarian

Sure, but I have to tell you that I've become a vegetarian. I don't eat any kind of meat.

Would you like to come over for dinner tonight?

杰克邀请好朋友安妮来吃晚饭，安妮告诉杰克她现在是素食主义者，所以饮食有特殊的要求。

Jack invites his good friend, Anny, to have dinner. Anny tells Jack she has become a vegetarian, so she has special requirements about food.

Jack: Would you like to come over for dinner tonight?

Anny: Sure, but I have to tell you that I've become a vegetarian. I don't eat any kind of meat.

Jack: When did you decide to become a vegetarian?

Anny: I saw a program a few months ago about how animals are raised for human consumption. I haven't been able to eat a single piece of meat ever since.

Jack: That's great! Do you find that you eat a lot more fruit and vegetables now?

Anny: Definitely. I've also been buying organic fruit and vegetables, which is more expensive, but much better for you because they don't have any pesticides on them.

Jack: You've really turned into a health nut, haven't you?

Anny: I guess you could say that. Eating fruit and vegetables helps keep you healthy. I've lost 5 pounds and I feel great!

杰克： 你今晚过来吃晚饭吗？

安妮： 好啊，但是我得告诉你我现在是素食主义者。我不吃任何肉类食品。

杰克： 你什么时候决定开始吃素的？

安妮： 几个月前我看了一个节目，讲的是为了向人们供应肉食，动物们是如何被饲养的。在那以后我再也吃不下一片肉了。

杰克： 这太好了。你有没有发现你现在吃的水果和蔬菜都比以前多了？

安妮： 一点没错。而且我现在开始买有机水果和蔬菜了，虽然价格贵了不少，但是对健康要好得多，因为上面没有农药。

杰克： 你真是开始变成一个保养迷了，是吧？

安妮： 我想你说对了。吃水果和蔬菜有助于保证身体健康。我已经减掉了5磅，感觉真是好极了。

Dialogue 3 经典影像观摩 The Emulation of Classical Movies

尼尔来到另一家燕麦店打工，大出女朋友凯特的意料。两人很不愉快地交谈，在此期间，尼尔接待了一位很有个人口味的顾客。

Neal works at another flake shop. His girlfriend Kate can't believe it. The two are talking very upset. Meanwhile, Neal serves a customer with a very particular taste.

Neal: Hi, Feral.

Kats: What are you doing here?

Neal: Same as you. Just needed a job, you know, now that Flakes is closed down. What is this, the new special? You buy three bowls of cereal; get a free Mr. P art smock?

Kats: I can't look at you in that hat.

Neal: Oh, will you excuse me for a moment?

Neal: Good morning, ma'am.

Customer: Good morning.

Neal: Can I help you?

Customer: Yes. I would like the Mix-a-Bunch with double maple granola, skim milk and crumpled boysenberry crumble.

Neal: Excellent choice.

Customer: Thank you.

尼尔： 你好啊，费罗。

凯茨： 你在这儿干嘛？

尼尔： 和你一样，只是讨份工作，燕麦店倒闭了。这是什么，新特制产品？只要你买上3盘，就能拿到一件P先生的艺术工作服？

凯茨： 你戴着帽子的滑稽样，我可看不下去。

尼尔： 介意我离开一会儿吗？

尼尔： 早上好，夫人。

顾客： 早上好。

尼尔： 有什么能帮您的？

顾客： 是的，我想要双份格诺兰拉麦片、脱脂牛奶和煎草莓干。

尼尔： 太有品位了。

顾客： 谢谢。

词句荟萃 Words and Sentences Gathering

throw ['θrəʊ] *vt.* 扔

delicate ['delɪkeɪt] *adj.* 精美的

colorful ['kʌləfl] *adj.* 色彩丰富的

resist [rɪ'zɪst] *vt.* 抵挡

suicide ['sjuːɪsaɪd] *n.* 自杀

vegetarian [ˌvedʒɪ'teərɪən] *n.* 素食者

pesticide ['pestɪsaɪd] *n.* 农药；杀虫剂

organic [ɔː'gænɪk] *adj.* 有机的

consumption [kən'sʌmpʃən] *n.* 消耗

hot pot 火锅

maple ['meɪpl] *n.* 枫树

skim [skɪm] *v.* 脱脂

crumple ['krʌmpl] *v.* 弄皱，压皱

crumble ['krʌmbl] *v.* 弄碎，压碎 *n.* 面包屑

132

疯狂链接 Interlinkage

制作饺子所需原料

炒菜油 cooking oil
橄榄油 olive oil
芝麻油 sesame oil
生姜 ginger
酱油 soy sauce
料酒 cooking wine
醋 vinegar
盐 salt
胡椒粉 ground pepper
大蒜 garlic
鸡蛋 egg

韭菜 Chinese chives
猪/鸡/牛/火鸡肉馅 pork/chicken/beef/turkey ground
胡萝卜 carrot
卷心菜 cabbage
洋葱 onion
面粉 wheat flour
淀粉 starch
饺子皮 wrapping
饺子馅 filling

chapter 3

住房用语一点通

House

你好，我预定过房间。
Hello, I have a reservation.

我现在想结账。请给我账单，好吗？
I'm checking out now. Can I have my bill, please?

请记在我的账里。
Please add to my account.

我们需要租一套新房子。
We need to rent a new apartment.

周围环境怎么样？
What about the surrounding area?

您可以接受什么价格范围的房子？
And what is your price range?

我想咨询一下你们搬家的价格。
I'm calling to ask how much your rates are for movers.

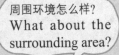

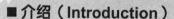 **■介绍（Introduction）**

在当今社会，住房问题已经和老百姓的命运紧密相关，那么无论你是要短期出门旅行，或是想租房、买房，还是装修房子，希望下面的表达都能助你一臂之力。

顺便问一下，你们可以提前把我的行李送到机场吗？
By the way, could you deliver my luggage to the airport in advance?

我房间里的抽水马桶好像出了点问题。
There seems to be something wrong with the toilet.

你能帮我租一间便宜的房子吗？
Can you help me to find a cheap apartment?

很好啊。交通便利吗？
That's good. Is the location easily accessible?

觉得新家怎么样？住进去还满意吗？
So what do you think of the place? Were you satisfied after you moved in?

只是些简单的装饰，我想为我住的地方增添一点个性。
It's just simple decorating. I just want to add personality to my living space.

您想怎么装修您的房屋？
How do you want to decorate your house?

采光好吧？
Is your house well lit?

经典句型

Section 1 宾馆

A: 早上好。这里是星星酒店，竭诚为您服务。
Good morning. Star Hotel, at your service.

B: 早上好。我想要预订一个房间。你们下周有空房吗？
Good morning! I'd like to make a reservation, please. Do you have any rooms available for next week?

Section 2 租房

A: 我打算另找一个地方住。
I am thinking about renting a new place.

B: 我有个朋友正想出租他的公寓呢。
I have a friend who wants to rent out his apartment.

Section 3 买房

A: 我们需要找个房地产经纪人。
We need to find a realtor.

B: 不需要。如果我们委托经纪人找房子，会比较贵。
Not necessarily. If we use a realtor to find a house, it will be more expensive.

Section 4 搬家

A: 您好，兄弟搬家公司。
Hello, Mover Brothers.

B: 我想咨询一下你们搬家的价格。
I'm calling to ask how much your rates are for movers.

Section 5　房屋设施

A：跑步完进来这里真不赖。
   It is nice to come in here after a run.
B：是呀，中央冷暖系统简直妙不可言。
   Yeah. The central heating and air-conditioner work like a charm.

Section 6　装修

A：我认为木制家具相对金属的看起来更高雅。
   I think wood furniture is much more elegant than metal furniture.
B：是的，你喜欢那种简约自然的风格，就像我一样。
   Yes. You like simple, natural styles, just like me.

Section 7　维修

A：为什么这里这么热？
   Why is it so hot here?
B：因为我们的空调坏了。
   Because our air-conditioner is broken.

Section 8　物业管理

A：我想知道什么时候收集垃圾？
   I was wondering when the trash collection day is.
B：星期二和星期五。
   It's on Tuesday and Friday.

Section 1

Good morning. Star Hotel, at your service.

■ 宾馆
Hotel

Good morning! I'd like to make a reservation, please. Do you have any rooms available for next week?

疯狂表达 Expressions

登记入住 Check In

我想要个房间。

I want a room.

你好，我预定过房间。

Hello, I have a reservation.

举一反三

What name is the reservation under?　您预订时用的名字是？

How long will you be staying?　您打算住多久？

Are you planning on checking out tomorrow?　您打算明天就离开吗？

And here is your key, Mr. Bradley. Your room number is 1420.

给您房间的钥匙，布拉德利先生。您的房间号码是1420。

It is on the 14th floor and the daily rate is $90.　房间在14层，每天的房费是90美元。

入住注意事项 Some Rules When Checking In

我会给您两套房间钥匙。

I'll give you two room keys.

请务必随时带着其中一个。

You must have one of them with you at all times.

如果您还需要毛巾或枕头，请给前台打电话。

Just call the front desk if you need any extra towels or pillows.

举一反三

I'm afraid you can't check in until after 4:00 pm.　恐怕您只能在下午四点以后才能入住。

Complimentary breakfast is served in the lobby between 8 and 10 am.

您可以在早晨8~10点到大厅享受住宿附送的早餐。

The dining room is on the main floor at the end of the hall.　餐厅在一层大厅最里面。

The weight room and sauna are on the top floor.　健身房和桑拿室在顶层。

填表 Filling out Forms

对了，我们这儿是有您预订的房间。

Yes, we do have a reservation for you.

请您把这份表填好，我同时就给您门卡，好吗？

Would you please fill out this form while I prepare your key card for you?

举一反三

What should I fill in under ROOM NUMBER?　"房间号码"这一栏我该怎么填呢？

I'll put in the room number for you later on.　过会儿我来给您填上房间号码。

You forgot to put in the date of your departure.　您忘了填写离店日期了。

续订 Extension Request

我的业务谈判进行得比我原先预料的慢了许多。

My business negotiations have progressed much more slowly than I had expected.

我想知道是否可以让我在这儿多待两天。

I wonder if it would be possible for me to extend my stay at this hotel for two days.

举一反三

Please make sure that you have it with you at all times.　请确保您一直随身携带着它。

I'll take a look at the hotel's booking situation.　我来查看一下本店房间的预订情况。

I'm happy to tell you that we'll be able to fulfill your extension request.

很高兴我们可以接受您延长住宿的要求。

But I'm afraid that you'll have to change rooms for the last two nights.

不过，恐怕最后两天我们得请您搬到别的房间去。

We have already lent your room to another gentleman.

我们已经把您住的房间租给了另外一位先生。

退房 Checking Out

我想现在结账。

I'd like to pay my bill now.

我现在想结账。请给我账单，好吗？

I'm checking out now. Can I have my bill, please?

举一反三

Excuse me. We're leaving today. I'd like to pay our bills now.

劳驾。我们今天要离开了。我希望现在就把账结清。

Can I pay by credit card?　我可以用信用卡支付吗？

Four nights at 90 US dollars each, and here are the meals that you had at the hotel.

That's a total of 665 US dollars.

4个晚上，每晚90美元，加上膳食费，总共是665美元。

退房注意事项 Some Rules When Checking Out

请问您的姓名和房间号码？

Your name and room number, please?

请问您今天早晨是否用过旅馆内的服务？

Have you used any hotel services this morning?

举一反三

Please sign your name here.　请您在这里签名。

By the way, the check-out time is 12:00 noon, sir.

先生，顺便告诉您，退房时间是中午12点。

What is the charge for the days you shared the room with your friend?

这几天您的朋友与您同住，费用怎么办呢？

Please add it to my account.　请记在我的账里。

投诉 Complaints

能给我换个房间吗？这儿太吵了。

Can you change the room for me? It's too noisy.

非常对不起，先生。

I'm awfully sorry, sir.

举一反三

My wife was woken up several times by the noise the baggage elevator made.

我妻子被运送行李的电梯发出的嘈杂声弄醒了几次。

140

She said it was too much for her.　她说这使她难以忍受。

The light in this room is too dim.　这房间里的灯光太暗了。

Please get me a brighter one.　请给我换个亮的。

The room is too cold for me, I'm rather cold at night.

这房间太冷了，我睡觉时感到很冷。

投诉处理 Dealing with Complaints

我向您道歉。

I do apologize.

好的，先生，我马上就回来。

Certainly, sir. I'll be back right away.

举一反三

We'll manage it, but we don't have any spare room today.

我们会尽力办到，但是今天我们没有空余房间。

Could you wait till tomorrow?　等到明天好吗？

And if there is anything more you need, please let us know.

如果还需要别的什么东西，请告诉我们。

酒店服务 Hotel Service

谢谢。先生，您在这里住得满意吗？

Thanks. Are you satisfied with your stay here with us, sir?

非常满意。房间很舒适，服务很周到。

Very much. The room was cozy and the service was jolly good.

举一反三

By the way, could you deliver my luggage to the airport in advance?

顺便问一下，你们可以提前把我的行李送到机场吗？

Sure. It will be taken care of, sir. Which flight are you taking?

当然可以。我们会办好的。您乘坐的是哪趟班机？

Flight 17. And my luggage should be delivered there by 4 o'clock.

第17号班机。我的行李需要在4点之前送到。

Got it, sir. It'd be great to see you again, sir.　没问题，先生。希望能再次见到您。

Dialogue 1 ● 预订 *Reservation*

一位美国教授丹要来史密斯的研究所参加为期一周的学术交流会。他的妻子也随他来到了中国旅游。丹是史密斯的老朋友，于是史密斯就打电话到酒店帮他预订房间。

An American professor, Dan, will go to the Smith's Institute to attend a one-week academic exchange meeting. His wife accompanied him to China to travel. Dan is an old friend of Smith, so Smith will call the hotel to help him book a room.

Waitress:	Good morning. Star Hotel, at your service.
Smith:	Good morning! I'd like to make a reservation, please. Do you have any rooms available for next week?
Waitress:	All right. Single-room or double-room?
Smith:	Double-room, please. It's for an American couple.
Waitress:	Hold on, please. Let me check the bookings. Yes, we have double-rooms available. What kind of room would you like, sir?
Smith:	I'd like a room with a nice view, please.
Waitress:	We have a nice garden-view room.
Smith:	Good. I'll take that one. Is there a bar in your hotel?
Waitress:	Yes, sir. And there is also a party each Saturday night in the bar till the next morning.
Smith:	Oh, really? Anyway, what's the room charge?
Waitress:	888 Yuan per night with breakfast. What's their arrival time?

Smith:	They'll turn up around 4 p.m. next Monday, and they'll check out next Sunday.
Waitress:	I see. May I have your name and phone number?
Smith:	Yes. 67101213. Smith.

服务生:	早上好。这里是星星酒店，竭诚为您服务。
史密斯:	早上好。我想要预订一个房间。你们下周有空房吗？
服务生:	有的。请问要单人间还是双人间？
史密斯:	双人间。我是为一对美国夫妇预订的。
服务生:	请稍等。让我查一下房间的预订情况。是的，我们有空的双人间。请问您要什么样的房间？
史密斯:	我想要一个带漂亮风景的房间。
服务生:	我们有一个面向漂亮花园的房间。
史密斯:	好的。我就要那一间了。酒店里有酒吧吗？
服务生:	有的。每周六晚上酒吧里都会有晚会，而且会一直持续到第二天早上。
史密斯:	哦，是吗？不管怎样，房间收费标准是怎样的？
服务生:	每晚888元，包早餐。他们什么时候到？
史密斯:	他们下周一下午4点左右入住，下周日离开。
服务生:	知道了。可以留一下您的名字和电话号码吗？
史密斯:	好的。67101213。史密斯。

Dialogue 2 入住 Check In

丹和史密斯在酒店门口见面。史密斯带丹夫妇到前台登记入住。来看一下具体情况吧。

Dan and Smith meet in front of the hotel. Smith takes Dan and his wife to the front desk to check-in. Let's look at the situation in detail.

Smith: Hi, Dan. Long time no see.

Dan: Hi. Nice to see you here. Oh, this is my wife Lena. Lena, this is Smith.

Lena: Nice to see you.

Smith: Nice to see you too. I've made a reservation for you guys. Wanna go and have a look?

Dan: Sure, you are the boss.

Waitress: Good afternoon. Can I help you, sir?

Smith: Well, I made a reservation last week for this American couple by the name of Smith. Here they are.

Waitress: One minute, please. Smith… Oh, yes, here it is. One double-room for a whole week, here is the registration card. Will you please fill this form out, sir?

Dan: Love to. Done. Here you are.

Waitress: Thank you. Now everything is in order. Your room number is 8715.

Dan: Is it on the 87th floor? Wow!

Waitress: No, sir. In China, 8 is only a lucky number. It's on the 7th floor.

Dan: Thank you.

史密斯：   嗨，丹，好久不见了。

丹：   嗨。见到你真高兴。哦，对了，这是我的妻子莉娜。莉娜，这是史密斯。

莉娜：   很高兴见到你。

史密斯：   我也很高兴见到你。我为你们预订了一个房间。现在想去看一下吗？

丹：   当然可以，听你的。

服务生：   下午好。有什么能为您效劳的吗？

史密斯：   上周我用史密斯这个名字为这对美国夫妇预订了一个房间。现在他们来了。

服务生：   请稍等。史密斯……哦，是的，这儿呢。一个双人间预订一周。这是登记卡。能麻烦您填一下吗？

丹：   非常乐意。填完了。给你。

服务生：   谢谢。全都处理好了。你们的房间号是8715。

丹：   房间在87层吗？哇噻！

服务生：   不，先生。在中国8只是一个幸运数字。房间在第七层。

丹：   谢谢你。

爱德华带维维安来到豪华的宾馆，并且为维维安叫了客房服务，可是维维安似乎对高档宾馆很陌生。当接待员送来饮料水果，等待维维安付给他小费时，维维安却不知道他想要什么。

Edward takes Vivian to a luxurious hotel and orders room service for Vivian. But Vivian seems very unfamiliar with luxury hotels. When the waiter brings fruit and drinks, and waits for Vivian to tip him, Vivian does not know what he wants.

Receptionist:	Good evening, Mr. Lewis.
Edward:	Hello. You have messages?
Receptionist:	Yes, we have several.
Edward:	Thank you. Could you send up some champagne and strawberries, please?
Receptionist:	Of course. Room service for Mr. Lewis, please.

(Someone is knocking the door.)

Vivian:	What is that?
Edward:	Champagne.
Vivian:	Oh! Well. Might as well make myself useful. Take a load off.
Waiter:	Good evening.
Vivian:	Hi.
Waiter:	Uh, where would you like it?
Vivian:	Where would we like it?
Edward:	Uh, over by the bar.
Vivian:	Excuse me!
Waiter:	It'll be on your bill, Mr. Lewis.
Edward:	Thank you.
Vivian:	What are you looking at? What is he looking at?
Edward:	Ah, yes. Here we go. Thank you very much.
Waiter:	Thank you very much, sir. Have a nice night.
Vivian:	Tip. Wow. I missed that one. Oh. Stupid.
Edward:	Don't worry about it.

接待员：	路易斯先生，晚上好。
爱德华：	你好，有我的信吗？
接待员：	是，有您几封。
爱德华：	谢谢你。请派人给我送点香槟和草莓。

接待员： 没问题。路易斯先生需要房间服务。

（有人敲门。）

维维安： 那是什么？

爱德华： 是香槟。

维维安： 这我可有事干了，我去开门。

服务员： 晚上好。

维维安： 嗨。

服务员： 哦，你想把它放在哪？

维维安： 放哪？

爱德华： 放吧台上吧。

维维安： 对不起。

服务员： 都记在账上了，路易斯先生。

爱德华： 谢谢你。

维维安： 你在看什么啊？他在那看什么？

爱德华： 噢，给你，非常感谢。

服务员： 多谢，祝你们度过一个愉快的夜晚。

维维安： 小费。噢，我……我居然没想到。真傻！

爱德华： 别往心里去。

词句荟萃 Words and Sentences Gathering

cozy ['kəʊzɪ] *adj.* 舒适的

fascinating ['fæsɪneɪtɪŋ] *adj.* 迷人的

reservation [ˌrezə'veɪʃn] *n.* 预订

couple ['kʌpl] *n.* 一对夫妻

registration [ˌredʒɪ'streɪʃn] *n.* 登记

traditional [trə'dɪʃənl] *adj.* 传统的

nationality [ˌnæʃə'nælɪtɪ] *n.* 国籍

forward ['fɔːwəd] *v.* 发送，寄发

passport ['pɑːspɔːt] *n.* 护照

signature ['sɪgnətʃə] *n.* 签名

departure [dɪ'pɑːtʃə] *n.* 离开

regulation [ˌregju'leɪʃən] *n.* 规章，规定，条例

negotiation [nɪˌgəʊʃɪ'eɪʃən] *n.* 谈判；磋商

extension [ɪk'stenʃən] *n.* 延长日期

forwarding address 转投地址

place of issue 发照地点

疯狂链接 Interlinkage

表示房间设施的词汇

床 bed
门 door
椅子 chair
镜子 mirror
桌子 table
抽屉 drawer
窗户 window
长沙发 couch

书架 bookshelf
壁炉 fireplace
壁橱 cupboard
扶手椅 armchair
橱柜 cabinet
折（叠）椅 folding chair
家具 furniture

Section 2

I have a friend who wants to rent out his apartment.

I am thinking about renting a new place.

■ 租房
Renting

疯狂表达 Expressions

租房计划 Making a Rental Plan

我们需要租一套新房子。

We need to rent a new apartment.

我们租什么样的房子?

What kind of place should we rent?

举一反三

In fact, I don't really care about the size of the apartment.

确切地说,对房子的大小我倒不是很在乎。

As long as it's close to the university so we don't have to get up so early.

离学校近就行,这样我们就可以多睡会儿了。

Neither do I. So a small place is OK, but we'll get a bigger one if it's not too expensive.

我也是。小的就行,当然,如果不贵的话,也可以找一个大一点儿的。

咨询中介 Consulting Estate Agent

你好,我要租间房。

Hello, I want a room.

好的，很高兴为您服务。

OK, my pleasure!

举一反三

Do you have rooms to let?　你那里有房间出租吧?

Can you help me find a cheap apartment?　你能帮我租一间便宜的房子吗?

If you get any information, please call me; this is my phone number.

如果你有什么消息，请打电话告诉我，这是我的电话号码。

通过广告租房 Renting a House by Advertisement

我想要一套只有一间卧室的公寓。

I want a one-bedroom apartment.

你看报纸上"房屋出租"的广告了吗?

Have you looked at the "For Rent" ads in the newspaper?

好主意，谢谢。

That's a good idea. Thanks.

举一反三

This city has a special paper that lists only rentals.　当地有一份报纸专门刊登房屋出租信息。

I'll go to the newsstand now and pick one up.　我这就去报摊买一份。

房屋要求 House Requirements

我们想要租一套七十到一百平米，两个卧室，有中央空调，新街口附近的新楼。

We want to rent a new two-bedroom apartment, around 70 to 100 square meters,

central heat and air conditioner, in the Xinjiekou area.

举一反三

I want a room with a double bed.　我要一间有双人床的房间。

Yes, just bed and breakfast.　只要床铺和早饭。

It must have a bathroom.　要有洗澡间。

Do you provide meals?　你们这里包饭吗?

Is it furnished?　有家具吗?

设施费用 Utility Fees

谁付水电费用?

Who pays utilities?

我们平摊煤气费、电费和水费。

We split the gas, electricity and water.

举一反三

Are all the utilities included?　各种费用都包括在房租里吗？

Electricity and water are included in the rent, but gas isn't.

房租包括电费和水费，但不包括煤气费。

How about the phone?　电话呢？

You may have your own telephone and phone bill.　你可以自己装电话，自己承担费用。

询问租金 Asking the Rent

租金是多少呢？

How much is the rent?

举一反三

What's the price per month?　每月房租多少啊？

What's the price per week?　按星期算房租是多少？

The price should be between 6000 and 8000 RMB.　房租价位在6000~8000人民币。

价钱偏高 Price Is High

房租有点贵啊。

It's a little expensive.

举一反三

That's quite a bit more than I was thinking of giving.　那比我本来想的价钱要贵一些。

Perhaps you have a less expensive room.　也许你们有比较便宜一些的房间吧。

看房 Checking Out the House

如果你们有一套这样的房子。今天下午可以去看一下吗？

If you do have one available now, could we go to look at it this afternoon?

举一反三

Could we go to check at the house next Monday?　下星期一去看房行吗？

Good. Let's go to the real estate agent's and see the house.

好的。我们现在就去房产中介那里看看房子。

房间合适 House Is Good

这对我来说很合适。

This is all right for me.

举一反三

I want the room today.　我今天就要来住。

I suppose I can move in at once, right?　我想我马上就能搬来吧，是不是？

签租约 Signing the Lease

我们要签一份租房契约。

We'll sign a lease.

我通常签1年的契约。

I usually only sign one year leases.

举一反三

Okay. If everything goes well, you can sign the lease quickly.

好的。顺利的话，你们很快就可以签约了。

Now, we can sign the lease.　现在，我们可以签约了。

Just sign your name and the date here.　在这儿写姓名和日期。

租房押金 Security Deposit

要交押金吗？

Do I need to pay a security deposit?

是的，要付一些。

Yes, you may pay some.

举一反三

Well, I think I'll take it. Can I write you a check for the security deposit now? $1200?

好的，我想我会租下的。现在写张支票交押金好吗？是1200元？

How will you return my security deposit?　我的押金要如何退还？

Yeah, and don't worry about the security deposit. If everything's all right when you move out, you'll get it back.

对，对于押金您不用担心，当你搬出的时候如果一切无恙，我会退还你的。

Dialogue 1 · 中介租房 Renting a House Through Agent

> I would like to rent an apartment.

> What do you need?

查理想要租套房子，由于对这个城市不熟悉，于是他去找中介帮忙。
Charlie wants to rent a house. Due to the fact that he's not familiar with this city, he turns to an agent.

Charlie: I would like to rent an apartment.

Agent: What do you need?

Charlie: A new two-bedroom apartment, around 70 to 100 square meters, central heat and air conditioner, in the Sanlitun area.

Agent: And what is your price range?

Charlie: 5000~8000 RMB.

Agent: We do have one available. Do you have time to go and look at it?

Charlie: Yes, I do. Shall we go now?

Agent: OK, let's go.

查理： 我想租个房子。

中介： 您有什么要求吗？

查理： 70到100平米，两个卧室，有中央空调，三里屯附近的新楼。

中介： 您可以接受什么价格范围的房子？

查理： 5000到8000块钱。

中介： 我们还真有一套这样的房子。您有时间去看一下吗？

查理： 有时间。我们现在就去吧。

中介： 好的。我们走吧。

Dialogue 2 · 计划租房 Wanting to Rent a House

I am thinking about renting a new place.

I have a friend who wants to rent out his apartment.

麦克打算另找地方住，莉莉有个朋友正想出租公寓。莉莉就向麦克介绍公寓的相关事宜。

Mike is thinking about renting a new place. One of Lily's friends wants to rent out his apartment. So Lily tells Mike about the new apartment.

Mike: I am thinking about renting a new place.

Lily: I have a friend who wants to rent out his apartment.

Mike: Where is it located? I don't want anything too far from my work.

Lily: It is near Xizhimen. It will only take you half an hour to cycle to work.

Mike: Really? Can you ask him the size of his apartment and the price?

Lily: Yes. It is an 100 m² apartment with three rooms. It costs 3500 RMB a month.

Mike: That's too much. Can he make it a little bit cheaper?

Lily: I can help you do the bargaining if you want to rent it.

Mike: What are the surroundings and the community like?

Lily: Not bad. The area is beautiful and it has all the facilities you need.

Mike: Can you take me to see your friend and the house tomorrow?

Lily: Okay. If everything goes well, you can sign the lease quickly.

麦克： 我打算另找一个地方住。

莉莉： 我有个朋友正想出租他的公寓呢。

麦克： 在什么位置？我不想住处离单位太远。

莉莉： 在西直门附近，骑自行车大约半小时就到单位了。

麦克： 能帮我打听一下公寓的大小和价钱吗？

莉莉： 是一套三居室的公寓，一百平米，每月3500元。

麦克： 价钱有点高，能便宜些吗？

莉莉： 如果你想租的话，我可以帮你砍砍价。

麦克： 小区以及周围的环境怎么样？

莉莉： 挺不错的，环境幽美，各种设施都很齐全。

麦克： 你明天带我去见见你的朋友，看看房子好吗？

莉莉： 好的。顺利的话，你们很快就可以签约了。

Dialogue 3 经典影像观摩 The Emulation of Classical Movies

乔伊带钱德勒参加同剧组演员的派对。该演员打算搬家，建议乔伊租下他现在的房子。

Chandler and Joey attend a party thrown by one of the other actors on Days of Our Lives. He happens to be moving out, so he offers to let Joey have his apartment.

Joey: Can you believe this place?

Chandler: I know. This is a great apartment.

Joey: I was just in the bathroom. And there're mirrors on both sides of you. So when you're in there, it's like you're peeing with the Rockettes.

Chandler: Well, there's my fantasy come true. No, seriously.

Joey: Hey, we were just saying, great apartment, man.

Actor: Thanks. You want it?

Joey: En?

Actor: Yeah. I'm moving to a bigger place. You should definitely take this one.

Joey: Can you see me in a place like this?

Actor: Why not? You hate park views and high ceilings? Come on. I'll show you the kitchen.

Chandler: Ah, that's all right, fellow. I saw a kitchen this morning. On TV. Stop talking, okay.

乔伊：   你相信这个地方吗？

钱德勒：   我知道，这个公寓很棒。

乔伊：   我刚去过浴室，两边墙上都有镜子，所以小便的时候，就好像有一排人在小便。

154

钱德勒: 我的梦想实现了。不，我是说真的。
乔伊: 我们正在赞美你的公寓，老兄!
演员: 谢了，你要吗?
乔伊: 嗯?
演员: 我要搬到一个更大的地方去，你真的应该租下来。
乔伊: 你看我会住这种地方吗?
演员: 有何不可呢? 你讨厌公园景观跟高天花板吗? 来吧。我带你去看厨房。
钱德勒: 不用了，兄弟，我今早在电视上看过一个厨房了。不要再说了。

词句荟萃 Words and Sentences Gathering

rent [rent] *v.* 租
estate [ɪ'steɪt] *n.* 财产；地产
consult [kən'sʌlt] *v.* 咨询
facility [fə'sɪlətɪ] *n.* 设施
sign [saɪn] *v.* 签
lease [liːs] *n.* 租约；租期

疯狂链接 Interlinkage

租房词汇

租金 rental price
押金 deposit
租家具 rent furniture
有线电视 cable
取暖 heating
消防通道 fire passage
公寓房间 apartment
租约，租契 lease
租金，租费 rent
房东 landlord

女房东 landlady
邻近地区 neighborhood
信用 credit
厨房 kitchen
客厅 living room
卧室，寝室 bedroom
浴室，化妆室，厕所 bathroom
保证金，不动产租赁押金 security deposit

Section 3

Not necessarily. If we use a realtor to find a house, it will be more expensive.

■ 买房
Purchasing a House

We need to find a realtor.

疯狂表达 Expressions

新房环境 Surroundings of New Houses

好啊。周围环境怎么样?

Great. How is the surrounding area?

举一反三

Very quiet and safe. And it's got a lot of trees and plants.
很安静，治安很好，而且绿化也很棒。

The neighborhood is nice too. There is a park nearby.
周围环境也不错，附近还有个公园。

Yes, and there are many houses nearby. I like neighborhoods that aren't full of apartment blocks.
是的，还有许多房子，我喜欢周围没有太多高层的公寓楼。

便利设施 Conveniences

很好啊。交通便利吗?

That's good. Is the location easily accessible?

嗯，挨着公车站。

Yep, it's near a bus stop.

举一反三

What sort of public transportation is nearby?　附近有什么公交系统?

There's a subway stop and a bus station is just around the corner.
附近有一个地铁站和一个公车站。

The schools in this area are very good. 这个地方的学校也很不错。

As far as other conveniences in the neighborhood, there's a grocery store just up the block, and there are lots of small shops nearby.
其他的便利设施还包括街区内的一个杂货店，附近还有很多小店铺。

买房咨询 Consulting of Buying House

我想询问你们在今天的报章中刊登有关唐厦的广告。

I would like to check out today's newspaper advertising on Tong House.

举一反三

Is the flat still available? 那个房子是否已经售出？

Can you tell me the size, layout and view of the house?
可否告诉我那套房子的面积、布局和观景如何吗？

Do you have the floor plan of the building? 你有没有这栋大厦的平面图？

咨询应答 Responses of Consulting

好的，太太，请坐。我想你所指的是定价450万港币的那个住宅。

Yes, Madam. Have a seat, please. I think you mean the one priced at four point five million Hong Kong dollars.

举一反三

Sure. The area of this flat is around nine hundred square feet. It has one living room, one dining room, one master bedroom and two bedrooms.
当然可以。房子面积约900平方英尺。有一个客厅、一个饭厅、一个主卧和两间客房。

Yes, here it is. For this unit, the efficiency rate is very high because the layout is very effective. Also, the owner keeps the house in a good condition.
有。这就是了。以这套房子而言，由于它的设计很实用，所以使用率很高。再者，业主把房子保持得非常好。

Maybe I can show you the house. 或者我先带您看看房子。

找房产经纪人 Finding a Realtor

我们需要找个好的房地产经纪人。

We need to find a good realtor.

不需要。如果我们委托经纪人找房子，会比较贵。你要付他们钱。

Not necessarily. If we use a realtor to find a house, it will be more expensive. You have to pay them.

举一反三

I still think we should have a realtor. We don't know all the laws of buying a house. And also, the realtor will inspect the house. He can tell us if the house has any problems.　我认为应该要找经纪人。我们不知道买房子的相关法律。而且经纪人也会检查房子。他可以告诉我们房子有没有问题。

And doesn't the person selling the house have a realtor?　那么卖房子的人不会找经纪人吗？

Sometimes they do, sometimes they don't. It's best to find someone who is selling by themselves.　有些会，有些不会。最好是找自己卖房子的人。

Why?　为什么？

Because if the seller has a realtor, his price will be higher. He has to pay a commission to the realtor.　因为如果卖主找经纪人，房价就会比较高。他必须付经纪人佣金。

贷款买房 Buying a New House by Loan

我很喜欢这套新房子，可是价钱太高了，我买不起。

I am very interested in this new apartment, but the price is really high, I really can't afford it.

可以用贷款买房。

You can buy it by taking out a loan.

举一反三

And we can take out a loan to pay the rest.　我们还可以贷款来付其余的钱。

He will pay in installments.　他将分期付款。

That surely will cost you a lot of money. Are you going to make a full payment?
那真得花掉你不少钱，你准备一次付清吗？

Do you think I am rich enough to do that? I am thinking about paying for the apartment in installments. The real estate agency says if I pay a 20% down payment, I can move in at once.　你以为我有那么多钱？我在考虑申请分期付款，房产商说如果我首付百分之二十房款就可以马上入住。

It sounds so tempting. Why not go to apply for a loan from the bank? They charge very low interest, so you can choose whether to pay off the balance in 10 or 20 years.
听上去好诱人啊。你何不到银行去申请贷款呢？他们的贷款利息收得很低，你还可以选择10年期或20年期还清。

讨论房价 Discussing Price of House

听说你买房了？

I heard that you bought a house, is that true?

唉，有这个想法，可是今年房价又暴涨了。

Oh, I always had the idea, but house prices have gone through the roof this year.

举一反三

Yes, house prices have escalated rapidly without any signs of reduction.
是的，房价一直在急速攀升，好像没有任何回落的迹象。

We are going to be mortgage slaves for life.　我们都快变成终身房奴了。

You can choose to rent a house instead of buying.　你可以选择租房，不买房啊。

Who doesn't want to have a house of his own?　谁不想拥有一套属于自己的房子啊！

Dialogue 1 · 找房子 Looking for a New House

> We should plan to move out of here before July. I'm tired of living in apartments.

> I think this spring is a good time for us to start looking.

亨利和珍妮已经厌倦住公寓了，计划在七月前搬入自己买的新房子。两人正在谈论着找新房子的事情。

Henry and Jeannie are tired of living in apartments and plan to move into their newly-bought house before July. They are talking about buying a new house.

Henry: I think this spring is a good time for us to start looking.

Jeannie: We should plan to move out of here before July. I'm tired of living in apartments.

Henry: I know, dear. Me too. But we've just been too busy to look for a house.

Jeannie: We need to find a realtor.

Henry: Not necessarily. If we use a realtor to find a house, it will be more expensive. You have to pay them.

Jeannie: So how can we find a house if we don't have a realtor?

Henry: It takes a little more time. We have to check the ads in the paper. Also there are probably special real estate magazines with ads. Then we have to drive to the houses and look at them.

Jeannie: Hmm. It all sounds very complicated.

Henry: It is. But buying a house is very important. So it takes time. That's why we haven't done it yet. It's very troublesome.

Jeannie: I want to read the papers today. Maybe we will see something we like.

Henry: Alright. I'll buy a newspaper when I go to the drug store.

亨利：　今年春天开始找房子是不错的时机。
珍妮：　我们应该计划在七月前搬走。我已经厌倦住公寓了。
亨利：　亲爱的，我知道，我也是。但是我们一直没时间去找房子。
珍妮：　我们需要找个房地产经纪人。
亨利：　不需要。如果我们委托经纪人找房子，会比较贵。你要付他们钱。
珍妮：　如果不找经纪人，我们要怎么找到房子呢?
亨利：　要花多一点时间。我们必须看看报纸上的广告。或许专门的房地产杂志上也有广告，
　　　　然后我们必须开车去看房子。
珍妮：　听起来挺复杂的。
亨利：　不过买房子很重要，所以要花时间。那就是为什么我们还没买，很麻烦的。
珍妮：　我今天要看报纸，或许可以找到喜欢的。
亨利：　好，我去药店的时候会买份报纸。

Dialogue 2　看房子 Viewing a New House

> Please come in and feel free to take a look around the house.

> Hello, Mr. Johnson, I am with Mrs. Chen to view your house.

陈太太签署看楼协议书后，物业代理詹姆士·威尔逊带陈太太到约翰逊先生的房子实地察看。他们按了门铃。

After Mrs. Chen signs the contract for viewing the new house, Agent James Wilson accompanies Mrs. Chen to see and inspect Mr. Johnson's house. They ring the door bell.

Agent:　　　Hello, Mr. Johnson, I am with Mrs. Chen to view your house.

Mr. Johnson:　Please come in and feel free to take a look around the house.

Agent:　　　Mrs. Chen, as you can see, the decoration is in perfect condition. The kitchen is on your left. Look! It is so big five people could sit here. The layout of the flat consists of one dining room, one living room, one master bedroom and two other bedrooms. The gross area of this unit is nine hundred and thirteen square feet.

Mrs. Chen: Does this apartment face south?

Agent: The living room faces south and the bedrooms face north. Mrs. Chen, what do you think of this unit? It has a beautiful hill view and a quiet environment. Also, Tai Koo Shing has many amenities such as a large shopping mall, wonderful playground, residents club, four standard tennis courts and a few supermarkets.

Mrs. Chen: Great!

Agent: Mrs. Chen, it's only because Mr. Johnson must go back to England that he has to sell this unit.

Mrs. Chen: I understand. The flat is in good condition and I won't have to redecorate it later. But, I've got to discuss it with my husband first. Mr. Wilson, how about I call you to make an appointment again?

Agent: Sure. Mrs. Chen. Although, I should remind you that you must be quick because I have other clients wanting to see this unit.

Mrs. Chen: Okay. I'll call you later.

Agent: Thank you, Mr. Johnson. I'll call you when I get back to the office.

Mr. Johnson: Thank you. I'll wait for your call. Bye.

Agent: Bye.

物业代理： 您好，约翰逊先生。这是陈太太，她来看看您的房子。
约翰逊先生： 请进来随便参观一下。
物业代理： 陈太太，这套房子装修挺好的，厨房就在左边。看，厨房可以容纳五个人。这套房子的基本设计为三室二厅，一个饭厅，一个客厅，一间主卧和两间客房。建筑面积是913平方英尺。
陈太太： 这房子是向南的吗？
物业代理： 客厅向南，卧室向北。陈太太，你觉得这套房子怎么样？这房子面向山景，风景不错，环境安静。而且太古城配套设施齐备，有大型购物商场、儿童游乐场、业主会所、四个标准网球场、超级市场等。
陈太太： 很好。
物业代理： 陈太太，因为约翰逊先生必须回英国，否则他可不愿意卖这房子的。
陈太太： 我明白，这房子基本情况很好，我不需要重新装修。不过，我要先和我先生商量。威尔逊先生，不如我再给你打电话再约吧？
物业代理： 没问题，陈太太。不过，我必须提醒您要快点决定，因为还有其他客户要求看这房子的。
陈太太： 好的，稍后我再给你打电话。
物业代理： 谢谢你，约翰逊先生，我回公司后再和你电话联络。
约翰逊先生： 谢谢。我等你的电话，再见。
物业代理： 再见。

摩妮卡和钱德勒打算买房，两个人正兴高采烈地谈论着新房。

Monica and Chandler intend to buy a new house and the two are talking about the new house excitedly.

Chandler:	Hey, hey.
Monica:	Hi, sweetie. Hey, you smell like perfume and cigarettes.
Chandler:	I was in the car with Nancy all day.
Monica:	Nancy doesn't smoke.
Chandler:	Well, at least the perfume's not mine. Be thankful for that.
Monica:	So, what did you think of the house?
Chandler:	It's perfect. It's everything we've been looking for.
Monica:	Isn't it? And what about the amazing wanes coating, the crown molding and the dormer windows in the attic?
Chandler:	And the wiggle worms and the zip zorps! What were the things you said?
Monica:	Don't you love the huge yard?
Chandler:	And the fireplace in the bedroom.
Monica:	And Nancy said it's really underpriced because the guy lost his job and has to move in with his parents.
Chandler:	This is bringing out a lovely color in you.
Monica:	So do you think we should get it?
Chandler:	I don't know. What do you think?
Monica:	I think we should.
Chandler:	I do too.
Monica:	This is huge. How bad you wanna smoke right now?
Chandler:	I don't know what you mean, giant talking cigarette.

钱德勒：	嘿，嘿。
摩妮卡：	嗨，亲爱的。你身上有香水和香烟的味道。
钱德勒：	我今天和南希在车里待了一天。
摩妮卡：	南希可不抽烟。
钱德勒：	至少那香水不是我的，你这点倒是不用担心。
摩妮卡：	那么，你认为那房子怎么样？
钱德勒：	简直太棒了，就是我们一直以来要找的。
摩妮卡：	是吗？那些漂亮的涂层，冠型屋顶，还有阁楼的天窗怎么样。
钱德勒：	还有蠕虫和爬虫。你刚刚说什么？

摩妮卡:	你不喜欢那个大院子吗？
钱德勒:	还有睡房里的壁炉。
摩妮卡:	南希还说这个价钱非常优惠，因为那家伙丢了工作不得不搬去和父母住，所以急于出手。
钱德勒:	看把你兴奋的。
摩妮卡:	你认为我们是不是应该把它买下来？
钱德勒:	我不知道，你怎么想？
摩妮卡:	我想我们应该买下来。
钱德勒:	我也这么想。
摩妮卡:	这是大事，现在想不想抽一支？
钱德勒:	你说什么？进言有功，奖励香烟。

词句荟萃 Words and Sentences Gathering

location ['ləʊkeɪʃən] *n.* 位置；场所

accessible [ək'sesəbl] *adj.* 可到达的

internal [ɪn'tɜːnl] *adj.* 内部的

efficiency [ɪ'fɪʃənsɪ] *n.* 效率；功能

effective [ɪ'fektɪv] *adj.* 有效的

layout ['leɪaʊt] *n.* 布局；安排

agent ['eɪdʒənt] *n.* 代理人

realtor ['rɪəltə] *n.* 房地产经纪人

commission [kə'mɪʃən] *n.* 委托；委任；佣金

contract ['kɒntrækt] *n.* 合同

inspector [ɪn'spektə] *n.* 检查员

关于买房词汇

买房 buy a flat/an apartment

房地产 real estate

按揭（指向银行借长期抵押贷款，用来买房子）mortgage

首付 down payment

现房（指已建好供销售的房子）completed apartment/flat

期房 forward housing delivery

二手房 resold apartment

经济适用房 affordable housing

房价 housing price

半独立式房子（一栋房子从中间隔开，成为两户人家，花园也用篱笆隔开）semi-detached house

独立式房子(一家拥有) detached house

连栋房屋(互相连接的一排房屋；两幢之间只有一层墙壁相隔) terraced houses/ row houses

篱笆 fence

房子前门 front door

车库 garage

车库通向马路的空地 driveway

公寓 flat/apartment

公寓楼 block of flats

第一层 ground floor

第二层 first floor

电梯 lift/elevator

楼梯 stairs

楼外的台阶 steps

阳台 balcony

Section 4

I'm calling to ask how much your rates are for movers.

■ 搬家
Moving

Hello, Mover Brothers.

疯狂表达 Expressions

准备搬家 Preparing to Move

不好意思，我就要搬家了。

I am sorry, I am going to move.

举一反三

I am planning something and about to make a move.　我正筹划搬家事宜呢!

I have got a job in Shanghai. I am preparing to move there soon.

我在上海找到了一份工作，这几天正准备搬过去呢!

When will you move out?　你什么时候搬家?

搬家进行中 Moving the House

你在做什么?

What are you doing?

我在搬洗衣机。

I am moving the washing machine.

举一反三

Let me help you move it.　我来帮你搬吧。

Thank you! Be careful!　谢谢！小心点。

咨询搬家公司 Consulting Moving Company

这是兄弟搬家公司，随时为您服务。

This is Mover Brothers company; we are happy to serve you anytime.

我想咨询一下你们搬家的价格。

I'm calling to ask how much your rates are for movers.

举一反三

The price depends on the amount of items to be moved, and which level they are to be moved to.　价格根据搬运物品的数量和楼层高低来定的。

The cost of moving depends on the floor you're moving to, the distance between the two places and the amount of furniture to move. We sign the contract with the customers to guarantee the stuff arrives safely.

费用是按照目的地的楼层、两地距离和搬运的家具数量来定的。我们会和客户签订合同，以确保物品安全到达。

搬家公司咨询客户 Moving Company Consulting Agent

您的东西多吗？

Do you have a lot to move?

你现在住几楼？从几楼搬到几楼？

Which floor do you live on now and which floor will you be moving to?

举一反三

First we sign the contract; you pay 50% of the cost in front, and the rest when we finish moving.　首先我们签订合同，您支付50%的费用，然后我们搬完之后再支付剩下的部分。

If any of the articles were damaged during the move, you may make a claim for compensation with our department.

如果您的任何物品在搬运过程中损坏，您可以向我们部门要求赔偿。

搬家感受 Moving Feelings

觉得新家怎么样?

So what do you think about the place?

住进去还满意吗?

Are you satisfied since you moved in?

举一反三

It's great! Unfortunately we are going to spend a fortune getting everything done.

好极了! 倒霉的是,为了把剩下的工作做好我们还得花上一大笔钱。

How old is your house then? 这房子盖了多久?

It was built two years ago. The style is still up to date.

两年前建的。我想风格上还是比较新的。

Sounds fascinating. 听起来真不错。

谈论新家 Talking about the New House

你的新家在哪里?

Where is your new house located?

靠近市中心。坐地铁很方便就能到了。

It is located nearby the downtown area. It's convenient to take the metro to get there.

举一反三

Do you have a big balcony? 你们有个大阳台吗?

It's bigger than our last one. So I can plant some flowers there.

比我们过去那个大了点。我可以在阳台养些花了。

Is your house well lit? 采光好吧?

Oh, yes. Our windows let plenty of natural lighting in. They're also wonderful views behind the house. 哦,挺好的。我们的窗户可以让很多自然光照进来,而且还能看到我们屋子后面的美景。

How many rooms does your house have? 你们家一共有多少间房子?

Right now there are three bedrooms, two bathrooms, a kitchen, a sitting room, a dining room and a living room. Would you like a tour of the house this weekend?

现在一共有三间卧室、两间浴室、一个厨房、一个起居室、一个饭厅和一个客厅。这个周末你来参观一下吧?

I'm up for that! 我真期待!

Dialogue 1 ● 向搬家公司咨询 *Consulting a Moving Company*

Hello, Mover Brothers.

I'm calling to ask how much your rates are for movers.

露西近期要搬家，打电话向兄弟搬家公司咨询相关事宜。
Lucy will move out soon, so she phones Mover Brothers to ask about moving.

David: Hello, Mover Brothers.

Lucy: I'm calling to ask how much your rates are for movers.

David: The price depends on the amount of items to be moved, and which level they are to be moved to. Generally it would be 150 yuan to 200 yuan within the city limits.

Lucy: I want to move from Xizhimen to Dongzhimen.

David: Do you have a lot to move?

Lucy: No. I have a television, a fridge, clothes and some smaller items.

David: Which floor do you live on now and which floor will you be moving to?

Lucy: Both are on the third floor.

David: That will be OK. When do you plan to move?

Lucy: I am not sure now, I am afraid it will be in three days.

David: OK, anytime, Call us when you are ready.

大卫：　您好，兄弟搬家公司。

露西：　我想咨询一下你们搬家的价格。

大卫：　价格根据搬运物品的数量和楼层高低来定的。市内单次一般在150元到200元之间。

露西：　我要从西直门搬到东直门。

大卫：　您的东西多吗？

露西：　不多。有电视机、冰箱、衣物和一些杂物。

大卫：　你现在住几楼？从几楼搬到几楼？

露西：　都是三楼。

大卫：　好的，您准备什么时候搬？

露西：　还不确定，恐怕要在三天之内吧！

大卫：　好的，随时都可以。你准备好之后，给我们打电话就成。

Dialogue 2 · 签订搬家合同 *Sign a Moving Contract*

> I've heard that you provide very good services, so when I need a mover, I call you guys first.

> Thanks a lot. Could you tell me more about what you need us to do?

苏珊与搬运工谈论搬家费用及赔偿问题。

Susan is talking with a mover about moving fees and compensation problems.

Susan:　I've heard that you provide very good services, so when I need a mover, I call you guys first.

Mover:　Thanks a lot. Could you tell me more about what you need us to do?

Susan:　Oh, you see, we are on the 8th floor, and moving into the 6th floor in another building. It is about 15 kilometers away.

Mover:　OK, the cost depends on the floor you are moving, the distance between the two places and the amount of furniture to be moved.

Susan: How much will it cost in that case?

Mover: Oh, let me see. It fits the second standard rates. Have a look at the contract, please.

(A little while)

Susan: Your charge is divided into two parts, the payment in advance and the rest. I thought that I would have to pay all of it before moving.

Mover: No, first we sign the contract; you pay 50% of the cost in front, and the rest when we finish moving.

Susan: The damage and compensation item confuses me. Could you explain it in detail?

Mover: OK. If any of the articles were damaged during the move, you may make a claim for compensation with our department.

Susan: Are you sure it will work if any of our valuables like the antique bookcase or the piano get damaged during the move?

Mover: You can rest assured! We are professional movers and we have adopted special protective measures.

Susan: OK, that's a relief.

Mover: Please trust us. We will sign the contract to guarantee your belongings arrive safely and our company cherishes its reputation above all. Shall we sign the contract right now?

Susan: OK.

苏珊： 听说你们的服务做得很好，所以现在我需要搬家，就先找你们了。

搬运工： 谢谢。您能详细说说都需要我们做什么吗？

苏珊： 你看，我们住在八楼，要搬到另一栋公寓的六楼，去那里有15公里的路程。

搬运工： 嗯，费用是按照目的地的楼层、两地距离和搬运的家具数量来定的。

苏珊： 如果那样的话需要多少钱？

搬运工： 噢，我来看看，这符合二号费率标准。请先看一下合同吧。

（过了一会儿）

苏珊： 费用是分两部分收取，预付和尾款。我还以为应该在搬运之前全部交清呢。

搬运工： 不是的，首先我们签订合同，您支付50%的费用，然后我们搬完之后再支付剩下的部分。

苏珊： 我对损坏和赔偿条款不太明白，能解释一下吗？

搬运工： 好的。如果您的任何物品在搬运过程中损坏，您可以向我们部门要求赔偿。

苏珊： 你确定如果我们的贵重物品像古董书柜和钢琴在搬运过程中损坏可以得到赔偿？

搬运工： 您可以放心。我们是专业的搬运公司而且我们有特殊的保护措施。

苏珊： 呃，好吧，我放心了。

搬运工： 请相信我们。我们签订了合同就会保证您的物品安全到达，我们公司最注重声誉。我们现在能签合同吗？

苏珊： 好的！

杰克和凯特在车上闲聊，两人谈起为什么搬离纽约的事情。

Jack and Kate are chatting in the car. The couple talks about why they moved away from the Village.

Jack: We had a lot of good times, didn't we?

Kate: Do you remember that place on Charles Street where we used to go?

Jack: Charles Street? What, in the Village? When we lived in Greenwich Village? Yeah. Yeah, Yeah, great times. Great place. Why did we ever leave?

Kate: You can't raise a kid in an apartment in the Village. And then there was that trek out to that hospital. You were great. But surviving the heart attack was one thing…

Jack: You had a heart attack?

Kate: Hey, Jack, stop that. I'm still mad at you. Who knows what would have happened if you hadn't stepped in at the store?

Jack: That's why I work for Big Ed. That's why I work for Big Ed, yeah. So we had a baby, Big Ed had a heart attack. Bought that house and I've been working for him ever since. Sayonara, Wall Street.

杰克: 我们有过很愉快的时光，对吧？

凯特: 记不记得查尔街那间餐厅？

杰克: 查尔街？你说纽约？那是我们住格林尼治村时的事。那时真愉快，那儿真棒。我们干嘛搬走？

凯特: 那地方不适合小孩成长，而且离医院太远。你当时真了不起。虽然心脏病大难不死……

杰克: 你有心脏病？

凯特: 杰克，别闹了，我气还没消。你要没接手，爸的店就完了。

杰克: 所以我才在大艾德上班？所以我才在大艾德上班，对。我们有了宝宝，大艾德心脏病。我们买了这房子，我去他公司。华尔街，再会了。

compensation [ˌkɒmpen'seɪʃən] *n.* 赔偿
confuse [kən'fjuːz] *vt.* 使糊涂
archaized ['ɑːkeɪɑɪzd] *adj.* 仿古的
protective ['prətektɪv] *adj.* 保护的
unfortunately [ʌn'fɔːtʃənɪtlɪ] *adv.* 不幸地，倒霉地
spend a fortune 花一大笔钱
natural lighting 自然采光
remote control 遥控器
a small cottage 小屋

疯狂链接 Interlinkage

电器和家具名称

电冰箱 fridge (refrigerator)	书架 bookshelf
煤气炉 gas stove	电视机 television/TV
煤气炉/电炉 (gas/electric) cooker	灯 lamp
微波炉 microwave oven	油画 painting
洗碗机 dishwasher	植物 plant
空调 air-conditioner	盆栽 potted plant
中央空调 central air-conditioner	水槽，洗碗槽 sink
电风扇 electric fan	洗脸盆 wash basin (sink)
暖气 radiator	洗碗机，洗碗的人 dishwasher
加热器 heater	烤面包机 toaster
洗衣机 washing machine	梳妆台 dresser/dressing table
干衣机 dryer	镜子 mirror
电炉 electric stove	衣柜，衣橱 wardrobe
音响 personal stereo (system)	橱柜 closet
热水器 (water) heater	淋浴 shower
百叶窗 shades/shutters	浴盆，浴缸 bath/bathtub/tub
沙发 sofa	盥洗室，马桶 toilet
扶手椅 armchair	写字台 writing desk
睡椅 couch	有线电视 cable television
咖啡桌 desk/coffee table	长椅 bench
电脑 computer	凳子 stool
地毯 carpet	高脚椅 high chair
小地毯，垫子 rug	
壁炉 fireplace	

Section 5

Yeah. The central heating and air-conditioner work like a charm.

■ 房屋设施
Household Facilities

It is nice to come in here after a run.

疯狂表达 Expressions

公寓设施 Apartment Facilities

我想我正好有间适合你的公寓。

I think I have just the right apartment for you.

可以，那公寓有一间卧室、一间大厅和一间设备齐全的厨房。

Yes. It has one bedroom, a large living space and a full kitchen.

举一反三

Two bedrooms, a nice living-dining area, a full kitchen, and a full bathroom.

有两个卧室，一个很好的餐饮区，一个完整的厨房和带浴室的卫生间。

Is it furnished or non-furnished?　是否配有家具？

It is a furnished apartment with the necessary home appliances.

这公寓配有家具及必备的家庭电器。

Is there an elevator?　有电梯吗？

Yes. It's a self-service elevator and operates twenty-four hours a day.

有，是自动电梯，一天24小时运行。

房间设施 Room Appliances

这是客厅，你看有很大的衣橱。

Here's the living room. You see there are big closets.

举一反三

What about the kitchen? 厨房怎么样?

It's a well furnished eat-in kitchen. The stove and the ice-box are in good working order, and the plumbing is OK, too.

厨房设施很全，可以在里面吃饭。炉灶和冰箱均正常，管道也没问题。

How about the bathroom? 浴室怎么样?

The bathtub in the bathroom is large enough for two people.

浴室的浴缸很大，足够两个人同时使用了。

公司设施 Company Facilities

你带那些客户参观了公司设施吗?

Were you able to give those clients a tour of the company facilities?

是的，我想已经给他们留下了深刻的印象。

Yes, I think it really impressed them.

举一反三

Great. First impressions count. 好极了，第一印象很重要。

I also thoroughly enjoyed the tour of your company facilities. It provided a great insight into the company that we will go into partnership with.

参观你们公司的设施也让我非常愉快，它让我们深入了解了我们将要打交道的贵公司。

Really? You have signed the contract? 真的吗? 你们已经签署了合同?

Yes, your company's professionalism and hospitality won me over.

是的，你们公司的专业性和热情款待把我打动了。

宾馆设施 Hotel Facilities

请进，就是这儿，503号房。这是客厅，带一个小厨房，虽然小，但设备齐全。有冰箱、微波炉、烤面包机和炉灶。

Come in, please. Here we are. Apartment 503.This is the living room with a kitchenette. It is small, but fully equipped with a refrigerator, a microwave oven, a toaster and a stove.

举一反三

Well, it's really nice. Is there central air conditioner and central heating?
真不错，有中央空调和供暖系统吗？

Yes, it's warm in the winter and cool in the summer.　有的，冬天很暖和，夏天很凉快。

Is there a washer and dryer?　有洗衣机和烘干机吗？

In the basement. You can use them anytime between 8 a.m. and 10 p.m., but we close it after that. People might be sleeping or studying, you know.
在地下室有，你在早上8点到晚上10点之间使用。过了时间不能用，因为有人睡觉或学习。

新家设施 New House Appliances

这地方不错，可你得弄些家具。

This is a nice place, but you need to get some furniture.

我们住的地方可以搬一些过来，而且还有一些在我父母家里。

I have some I can bring from our place, and there's some more out at my parents'.

举一反三

Do you have a bed?　你有床吗？

Yeah. I have one from college at my parents' house.　有啊，我父母家有一张我大学时代就用过的床。

Can I take a shower?　我可以洗个澡吗？

Sure, but I don't have hot water, yet.　当然可以，可是还没有热水。

Really?　是吗？

Yes. They're coming tomorrow morning to turn the gas on. The phone should be working then, too.
是呀，他们要明天才来帮我把煤气接上，电话也到时才可以用。

Dialogue 1 · 暖气和空调 Heating and Air-Conditioner

王芳的家安装了中央冷暖系统，虽然很费钱，可是住起来很舒服。

Wang Fang has installed central heating and air-conditioner. Though it cost a lot, it could make her more comfortable.

Chen Hao: Wow, you keep this place cool.

Wang Fang: Yep. It's cool in the summer, warm in the winter.

Chen Hao: Your electricity bills must be enormous.

Wang Fang: Yeah, well, in my mind, it's a small price to pay to be comfortable.

Chen Hao: It is nice to come in here after a run.

Wang Fang: Yeah. The central heating and air-conditioner work like a charm.

Chen Hao: I usually don't use it unless it gets really hot. I just open up some windows, and I'm fine.

Wang Fang: My friend's family does the same thing. I could never get used to that, though.

陈浩：哇，你这个地方真够凉快的。

王芳：是。冬暖夏凉。

陈浩：你的电费可不得了吧。

王芳：是呀，可是，我觉得要住得舒适这点钱不算什么。

陈浩：跑完步进来这里真不赖。

王芳：是呀，中央冷暖系统简直妙不可言。

陈浩：除了非常热的时候，否则我是不会用（空调）的。就把窗户打开，这样就很好了。

王芳：我朋友家里也是这样。可是我很不习惯。

This is supposed to be your vacation; we'd like you to just relax.

Cooking relaxed me. So, what are we cooking?

琳达来到女儿家帮忙，可是女婿却总是叫她休息，最后琳达还是要到厨房帮忙。

Linda goes to her daughter's house to help out. However, her son-in-law always asks her to relax. In the end, Linda manages to help in the kitchen.

David:	Jane will be back soon. I'm going to start making dinner. You can just watch some TV in the TV room if you like. We just bought a new TV with an LCD screen. The remote control is on the coffee table next to the armchair.
Linda:	Would you mind if I helped out in the kitchen instead? I do enjoy cooking.
David:	This is supposed to be your vacation; we'd like you to just relax.
Linda:	Cooking relaxed me. So, what are we cooking?
David:	OK, well, we're going to make a pan of lasagna, a salad, and some garlic bread. Here's the recipe. Do you want to get the ingredients we need out of the cupboard?
Linda:	Sure. We should probably pre-heat the oven right away, too.
David:	That's a great idea. Can you set the oven to 200 degrees Celsius?
Linda:	That's a bit high for lasagna. I'll set it at 180 degrees and we can go from there.
David:	Fine. I'll just get out the casserole dish, the saucepan, the salad bowl, and the baking sheet.

大卫： 简快回来了。我该准备晚饭去了。如果想看电视的话，你可以去电视机房看。我们刚刚买了台新电视，是液晶屏的。遥控器就在扶手椅旁边的咖啡桌上。

琳达： 你介不介意我去厨房帮忙？我很喜欢做饭。

大卫： 你是来度假的，我们希望你能好好休息。

琳达： 做饭对我来说就是休息。那么，咱们晚饭做什么？

大卫： 好吧，呃，我们打算做一锅意大利宽面，一份沙拉还有些大蒜面包。这儿有菜谱。你能把咱们需要用的配料从橱柜里拿出来吗？

琳达： 没问题。我们应该现在就把烤箱预热上。

大卫： 好主意。你可以把烤箱调到200摄氏度。

琳达： 做意大利宽面这温度有点太高了。我想调到180度，现在我们可以开始做饭了。

大卫： 好的。我要拿一下砂锅、平底锅、沙拉碗和烤盘。

Dialogue 3 经典影像观摩 *The Emulation of Classical Movies*

戴西小姐的儿子伍森先生来看他的妈妈，他正在和女仆艾戴拉谈论关于吸尘器的事情。

Miss Daisy's son, Mr. Werthan, goes to see his mother. He is talking with the maid, Idella, about the vacuum cleaner.

Mr. Werthan:	How are you, Idella?
Idella:	Living.
Mr. Werthan:	Where's the new vacuum cleaner?
Idella:	In the closet.
Mr. Werthan:	She won't touch it.
Idella:	It gives me a shock every time I'm near it.
Mr. Werthan:	It works for me.
Idella:	Good! Then you clean and I'll go down and run your office.

伍森先生：	你好吗，艾戴拉？
艾戴拉：	还活着。
伍森先生：	我拿来的新吸尘器在哪里？
艾戴拉：	在柜子里。
伍森先生：	她不肯碰它了。
艾戴拉：	如果我靠近它不会每次被电到，我就会用。
伍森先生：	我用得好好的。
艾戴拉：	那好！那你打扫，我去替你管理公司。

shower ['ʃaʊə] *n.* 淋浴；淋浴器；淋浴间
pliers ['plaɪəz] *n.* 钳子
central heating 中央系统暖气
air-conditioner 空调
vacuum cleaner 吸尘器
LCD screen 液晶屏
remote control 遥控器
casserole dish 砂锅
saucepan 平底锅
salad bowl 沙拉碗
baking sheet 烤箱垫
screw driver 螺丝刀
It's a small price to pay. 这点钱不算什么。

疯狂链接 Interlinkage

房屋设施名称

CD机 CD player	水龙头 tap
地毯 carpet	茶壶 teapot
咖啡桌 coffee table	水壶 kettle
沙发 sofa	打蛋器 whisk
扶手椅 armchair	磅秤 scale
窗帘 curtain	开罐器 tin opener
书架 book shelf	砂锅 casserole dish
靠垫 cushion	平底锅 saucepan
壁炉 fireplace	烤箱手套 oven glove
封闭式扬声器 closed enclosure	蔬菜削皮器 vegetable peeler
遥控器 remote control	吸尘器 vacuum cleaner
壁炉架 mantelpiece	桶 bucket
烤面包机 toaster	拖把 mop
橱柜 cupboard	扳子 spanner
洗碗器 dishwasher	手电筒 torch
冰柜 freezer	老虎钳子 pliers
电冰箱 fridge	熨衣板 ironing board
微波炉 microwave oven	剪刀 scissors
插头 plug	螺丝刀 screwdriver
洗涤槽 sink	液晶电视 liquid crystal display(LCD)

Section 6

Yes. You like simple natural styles, just like me.

I think wood furniture is much more elegant than metal furniture.

疯狂表达 Expressions

装修设想 Decoration Design

你打算如何装饰你的公寓呢？

How are you going to decorate your apartment?

我觉得我们只要整修一下这木地板就可以了，然后粉刷一下墙面。

I thought we'd just fix up the wood floor, and use some paint for the walls.

举一反三

Well, it would be spacious and located next to a park, because a nice view is important to me.

嗯，它应该非常宽敞，而且紧挨着公园。因为能欣赏到窗外的美景对我非常重要。

I'm taking some measurements for new curtains.　我正在量新窗帘的尺寸。

What about measuring the floor for new carpet, and the walls for new wallpaper?

那咱们把地板和墙壁也量一量吧，然后换上新地毯和新壁纸。

Good idea. I was thinking about the same thing myself.　好主意，我跟你想的一样。

装修进程 Decoration Process

也许我们应该先画个蓝图。

Maybe we should make a blueprint first.

嗯，然后就去准备材料。

Yeah, then go to prepare for the material.

举一反三

Well, I'm going to buy some new curtains tomorrow.　嗯，我明天要去买些新窗帘。

What about the floor?　那地板呢？

I'm going to buy some durable rugs.　我要去买一些耐磨的地毯。

购买材料 Buying Material

下午好，先生。很高兴您能来我们这儿，您是在找装潢材料吗？

Good afternoon, sir. I'm pleased to have you here. Are you looking for some particular type of decoration material?

嗯，我刚买到一套新房子，我想装修一下。

Well, I've got a new flat and I want to decorate it.

举一反三

I see. If you will allow me, I would be happy to show you around and explain any product to you.

我明白了，如果您愿意的话，我乐意带您到周围看看，为您介绍一些产品。

That's very kind of you.　谢谢你了。

装修风格 Decoration Style

你家装修挺棒的，我喜欢。

Your home decor is superb. I like it.

你喜欢？你知道，我父母非常反对我这个设计，说这个色调太冷了。

You do? You know my parents are totally against my design. They said the color is too cold.

举一反三

What about repainting the living room in primrose yellow?　你觉得把客厅刷成淡黄色怎么样？

Good idea. I like a rustic style.　好主意，我喜欢乡村风格的。

I see. If you lived in an old house, would it be decorated in a modern way?

我知道了。如果你有一套老房子，你会把它装修得很现代吗？

No, I'd definitely try to restore it to its original state.　不会。我会尽力把它装修成原来的样子。

装修费用 Decoration Cost

这次我们装修房子花了近300000元。

We spent nearly 300000 yuan on sprucing up the house.

举一反三

They decorated the house regardless of the cost.　他们不计费用多少，把房屋装修一新。

We got a home improvement grant from the local council.

我们从当地市政会得到一笔装修房屋的补助。

I am thinking about redecorating our house.　我想要重新装修一下我们的房子。

That would cost a lot of money. But we do need a little change to live up the house.

那会花很多钱的。不过我们确实是要做点改变来激活这个房子。

贷款装修房子 Loaning for Home Improvement

我想借10万元，贵行可有这类贷款计划？

I want to borrow about one hundred thousand yuan. Does your bank have such loan

plans?

哦，有的。你的贷款是什么用途？

Oh, yes. What would you like to use it for?

房屋装修。

Home improvement.

举一反三

I see. Would you mind telling me your monthly salary?　您能否告诉我您的月薪是多少？

Four thousand yuan per month.　每月四千元。

Yes, sir. I suggest you apply for our "Personal Loan Scheme" which offers you a high

credit amount.　是的，先生。我建议您申请"个人贷款计划"，这个贷款额较高。

Well, how much can I borrow?　我可以借多少？

The maximum loan is 20,000 yuan.　最高可借20000元。

Dialogue 1 • 装修风格 *Style of Sprucing Up*

Yeah. I am trying to decorate my house.

What are you doing? You look as busy as a bee.

　　麦克刚刚搬入新家，好朋友莉莉来拜访麦克，看到麦克正在装饰房子，两人谈论起关于装修风格的问题。

　　Mike moved into a new house lately. His good friend, Lily, comes to visit him and sees Mike decorating his house. They then talk about the style of redeeming the house.

Lily: What are you doing? You look as busy as a bee.

Mike: Yeah. I am trying to decorate my house.

Lily: Really? That's cool. Let me see what you've done.

Mike: But actually it's not done yet. I am going to get a special pendent lamp.

Lily: It's all right. It's all right. Let me see, oh, the vase is so unique. And it is so creative to have a picture display here. What gave you the idea?

Mike: It's just simple decorating. I just want to add personality to my living space.

Lily: I noticed that most of your furniture is very traditional. You like wood furniture, don't you?

Mike: Yes. My wife and I prefer wood furniture to metal furniture.

Lily: I think wood furniture is much more elegant than metal furniture.

Mike: Yes. You like simple natural styles, just like me.

莉莉： 你在干嘛呢？你好像很忙。

麦克： 是的，我正在装修我的房子。

莉莉： 真的吗？太棒了，让我看看你都做了些什么。

麦克： 不过没弄完呢。我正打算去买一种特别的吊灯。

莉莉： 没关系，没关系。让我看看，噢，这个花瓶真别致。还有在这里放个照片陈列真是太有
　　　 创意了。你是怎么想出来的？

麦克： 只是些简单的装饰，我想为我住的地方增添一点个性。

莉莉： 我发现你大多数家具都很传统。你喜欢木制家具，是吗？

麦克： 是的，我妻子和我都更青睐木制家具，而不是金属家具。

莉莉： 我认为木制家具看起来更高雅。

麦克： 是的，你喜欢那种简约自然的风格，就像我一样。

Dialogue 2 ● 新居装饰 Decoration of a New House

> It's so great to be here! I'm so excited to help you and my daughter with your new home!

> We're glad that you're here. Would you like a tour of the house?

　　狄伦的岳母莉莉来女儿家帮忙收拾新居，她好像对客厅的窗帘很不满意，可是这却是狄伦父
母送的礼物。莉莉觉得尴尬极了，那她会怎么说呢？让我们一起来看看吧

　　Lily, Dylan's mother-in-law, goes to her daughter's new house to help out. It seems that
she is quite unsatisfied with the curtain in the living room. But it was a gift given by Dylan's
parents. Lily is very embarrassed. What will she say? Let's see together.

Lily: It's so great to be here! I'm so excited to help you and my daughter with your
　　　 new home!

Dylan: We're glad that you're here. Would you like a tour of the house?

Lily: That would be great, but could I have a cup of tea first?

Dylan: Sure, I'll go to put the kettle on. Why don't you have a seat on the sofa and I'll go and take care of things in the kitchen.

Lily: That would be lovely, thanks.

Dylan: Do you take milk or sugar with your tea?

Lily: I'll take a little milk, but no sugar, please. Make sure you let the tea steep a few minutes before you take the tea bag out of the cup.

Dylan: OK. What do you think about our living room?

Lily: Well, I do like the mantelpiece and the coffee table, but I don't really care for the curtains. Did you get them at a yard sale? They look ancient.

Dylan: My parents gave them to us as a house warming gift.

Lily: Oh dear. Well, I suppose they will do for now. Do you ever dust in here? It seems a bit dusty in here.

Dylan: Your daughter usually does the dusting, and I do the vacuuming.

Lily: I see. Well, I can help with the chores while I'm here. You two could probably use my help.

Dylan: That's very nice of you to offer. Here's your tea. Be careful, it's still quite hot.

莉莉：来这儿真是不错！我很高兴能帮你和我女儿收拾新房。

狄伦：我们很高兴您能来。想不想参观一下我们的房子？

莉莉：太好了。我能不能先喝杯茶？

狄伦：当然可以，我去烧壶水。您先在沙发上坐一会儿，我到厨房准备准备。

莉莉：那可太好了，谢谢。

狄伦：茶里放奶还是糖？

莉莉：请给我一点牛奶。但是不放糖。茶包多沏一会儿再拿出来。

狄伦：好的。您觉得我们的客厅怎么样？

莉莉：嗯，我很喜欢壁炉和咖啡桌，但是我觉得窗帘可不怎么样，你们是在大甩卖的时候买的吗？看起来很旧了。

狄伦：那是我父母送我们的新居礼物。

莉莉：我的天。其实，我觉得挺不错。你们打扫过这里吗？这儿看起来有点儿脏。

狄伦：一般是你女儿擦掉尘土，我来用吸尘器吸尘。

莉莉：我知道了。我在这儿的时候可以帮你们做点杂务。让我帮忙干什么，你们尽管跟我说。

狄伦：您能来帮忙实在是太好了。这是您的茶，小心，还有点儿烫。

乔伊带朋友们参观他的新住处，不幸的是新房子是由他亲自设计装修的。
Joey shows his friends his new apartment, which, unfortunately, he decorated himself.

Joey: Well, so what do you think? Casa de Joey. I decorated it myself.

Ross: Get out.

All: No.

Monica: Wow, Joey, this is …

Joey: Art.

Monica: Art it is.

Ross: Look, check this out! Is it a coffee table? Is it a panther? There's no need to decide.

Rachel: Hey, nice pillow. So now tell me, is this genuine Muppet skin?

Phoebe: Hey, excellent! Excellent water, table thing.

Joey: Thanks, yeah I love this. But you know what, it makes me wanna pee.

Phoebe: Yeah, well me too, yeah. I think that's the challenge.

乔伊: 你们觉得怎么样？乔伊的窝。我自己布置的。

罗斯: 少来。

朋友们: 不。

摩妮卡: 乔伊，这个是……

乔伊: 艺术。

摩妮卡: 就是艺术。

罗斯: 哦，这是一张咖啡桌呢？还是一只豹？都无所谓。

瑞秋: 好漂亮的枕头。这是真的布偶皮吗？

菲比: 好极了，桌上很棒的大水瓶子。

乔伊: 谢了，我很喜欢这个东西。你知道吗？它会让我想尿尿。

菲比: 对呀，我也是。对呀，我想挑战就在那儿。

decoration [ˌdekəˈreɪʃən] *n.* 修饰；装修

occupancy [ˈɒkjʊpənsɪ] *n.* 占有；居住

spruce [spruːs] *v.* 打扮

pendent [ˈpendənt] *adj.* 悬垂的；吊着的

unique [juːˈniːk] *adj.* 唯一的；特别的

mother-in-law 岳母，婆婆

embarrass [ɪmˈbærəs] *v.* 使窘迫

mantelpiece [ˈmentlpiːs] *n.* 壁炉架；壁炉

ancient [ˈeɪʃənt] *adj.* 古老的

vacuum [ˈvækjʊəm] *n.* 真空；真空吸尘器；*v.* 用吸尘器打扫

疯狂链接 Interlinkage

装修家具常用词汇

铝 aluminum

脚轮滑道 ball bearing slide

螺栓插销 bolt pin

家具用螺钉，螺帽 bolts and nuts for furniture

铜 brass

框架，架子 carcase

小脚轮 castor

天花板 ceiling

中央铰链铬 central hinges chrome

各种类型的抽屉滑道 complete range of drawer slide

零配件，元件 component

内藏铰链 concealed hinge

柜门锁 cupboard-lock

家具金边饰条 decorative trims for furniture

门窗 door & window

抽屉锁 drawer-lock

抽屉滑槽 drawer runner

表面处理工具 equipment for surface treatment

部分开式滑道 extension slide

水龙头 faucet

固定装置 fixture

全开式滑道 full extension slide

家具五金 furniture fittings/furniture hardware

家具零配件 furniture parts

家具结构零件 furniture structural parts

气压棒底盘 gas lift chassis

玻璃门铰链 glass door hinge

承重式滑道 heavy duty slide

钩锁 hook lock

键盘板滑道 keyboard slide

大头型 large head type

定位榫钉 locating dowel

安锁冒头 lock rail

磁性拉手 magnetic catch

磁锁 magnetic-lock

磁性撞锁 magnetic push latch

原材料 material

金属配件 metal fittings

金属拉手 metal handle

模具 mold

办公椅中管配件 office chair central tube accessories

办公椅五金配件 office chair hardware accessories

外盖型套轮 out set

板料 panel veneer

塑料 plastic

塑料螺帽及牙轴 plastic bolt and threaded axis

柜门滑道 pocket door slide

防止旋转脱落 prevent falling off due to turning

暗铰 secret-hinge

家具半成品及配件 semifinished furniture product and accessories

装潢用半成品 semifinished product for interior fittings

简单五金配件 simple connecting fittings

单项产品 single item

推拉门用轮系列 sliding door roller series

企口锁 straight-lock

板面上胶 surface gluing

薄片整修 veneer trimming

直挂格 vertical upright

木纽 wood-button

木制配件 wood components

车件 wooden bar

木塞 wooden cork

木制窗帘杆及吊环 wooden curtain rod and ring

木螺钉 woodscrew

扭弯扶手 wreathed hand-rail

Section 7

> Because our air-conditioner is broken.

■ 维修
Maintenance

> Why is it so hot here?

疯狂表达 Expressions

家庭设施问题 Household Facilities Problems

你好，是物业处吗？我是住在35号楼1901室的业主，我厕所的下水道堵了。

Hello, is this the property management office? I am the owner of building 35, room 1901. My toilet's pipes are clogged.

举一反三

It's not flushing properly, right?　不好冲，是吗？

Yes, the water is about to spill out of the toilet; please send somebody over to check it. 是啊，水都快流出来了，麻烦派人过来看看吧。

The toilet won't flush.　抽水马桶不放水了。

The pipe in my bathroom is broken, and now the water won't flow because there is no pressure.　我厕所的水管坏了，现在水因为缺压流不出来。

No problem. He'll be there in 10 minutes.　没问题，他10分钟就到。

There seems to be something wrong with the toilet.　我房间里的抽水马桶好像出了点毛病。

The faucet drips all night long.　水龙头一整夜滴水。

家用电器问题 Household Appliance Maintenance

噢，电视机好像有些毛病。

Ah, I'm afraid there's something wrong with the TV.

图像不稳定。

The picture is wobbly.

电视机有毛病了。

The TV set is not working well.

举一反三

Something has gone wrong with my computer. It always restarts.

我电脑出了点儿问题，总是自动重启。

Sounds like a virus.　好像是中病毒了。

Our washing machine just bit the dust. It doesn't work at all.

咱们的洗衣机报销了。根本不能用。

约定维修 A Maintenance Appointment

喂，是维修部?

Hello? Is this the Maintenance Department?

对，有什么事?

Yeah. It is. What can I do for you?

举一反三

我们的打印机有很多问题。你能下午过来看看吗?

We're having a lot of trouble with our printer. Could you come and take a look at it

sometime this afternoon?

让我看看，好，没问题。我大约两点钟过去。

Let me see. Yeah, all right. I'll be over around two.

应答 Responses

好，您什么时候有时间?

All right, what time is convenient for you?

好，我们尽快派个修理工过去。

OK, we will send a repair man as soon as possible.

举一反三

We'll send someone to repair it immediately.　我们会马上派人来修的。

I'm sorry, May I have a look at it?　很遗憾，我可以看看吗?

I'll send for an electrician from the maintenance department.　我去请维修部的电工来。

We can have it repaired.　我们能找人修理。

Please just wait a few minutes.　请稍等几分钟。

我不清楚具体状况。但重装是个办法，或者装个杀毒软件。

I don't know the details of your situation. Reinstalling is an option, or you can install some anti-virus software.

举一反三

Good morning. I understand that you've got a problem with your washing machine. I'm from the repair company.　早上好，我是修理公司的。公司通知我说你的洗衣机出毛病了。

Excellent. Come in please. The washing machine is in the bathroom upstairs.
太好了。请进。洗衣机在楼上的浴室里。

When did it first break down?　第一次出问题是什么时候？

About ten days ago.　大概十天前。

A part needs to be replaced. I will be back soon.　有个零件要换了。我片刻就来。

Let me see. Oh, it's clogged.　让我看看。噢，堵住了。

OK. I'll start by looking at the motor. You'd better go sit down. This could take a while.
好的，我先要查看一下发动机，你最好先坐下来，要等一会儿。

Okay, I will. Is this visit free?　可以，请尽快吧。请问一下修理是免费的吗？

保修期 Warranty Period

还在保修期吗？

Is it still under warranty?
是的，还在。

Yes, it's still under warranty.

举一反三

How long is the warranty good for?　保修期是多长时间？

One year. The maintenance store location and telephone numbers are on the warranty card.　一年。维修地点和电话都在保修卡上。

And what about your customer service?　售后服务怎么样？

We provide free delivery and installation, along with a one-year warranty.
我们提供免费的送货和安装，还有一年的保修期。

What if it doesn't work well, I mean in case?　要是坏了怎么办啊？我是说万一。

The guarantee provides for free service and parts. But judging from my experience, I'd say you'll never have to use that.
保修期内提供免费的服务。根据经验，您永远都不需要使用这个（指维修）。

How long is it guaranteed for?　保修期有多长？

Three years. And you can exchange it provided there is no damage to the product.
三年。只要没有受到损伤，你可以随时拿来调换。

疯狂对话 Dialogues

Dialogue 1 传真机坏了 Fax Machine Is Broken

> Not really, Betty. What do you need?

> Excuse me, Richard. Are you busy at the moment?

贝蒂的传真机坏了，她需要理查德的帮忙。不过理查德好像很忙，那他是怎么回答贝蒂的呢？

Betty's fax machine is broken. She needs Richard's help. But Richard seems very busy. How does Richard answer Betty?

Betty:	Excuse me, Richard. Are you busy at the moment?
Richard:	Not really, Betty. What do you need?
Betty:	My fax machine is on the blink. Would you take a look at it?
Richard:	Sure. I just need to do some other jobs first. How about if I come up around 11:30?
Betty:	OK. Thank you very much.

贝蒂：	打扰了，理查德。你这会儿忙吗？
理查德：	不太忙，贝蒂。有事吗？
贝蒂：	我的传真机快坏了。你能帮我看看吗？
理查德：	好。我还有一件事先要做。我大约11:30上去怎么样？
贝蒂：	好的。十分感谢。

Because our air-conditioner is broken.

Why is it so hot here?

董事长尼克和经理正在谈论办公室设施维修问题。

The President Nick is talking with the manager about office equipment repair problems.

Manager: Why is it so hot here?

Nick: Because our air-conditioner is broken.

Manager: Call the maintenance people in to repair it then.

Nick: Don't worry, it has already been done. Also, while on the topic of office conditions, I want to ask you what's going on with our office cleaning company.

Manager: What about them?

Nick: Well, lately when I arrive at work in the morning, I've noticed that the office isn't as clean as it used to be. I think we might need to find another cleaning company.

Manager: OK, I'll have a word with the current company and give them a second chance to pick up their act, if not, I'll replace them with someone else.

Nick: Also I think you need to have a word with our catering company about the quality of the food lately in the cafeteria. I've been receiving a lot of complaints lately.

Manager: Is anything around here still not up to standard? Yes. I'll get on that as well. Anything else?

Nick: Unfortunately yes, I just called our Internet service provider to find out why our net service is down. It dropped out this morning at about 9 a.m. and has been off ever since.

经理：为什么这里这么热？

尼克：那是因为我们的空调坏了。

经理：那赶紧叫维修工来修啊。

尼克：别担心，已经叫了。此外，说到办公条件这个话题，我想问问你保洁公司是怎么了？

经理：他们有什么问题吗？

尼克：嗯，最近我早上到公司时发现办公室没以前干净了，我认为我们也许有必要另找一家保洁公司。

经理：我会和目前的这家公司谈谈，然后再给他们一次改正的机会。如果还不行的话，我会另外找人换掉他们。

尼克：此外，我认为你有必要和为我们提供餐饮的公司就食堂的质量问题谈一谈，最近我听到好多抱怨。

经理：还有其他不达标的事情吗？这我也会处理的。还有别的吗？

尼克：很遗憾还有问题。我刚刚打电话给我们的互联网服务询问为什么网络服务掉线了，从今天早上九点钟断线后一直没有连上。

Dialogue 3 · 经典影像观摩 The Emulation of Classical Movies

克莱尔换了个新冰箱，不过她要重新修理放冰箱的架子，这事拖了很久，一直令她头疼。

Claire changes to a new refrigerator, and she has to rebuild the cabinets that hold the fridge. It takes a long time and really bothers her.

Sam:	So, Claire, is there a problem?
Claire:	I was tossing and turning last night. You know what that's like, Sam, because I realized I'm never going to fit my platters in the refrigerator we ordered, and when I give parties, I always put in platters. So I thought I would get the Sub-Zero refrigerator instead. The only problem...
Man 1:	We have to redo all the cabinets.
Sam:	We'll be into this wall.
Man 1:	That's a bearing wall.
Man 2:	That's a delay, Claire, of-Two, three-
Sam:	Five, six-
Man 1:	Twelve weeks.
Claire:	I don't mind. The important thing is to get it right.
Sam:	Absolutely.
Claire:	Your words. I've got to rush. La décorateur calls. Bye!
Three men:	Bye-bye.
Man 1:	Well, this is fate. She's divorced. We don't want to redo the cabinets, and you need a wife. What do they call that when everything intersects?
Sam:	The Bermuda Triangle.

萨姆:	克莱尔，有什么问题吗？
克莱尔:	我昨晚失眠，你知道那滋味，萨姆，因为冰箱放不下盘子，我一向用盘子盛点心待客，我就换了个冰箱，唯一的问题是……
男人一:	架子得重订。
萨姆:	得嵌进壁里。
男人一:	那是承重墙。
男人二:	克莱尔，已经拖了……二……三……
萨姆:	五……六……
男人一:	12周了。
克莱尔:	我不管，做好才重要。
萨姆:	当然。
克莱尔:	是你说的，我和设计师还有约，再见！
三个男人:	再见。
男人一:	这是命啊，她离婚了，我们不想重做，你少个老婆。倒霉事搅成一团怎么形容？
萨姆:	百慕大三角洲！

词句荟萃 Words and Sentences Gathering

maintenance ['meɪntɪnəns] n. 保持，维修

household ['haʊshəʊld] adj. 家庭的，家族的，普通的

facility [fə'sɪlətɪ] n 设备；工具；设施

appliance [ə'plaɪəns] n. 器具；用具；器械

toilet ['tɔɪlɪt] n. 抽水马桶

flush [flʌʃ] v. 奔流；奔涌

clog [klɒg] v. 妨碍；塞满

tap [tæp] n. 水龙头

wobbly ['wɒblɪ] adj. 摆动的；不稳定的

electrician [ˌɪlek'trɪʃən] n. 电工；电学家

fax [fæks] n. 传真

blink [blɪŋk] n.&v. 眨眼；闪烁

cafeteria [ˌkæfɪ'tɪərɪə] n. 自助食堂；餐厅

cater ['keɪtə] v. 备办食品；提供酒食或服务

pick up 好转；改进

drop out 断线

up to standard 符合标准

How about...? ……怎么样？

I'll get on that as well. 我会处理的。

Anything else? 还有别的吗？

关于房屋和房屋类型的词汇

公寓 apartment

阳台 balcony

浴室 bathroom

卧室 bedroom

厨房 kitchen

客厅 living room

储藏室 storeroom

卫生间 bathroom

厨房 kitchen

小厨房 kitchenette

书房 study/library

卧室兼客厅 bedsitter/bedsit

早餐室 breakfast room

餐室, 食堂 dining room/hall

阁楼 attic

储藏室 store room/house

走廊 hallway/corridor

洗衣室 laundry room

花园 garden

游泳池 (swimming) pool

网球场 tennis court

明亮的 bright

双人的 double

富丽堂皇的 palatial

简陋的 simple and crude

单人的 single

小的 small

宽敞的 spacious

空的 vacant

Section 8

It's on Tuesday and Friday.

■ 物业管理
Property Management

I was wondering when the trash collection day is.

It's on Tuesday and Friday.

疯狂表达 Expressions

报修 Reporting Problems

你好，物业中心。

Hello, management office.

你好，我们家电表好像坏了，你能派人来看一下吗？

Hi, our ammeter doesn't work. Could you send someone here to check it out?

举一反三

Can you please tell us the situation first? How come it doesn't work?

你能先说一下情况吗？怎么坏了？

Well, I put in the electricity card and it doesn't work. We have no electricity right now.

插上电卡，电表不走，家里也没有电。

How long has it been like that?   出现这种情况有多长时间了？

I noticed it was broken this morning.   今天上午刚发现坏的。

OK, we'll send a repairman to your house as soon as possible.

好的，我们会尽快派维修人员上门查看的。

社区安全 Community Security

这个地方安全吗？

Is this area safe?

还好。几个月前我们抓到一个家伙。

It's OK. We caught a guy a couple of months ago.

举一反三

I am worried so much about the security of this community because my house has been burgled twice before.　我非常担心这个社区的安全问题，因为我们家以前被盗过两次。

Oh, don't worry about that here. There are security guards on duty 24 hours a day and they patrol all over the neighborhood. You know, they are all very strong.

噢，在这儿不用担心。这儿一天24小时都有保安值班，他们会在社区里巡逻，而且他们都非常强壮。

Oh, well, you should lock the doors and turn the security system on when you leave.

哦，当你离开家的时候要锁好门，并且打开安全系统。

Is the neighborhood trying to do anything about the security?

对于安全问题，这儿的邻里有没有任何措施？

Well, we've set up a neighborhood watch program.　噢，我们建立了一个邻里监督项目。

And the superintendent won't let any strangers in.　而且物业不会让陌生人进来的。

投诉争端 Complaint Dispute

你好，我是警察。我来这里有几个问题问你。你的邻居向我投诉，说你在这个社区制造噪声。

Hello, I am from the police station. I've come to ask you a few questions. Your neighbor has complained to me that you are creating a nuisance in the vicinity.

警官，你可以说得更详细点吗？

Could you be more specific, sir?

他打电话告诉我们你经常在家里开派对。声音大得很，足以吵醒死人。

He called to tell us that you often hold parties in your house. The noise is loud enough to wake up the dead.

198

As a matter of fact, I have parties at times, but not frequently. In addition to that, we didn't play the music very loudly. Just loud enough for us to hear.

事实上，我偶尔开派对，但并不是很频繁。再说，我们的音乐声并不大，只是我们自己能够听到而已。

Not frequently? He said you have parties every weekend into the wee hours.

还不频繁？人家说你每周末都在开派对，持续到凌晨一两点。

Sir, I have to admit I do have parties sometimes on the weekend, but not every week. Besides, every time we end the party around half past 10 p.m.

是的，先生，我不得不承认，我确实有时候在周末开派对，但不是每周都开。除此之外，每次我们都在大约10点半左右结束了。

In any case, you are forbidden to do that in a residential area. You can take your friends to public places and entertain them there.

无论如何，你也不该在居民区开派对。你可以带你的朋友们去娱乐场所，在那里款待他们。

I can't agree with you more, sir. I promise that it won't happen again. Thanks .

我完全同意你的观点，警官。我保证再也不会发生这种事了。谢谢。

社区服务 Community Services

要收集垃圾可以找谁？

Who do I call for trash collection?

把它放在路边好了，会有人来收的。

Just leave the stuff by the curb. And someone will come to take it.

举一反三

I left my keys inside so I called the superintendent to break the lock.

我把钥匙落在里面了，所以我叫了物业来把锁砸开。

What's up, Bro? What's in the bulletin?　怎么啦？兄弟。布告栏上面说的是什么？

It says that there will be a blackout from 5 p.m. to 7 p.m. in our neighborhood today.

布告栏上说社区今天晚上5点到7点要停电。

Dialogue 1 社区服务 Community Services

> Oh, hi, Mary, what can I do for you?

> Hi, John, this is Mary, your tenant up in Lincoln Park.

玛丽最近租了林肯公园的房子，正在打电话询问收垃圾的时间及倒垃圾的地点。

Mary rents one of the houses in Lincoln Park and is calling to ask the trash collection time and where to dump the trash.

Mary:	Hi, John, this is Mary, your tenant up in Lincoln Park.
John:	Oh, hi, Mary, what can I do for you?
Mary:	I was wondering when the trash collection day is.
John:	It's on Tuesday and Friday.
Mary:	Great.
John:	You could save a couple of dollars by taking it to the dump yourself, though.
Mary:	Oh, OK. Where's that?
John:	It's at the corner of that street.
Mary:	Thanks. Who do I call for trash collection?
John:	Just leave the stuff by the curb. The company will send a guy out next month to give you the bill.
Mary:	All right. Thanks a lot.
John:	No problem.

玛丽：你好，约翰。这是玛丽，是租你林肯公园房子的人。

约翰：噢，你好，玛丽，有什么可以为你效劳的？

玛丽：我想知道什么时候收集垃圾？

约翰：星期二和星期五。

玛丽：好的。

约翰：如果你自己扔到垃圾站的话还可以省几美元。

玛丽：噢，好的。垃圾站在哪儿呢？

约翰：在那条街的拐角。

玛丽：谢谢。那要求收集垃圾可以找谁呢？

约翰：就把垃圾扔到路边。下个月（垃圾收集）公司会派人把账单给你。

玛丽：好的，非常感谢。

约翰：没事。

Dialogue 2 ● 新邻居 New Neighbor

Hi, Shirley. I'm Sam. It's nice to meet you.

Hello, let me introduce myself. I'm your neighbor. My name is Shirley.

隔壁搬来了新邻居，雪莉决定去拜访新邻居，那么她会和新邻居谈些什么呢？

There is a new neighbor next door. Shirley decides to visit the new neighbor. What will they talk about?

Shirley: Hello, let me introduce myself. I'm your neighbor. My name is Shirley.

Neighbor: Hi, Shirley. I'm Sam. It's nice to meet you.

Shirley: Nice to meet you, too.

Neighbor: Please come in.

Shirley: Here is a little gift for your family. It's a calendar with all the community events on it. I hope it's helpful.

Neighbor: I really appreciate it.

Shirley: Since we are neighbors, if you need any help or anything, please come to me.

Neighbor: I will. Actually, I am worried so much about the security of this community because my house has been burgled twice before.

Shirley: Oh, don't worry about that here. There are security guards on duty 24 hours a day and they patrol all over the neighborhood. You know, they are all very strong.

Neighbor: Really? That's good. Are there any supermarkets in our neighborhood?

Shirley: Of course. There is a Carrefour near the neighborhood. I'll show you the way if you want.

Neighbor: That would be terrific!

Shirley: By the way, a party will be held for new neighbors the day after tomorrow; I hope to see you there.

Neighbor: Yeah, and we can get to know each other better at the party.

Shirley: That sounds good! I've got to go.

Neighbor: OK, come and visit anytime.

Shirley: Thanks for the invitation. I will!

雪莉： 你好，首先让我做个自我介绍。我是你的邻居，我叫雪莉。

邻居： 你好，雪莉，我叫山姆。见到你非常高兴。

雪莉： 我也非常高兴见到你。

邻居： 请进。

雪莉： 这是给你们家的一点小礼物。是一本台历，上面列出了所有的社区活动。希望这能对你们有帮助。

邻居： 非常感谢。

雪莉： 既然我们是邻居，如果你需要任何东西或帮助，都可以来找我。

邻居： 我会的。事实上，我非常担心这个社区的安全问题，因为我们家以前被盗过两次。

雪莉： 噢，在这儿不用担心。这儿一天24小时都有保安值班，他们会在社区里巡逻，而且他们都非常强壮。

邻居： 是吗？那太好了。那我们社区里有超市吗？

雪莉： 当然有啊。在我们社区附近有个家乐福超市。你要想去的话，我带你去。

邻居： 那太棒了！

雪莉： 顺便说一声，后天会有一个为迎接新邻居而开的晚会，希望你能参加。

邻居： 好啊，在晚会上我们可以相互了解。

雪莉： 听起来不错。我要走了。

邻居： 好的，欢迎随时来访。

雪莉： 谢谢你的邀请。我会的！

莫妮卡和瑞秋为了省钱，做了些饼干代替圣诞节小费，支付给报童、邮差和管理员等。结果她们的暖气关不掉了，管理员不能来及时修理，她们疑心他在为没收到钱而生气。

Monica and Rachel, low on funds, make cookies to give instead of cash as holiday tips to the paperboy, the mailman, the superintendent, etc. Then when their heater won't turn off and the super couldn't come to fix it in time, they fear he's upset about not getting cash.

Rachel:	Oh, gosh! It's hot in here!
Monica:	Rachel, get the heat. Ross, could you turn the heat down, please.
Ross:	Sure. By the way, there is a difference between being obsessive and …
Monica:	Ross, the heat!
Ross:	Okay! Heat, heat, heat! And I'm the obsessive one. OK, this way is on. So this is…off.
Rachel:	Did you just break the radiator?
Ross:	No, no. I was turning the knob and …here it is.
Monica:	Well, put it back!
Ross:	Uh, it won't go back.
Rachel:	I'll call the super.
Monica:	Here, let me try.
Ross:	Oh, oh that's right. I forgot about your ability to fuse metal.
Monica:	Hey, it's Funny's cousin. Not Funny!
Rachel:	Hi, Mr. Treeger? Hi. It's Rachel Green from upstairs. Yes, somebody broke our knob on the radiator and it's really hot in here. Yes, it's, it's hot enough to bake cookies. Well, would you think we could have a new one by 6? What? No, no. Tuesday? We can't wait until Tuesday, we're having a party tonight.
Ross:	Okay, tip the man.
Monica:	No. If he doesn't like our cookies, too bad, I'm not gonna be blackmailed. Look, if worse comes to worse, it gets a little warm, we'll call it a theme party.
Ross:	Here's a theme: "Come on in, live like bacon!"

瑞秋:	天啊，这里怎么这么热啊？
莫妮卡:	瑞秋，麻烦把暖气关小。罗斯，把暖气关小。
罗斯:	好的。顺便问一下，两者之间的差别……
莫妮卡:	罗斯，暖气！
罗斯:	好，暖气、暖气、暖气！还说我钻牛角尖？好吧，往这边是开，往这边是……关。

瑞秋： 你是否把暖气机弄坏了？

罗斯： 没有，我不过是转了开关……结果就这样了。

莫妮卡： 那就装回去啊！

罗斯： 装不回去了。

瑞秋： 我打电话给管理员。

莫妮卡： 我来试试。

罗斯： 对了，我忘了你融合金属的能力了。

莫妮卡： 和好笑相反……不好笑！

瑞秋： 崔先生？我是楼上的格林·瑞秋。对，有人弄坏我们暖气的开关，我们这里好热。
是的，热到可以烤饼干了。你想你能在6点以前修好吗？什么？不，不，星期二，我们等不到那个时候，我们今晚有派对。

罗斯： 好吧，给他小费。

莫妮卡： 不，不喜欢我们的饼干就算了吧，我才不要任人勒索呢。看，如果事情越来越糟，这里有点热，就改成主题派对好了。

罗斯： 这下有主题了："请进，我们是热锅上的蚂蚁。"

词句荟萃 Words and Sentences Gathering

ammeter ['æmɪtə] *n.* 电表

convenience [kən'viːnɪəns] *n.* 便利设施；方便的用具

tenant ['tenənt] *n.* 房客；佃户；承租人

trash [træʃ] *n.* 废物，垃圾

dump [dʌmp] *v.* 倾倒，抛弃；垃圾堆放处

calendar ['kælɪndə] *n.* 台历

burgle ['bɜːgl] *vt.* 偷窃

patrol [pə'tʃəul] *vi.* 巡逻

nuisance ['njuːsəns] *n.* 损害；公害

superintendent [ˌsjuːpəɪn'tedənt] *n.* 管理者；主管

bulletin ['bulɪtɪn] *n.* 公告栏

tip [tɪp] *n.* 小费

radiator ['reɪdɪeɪtə] *n.* 暖气

obsessive [əb'sesɪv] *adj.* 萦绕于心的，有执着想法的

knob [nɒb] *n.* 手柄；把手

fuse [fjuːz] *v.* 熔合；溶化

bacon ['beɪkən] *n.* 咸肉；熏肉

security system 安全系统

around the corner 在附近

If worse comes to worse... 如果事情越来越糟……

物业管理词汇

住宅小区 residential estate

停车场 car park

室内体育馆 covered stadium

健身 body-building

私人住房 private houses

水塔 water tower

煤气公司 gas company

游泳池 swimming pool

羽毛球场 badminton field

公用设施 public utilities/services

设计 design

建造 construction

前期参与 earlier involvement

正常运转 smooth operation

居民 resident

管理经费 operating charges

资金 funds

好处 benefit

管家 housekeeper

衡量 measure

chapter 4

行 Transportation

出行用语一点通

对不起，我也是外地的。
I'm sorry. I'm a stranger here.

早上好，先生。能给我看一下您的登机牌吗？
Good morning, sir. Can I see your boarding pass, please?

请问，附近有超市吗？
Is there a supermarket nearby?

对不起，请问我在地图上的什么地方？
Excuse me, Where am I on this map?

你不能把车停在这儿。会罚款的。
You can't park here! You'll be fined!

离这儿有多远？
How far is it from here?

你可以叫一辆出租车。
You could get a taxi.

■介绍（**Introduction**）

随着信息时代的到来，我们与世界的联系越来越紧密，人们出行的机会也越来越多。无论你是出国留学，还是外出旅行，或是因公出差，你的英文水平能否让你各个场合表达自如呢？希望下面的表达能让你在出行的各种场合避免尴尬，自如交流。

今晚8点的夜车下铺车票一张。
A lower bunk ticket for the night train at eight o'clock tonight.

你去那边有什么事？
What are you going there for?

下雨天出车祸往往引起堵车。
These accidents always cause traffic jams on rainy days.

你使用计价器吗？
Do you use the meter?

两块钱。单一票制，可以乘坐全部的地铁线路。
Two yuan. A flat fare with unlimited transfers throughout the entire system.

对，很漂亮。可是颜色之所以这么红是因为空气污染。
Yeah, it's pretty nice, but it's so red because of air pollution.

假如一路绿灯的话，我们能赶到的。
We should be OK if the lights are with us.

我去那里只是观光而已。
I go there just for sightseeing.

Section 1 指路

A: 最近的公共汽车站在哪?
Where is the nearest bus-stop?

B: 直走,在第二个路口处右转。你肯定能找到的。
Go straight ahead and turn right at the second intersection. You can't miss it.

Section 2 公交地铁

A: 爸爸,你知道我们坐哪路车吗?
Dad, do you know which bus we should take?

B: 当然啊,嗯,让我先看一下公车牌。
Of course, er, let me check the bus schedule first.

Section 3 出租车

A: 师傅,请在下一个路口右转。停在出租车站牌那边好了。
Sir, please turn right at the next corner. And stop at the taxi stand.

B: 好的!
OK!

Section 4 私家车

A: 我们小区的停车场太拥挤了,不是吗?
The car park in this community is over-crowded, isn't it?

B: 是啊,私家车越来越多了。人们应该试着使用公共交通。
Yeah, there are more and more cars. People should try to take public transportation.

Section 5 火车

A: 当我们到站时你能提醒我一下吗?
   Will you tell me when we get there?
B: 您可以听车上广播。我们到站时广播公告会提醒您。
   You can listen to the announcement on the train, and it will tell you when we get there.

Section 6 飞机

A: 早上好,美国联合航空公司。我能为您做些什么?
   Good morning. United Airlines. What can I do for you?
B: 是的,我想订一张下周飞往波士顿的机票。
   Yes, I'd like to make a reservation to go to Boston next week.

Section 7 轮船

A: 你们打算乘飞机还是乘船旅行?
   Will you travel by sea or by air?
B: 可能坐船, 便宜些。
   We may travel by sea. It's cheaper.

Section 8 出入海关

A: 请告诉我你到英国来的目的, 好吗?
   Would you mind telling me the purpose of your visit to the U.K.?
B: 我是到大学读书的。
   I am here to study at a university.

Section 1

Where is the nearest bus-stop?

■ 指路
Giving Directions

Go straight ahead and turn right at the second intersection. You can't miss it.

疯狂表达 Expressions

问路时礼貌用语 Polite Expressions When Asking the Way

打扰一下，你能告诉我去警察局的路吗？

Excuse me. Could you tell me the way to the police station?

举一反三

Excuse me. Would you please tell me if there is a hospital nearby?
对不起，打扰了。请问附近有医院吗？

Pardon me, but can you tell me how to get to the zoo?
对不起，打扰了，请问去动物园怎么走？

I beg your pardon, but could you tell me the way to Liu Lichang?
对不起，打扰了，能告诉我去琉璃厂怎么走吗？

Sorry to bother/trouble/disturb you, but could you tell me how to get to the park?
对不起，打扰了。劳驾能告诉我去公园怎么走？

问去某地的路 Asking the Way to Some Places

请问，去奥林匹克公园怎么走？

Excuse me, could you tell me how to get to the Olympic park?

举一反三

Excuse me. How can I get to the History Museum, please?
打扰一下，请问我怎样能到历史博物馆？

Excuse me. Where is the Blue Sky Hotel?　打扰一下，请问蓝天大酒店在哪儿？

210

How do I get to the station?　去车站怎么走?

Excuse me, where can I find the library?　请问，怎么去图书馆?

问去某地最近的路 Asking the Fastest Way to Some Places

请问哪条路去邮局最近?

Could you please tell me the fast way to the post office?

举一反三

Please tell me the shortest way to the library.　请问去图书馆的近路怎么走?

What is the quickest way to get to the stadium, please?　请问去体育场最近的路怎么走?

Is there a shortcut to the airport, please?　请问去飞机场有近路吗?

Which is the best way to get to the railway station?　哪条路去火车站最近?

问去最近的某地的路 Asking the Way to the Nearest Places

打扰一下，请问最近的邮局在哪里?

Excuse me. Where is the nearest post office?

举一反三

Excuse me, where is the nearest bus station?　请问，最近的公共汽车站在哪儿?

Could you tell me where the nearest ladies' room is?　请问离这最近的女卫生间在哪?

Do you know where the nearest food market is, please?　你知道最近的菜市场在哪吗?

问地点 Asking Places

打扰一下，这附近有医院吗?

Excuse me. Is there a hospital near here?

举一反三

Is there a supermarket nearby?　请问，附近有超市吗?

Excuse me. Where am I on the map?　对不起，请问我在地图上的什么地方?

What's the name of this street?　这条街叫什么名字?

Excuse me, but I'm trying to find a drug store.　对不起，我要找一家药店。

问距离 Asking How Far

离这儿有多远?

How far is it from here?

举一反三

Is it near here?　是在附近吗?

Is the zoo far from here?　动物园离这儿远吗?

It's quite away.　很远。

It's a long way/distance from here.　离这里很远。

It is three miles to the lake.　这儿离湖有3英里的路程。

The post office is two blocks away.　邮局离这儿两个街区的距离。

It's about 700 metres from here.　离这儿大约有700米。

问时间 Asking How Long

去公司要多长时间?

How long does it take to get to the company?

举一反三

Will it take long to get to the airport?　去机场要很长时间吗?

It's about ten minutes' walk.　步行大约要十分钟。

It's about fifteen minutes by taxi.　乘出租车大约十五分钟。

问交通方式 Asking about Modes of Transportation

我怎么去那里?

How can I get there?

我可以坐公共汽车吗?

Can I take a bus?

举一反三

Hello! Which bus should I take to get to the railway station?

你好! 请问到火车站，我该坐哪路车?

You can take the No. 22 bus here.　您可以在这儿乘坐22路公共汽车。

Where am I supposed to change?　我应该在哪站换车?

At University street.　在学院路换车。

You'd better take No. 92.　你最好乘92路车。

Take the No. 46 bus, and get off at the square.　坐46路公共汽车，在广场下车。

You could get a taxi.　你可以叫一辆出租车。

指路 Giving Directions

直走。

Go straight.

向右拐。

Turn right.

举一反三

Keep straight on until you get to the bus stop.　一直走，走到公交站。

Go straight ahead and turn right at the second traffic lights.

一直往前走，在第二个红绿灯处右转。

Turn right at the crossroads.　在十字路口右转。

Walk along the road, and turn left at the third curve.

沿着这条路走，在第三个拐弯处向左拐。

Go along the street until you come to the traffic light.　沿这条路一直走到红绿灯那儿。

Keep going for 50 yards before you come to a fork in the road.

继续走 50 码, 直到你走到一个三岔路口。

指明地点 Pointing to the Location

有的，就在那儿。

Yes, it's just over there.

地点就在街的尽头，你会看到的。

It's at the end of the street. You can't miss it.

举一反三

There is a Bank of China over there.　那边有一家中国银行。

The post office is between the factory and the hotel.　邮局在工厂和旅馆之间。

It's next to Zhongshan Park.　它在中山公园旁边。

It's on the corner of Huaihai Street and Xizang Road.　在淮海路和西藏路的路口。

Simpson Hall is on the corner of Bellflower Boulevard and Atlantic Avenue.

辛普森楼位于贝尔弗劳尔大道和大西洋街的街角上。

You will see a BP gas station on your left.　在你的左手边你会看到一个 BP 加油站。

无法指路 Not Knowing Directions

对不起，我也是外地的。

I'm sorry. I'm a stranger here.

举一反三

Sorry, I don't know. I'm new here, too.　对不起，我不知道。我也是刚到这儿的。

I am sorry I can't help you. I'm a stranger here myself.　对不起，我也不知道如何走。我对这里不熟。

I'm sorry, I'm not sure. You'd better ask the policeman over there.

对不起，我不能确定，你最好问那边的警察。

感谢和应答 Thanks and Responses

谢谢。

Thank you very much. / Thanks a lot.

仍然要谢谢你。

Thank you all the same.

举一反三

Thank you for your help.　多谢你帮忙。

My pleasure.　乐意效劳。

You are welcome.　不客气, 不用谢。

That's OK.　不用谢。

Dialogue 1 ● 问路 Asking for Directions

> Er, let me see. Oh, look, you're right here. Pretty close to the Olympic Park.

> Excuse me, I'm lost. Can you show me where I am on this map?

今天是周末，小丽和弟弟一起出去玩。在路上，姐弟俩碰见了一个迷路的外国人。他想去逛琉璃厂，姐姐热情地给他指路。

It is the weekend. Xiaoli and her little brother go out to play. On the road, they meet a lost foreigner. He wants to look around Liulichang. Xiaoli gives him directions.

Foreigner: Excuse me, I'm lost. Can you show me where I am on this map?
(He holds a map in his hand.)
Xiaoli: Er, let me see. Oh, look, you're right here. Pretty close to the Olympic Park.
Foreigner: That's great! It's not my day. I have a very bad sense of direction.
Xiaoli: Is this your first time here? Where are you going?
Foreigner: I am supposed to go to Liulichang.
Xiaoli: Oh, there are many Chinese antique stores there. They have paintings, too. Are you interested in paintings?
Foreigner: Yes. Yes. Can you tell me how to get there?
Xiaoli: Wow, it is quite far away from here. I'm afraid you're gonna have to take Bus No.713.
Foreigner: Where is the nearest bus-stop?
Xiaoli: Go straight ahead and turn right at the second intersection. You can't miss it.
Foreigner: Thanks a lot.
Xiaoli: You are welcome.

外国人：　　你好，我迷路了。你能告诉我我现在处于地图上的哪个位置吗？
（他手里拿着一张地图。）
小丽：　　　呃，让我看看。哦，看，你就在这里。离奥林匹克公园很近。
外国人：　　真是糟糕！今天真不顺。我的方向感的确很差。
小丽：　　　这是你第一次到这里吧？你想去哪里？
外国人：　　我想去琉璃厂。
小丽：　　　哦，那里有很多中国古董店，也有中国画。你对那些感兴趣吗？
外国人：　　是的，是的。你能告诉我怎么去那里吗？
小丽：　　　哇，那离这里很远呢。恐怕你得乘713路公交才能到。
外国人：　　最近的公共汽车站在哪？
小丽：　　　直走，在第二个路口处右转。你肯定能找到的。
外国人：　　非常感谢。
小丽：　　　不客气。

Dialogue 2 ● 杰克告诉凯特怎样去警察局
Jack Directs Kate to the Police Station

And the police station is next to that. Is that clear?

I think so.

　　凯特不知道去警察局的路怎么走，向路人杰克询问，杰克能否给凯特正确指出去警察局的路呢？

　　Kate doesn't know how to get to the police station and asks a passer-by, Jack, about it. Could Jack point out the right way to the police station?

Kate:　　Excuse me.

Jack:　　Yes.

Kate:　　Is there a Police Station near here?

Jack:　　Ah, police station? Yes, there is. Yes. Let me just think. You'll go straight down this road for about a mile.

Kate: Uh-huh.

Jack: And then you turn right at the traffic light, yes, traffic light, turn right. Go straight on, and then you turn left at a roundabout. There's a big church on the corner.

Kate: Ah.

Jack: And the police station is next to that. Is that clear?

Kate: I think so.

Jack: OK, good bye.

Kate: Thanks, bye.

凯特：对不起，打搅一下。

杰克：啊？

凯特：这附近有警察局吗？

杰克：啊，警察局？有的，有一个，我想想。你沿着这条路一直走，大约一英里。

凯特：好的。

杰克：然后在信号灯处向右拐，信号灯，向右。一直走，在环岛向左。拐角处有一个大教堂。

凯特：啊。

杰克：警察局就在它旁边。清楚了吗？

凯特：知道了。

杰克：好，再见。

凯特：谢谢，再见。

Dialogue 3 经典影像观摩 The Emulation of Classical Movies

　　商业巨子爱德华在比弗利山迷路了，他邂逅了妓女维维安。维维安主动要求给理查德指路，于是他们一起到了酒店。

Business giant Edward is lost in Beverly Hills. He meets a prostitute Vivian. Vivian actively offers directions to Edward, so they go to the hotel together.

Vivian: Hey, sugar, are you looking for a date?

Edward: No! I wanna find Beverly Hills. Can you give me directions?

Vivian: Sure, for five bucks.

Edward: Ridiculous!

Vivian: Price just went up to ten.

Edward: You can't charge for directions.

Vivian: I can do anything I want to, baby, I'm not lost!

Edward: All right, OK? All right, you win, I lose, got change for a twenty?

Vivian: For twenty I will show you personal. Even show you where the stars live.

Edward: Oh, that's all right, I have been to the Stallone's.

Vivian: Great. Down the streets make a right.

维维安: 嘿，亲爱的，想找个伴吗？

爱德华: 不，我想去比弗利山，能告诉我怎么走吗？

维维安: 可以，五美元。

爱德华: 太荒谬了！

维维安: 现在是十美元了。

爱德华: 指路也要收费？

维维安: 我会做任何事情，亲爱的，但我可没有迷路！

爱德华: 好了，你赢了，我输了！ 二十美元有找吗？

维维安: 二十美元我会亲自带你去并告诉你明星住在哪里。

爱德华: 好吧！ 我刚到史泰龙的家。

维维安: 好，往前开然后再右转。

词句荟萃 Words and Sentences Gathering

lost [lɒst] *adj.* 迷失的
sense [sens] *n.* 感觉
antique [æn'ti:k] *n.* 古董
straight [streɪt] *adj.* 直的 *adv.* 一直，笔直地
intersection [ɪntə'sekʃən] *n.* 十字路口
close to 离……很近
suppose to 想做
to be interested in 对……感兴趣
far away from 离……很远
gonna 等同于going to

疯狂链接 Interlinkage

表示交通工具的词汇

出租车 taxi	自行车 bike
吉普车 jeep	跑车 sports car
船 ship	卡车 truck
小船 boat	消防车 fire engine
飞机 plane	救护车 ambulance
火车 train	独木舟 canoe
公交车 bus	

Section 2

> Of course, er, let me check the bus schedule first.

■ 公交地铁
Taking a Bus or Subway

> Dad, do you know which bus we should take?

疯狂表达 Expressions

候车 Waiting for the Bus

下一趟车要等多久才来?

How long do I have to wait for the next bus?

举一反三

There is a bus every five minutes here. 这车五分钟一趟。

The buses on this line run every 10 minutes. 这路车十分钟一趟。

What time do the first and last bus on this line start? 这路车的首班车和末班车各是几点?

The first bus starts at 6:00 a.m. and the last at 10:30 p.m.
首班车早上六点开，末班车晚上十点半开。

上车 Getting On the Bus

乘坐公车先下后上。

Let the people get off the bus before you get on.

请排队上车。

Please get on the bus in a line.

举一反三

You have to wait in line like everyone else. 你必须和其他人一样排队等候。

Move towards the back when you get on the bus. 上车后请向后走。

Can't you see there's a line? 你没有看到有一条线吗?

Besides, you should let old people get on first. 除此之外，你该让老人先上车。

在车上 On the Bus

请买票。

Fares, please.

请往后走。

Move to the rear of the bus.

请投币一元。

Drop one yuan in the box.

举一反三

Please let us know when we reach our stop.　请到站时告诉我们一声。

When you're ready to get off, remember to press the button near your seat.

当你要下车的时候，别忘了按你座位旁的按钮。

Then how far ahead of time do I need to ring the bell for you to stop the bus?

我应提前多久按铃请你停车呢？

One minute is OK.　提前一分钟就可以了。

车费 Bus Fare

车费多少钱?

How much is the fare?

成人每人80美分，12岁以下的小孩每人35美分。不要用纸币，上车之后把钱数正好的硬币投入投币箱中。

It's eighty cents for adults and thirty-five cents for children under twelve. Don't use bills, and drop the exact fare into the money box after getting on the bus.

举一反三

Does it cost money to transfer?　换乘要钱吗?

Yes. When you get on the transfer bus, just show the bus driver the ticket stub. You will only have to pay ten more cents for yourself and a nickel for your child.

要。当你上了转乘的公共汽车时，就把这张票根给司机看。你只需另外再付十美分，而你的孩子只需再付五美分。

公交卡 Bus Card

不好意思，我的一卡通坏了。该去哪儿换啊?

Excuse me, my metro card is broken. Where can I get it replaced?

这儿换不了。你得到西单站去换。

We can't replace your card here. You will need to go to Xidan Station to replace it.

举一反三

Can I have the value of the card refunded?　能退卡的工本费吗?

If the card is damaged, the value of the card cannot be refunded.

如果卡有损伤，卡的工本费就不能退了。

What about the balance on my current card?　那卡里的余额呢?

The balance of your current card will be transferred to your new card.

卡里的余额会转到你的新卡里。

如何乘坐地铁 How to Take the Subway

打扰一下，请问去华尔街坐地铁怎么走?

Excuse me, how do I get to Wall Street by subway?

坐往南开的A 列车到自由大街站。在那儿你就可以找到了。

Take the A train south to the Liberty Ave stop. You should be able to find it from there.

抱歉。我如何知道地铁是往南开的呢?

I'm sorry, but how do I know the subway train is going south?

往南开的A列地铁上写着 "布鲁克林"。

The southbound A trains say Brooklyn.

举一反三

Oh, I just can't figure out the subway system at all.　哦，我不知道该怎么坐。

But it's easy to get to Wangfujing from here by the subway. You take the downtown Line 5 train and get off at Dongdan. Dongdan station is a transfer station. Then you take the Line 1 train and get off at Wangfujing.

可是从这儿乘地铁到王府井很方便。你坐开往市中心的5号线列车，在东单下车。东单站是个换乘站。然后坐1号线在王府井下车。

Is this the right subway to Dongdan?　这就是去东单的地铁吗?

Yes, you take the train Songjiazhuang direction, and go nine stops.

是的，你坐开往宋家庄方向的列车，一共九站路。

You take the uptown R train and get off at 42nd street.　您乘北线方向的R路车到第42街下车。

Yes, you take the D train on the downtown platform, and go three stops.

是的，您在市中心站乘坐全景观列车，一共三站路。

How do I get off the platform after I get off the train?　我下车后怎么出站台呢?

That's very easy. The exits are always open, and there are signs.

那很容易，出口处总是敞开着，也有标识。

Remember, the D train, the downtown platform.　记住，D路车，南线站台。

地铁车票和辅币 Subway Tickets and Token

车费多少?

How much is the fare?

两块钱。单一票制，可以乘坐全部的地铁线路。

Two yuan. A flat fare with unlimited transfers throughout the entire system.

举一反三

What should I do with the token?　我该怎么用这个辅币呢?

You put it in the slot at the turnstile and then push the turnstile to get on the platform.

您把它投入旋转栅门的缝槽里，然后推动旋转栅门就可以进入站台了。

Dialogue 1 · 公交车路线 *Bus Route*

> **Dad, do you know which bus we should take?**

> **Of course, er, let me check the bus schedule first.**

今天是周末，爸爸带着凯特去西单图书大厦购买图书，但是走到了公交车站牌处却忘记了具体的路线，那么最后他是怎么解决这个问题的呢？

It is the weekend. Dad takes Kate to the Xidan Book Building to buy books. But when they get to the bus station, dad forgets the route. How does he end up solving the problem?

Kate:	Dad, do you know which bus we should take?
Dad:	Of course, er, let me check the bus schedule first.
Kate:	Be quick, please!
Dad:	Why can't I find the bus your mother told me about yesterday?
Kate:	Mom gave you the directions 3 times yesterday.
Dad:	But I was watching "American Idol" at the time.
Kate:	We need to ask someone else.

(Here comes Bus 29)

Dad:	Excuse me? Does this bus go to the Xidan Book Building?
Conductor:	No, it doesn't. You need to take Bus 52.

Kate:	Do I have to change to some other bus on the way?
Conductor:	No.
Dad:	I see. Thanks. Oops! The Bus 52 is coming. Kate, come on. Let's go.

凯特:	爸爸，你知道我们坐哪路车吗？
爸爸:	当然啊，恩，让我先看一下公车牌。
凯特:	快点吧！
爸爸:	为什么我没有看见你妈妈昨天跟我说的那路公车呢？
凯特:	妈妈昨天跟你说了三次公交路线。
爸爸:	但是那个时候我在看《美国偶像》啊。
凯特:	我们要问问其他的人。

（来了一辆29路车）

爸爸:	你好，请问一下这车到西单图书大厦吗？
售票员:	不到。你应该乘52路。
凯特:	那我还需要转车吗？
售票员:	不需要。
爸爸:	我知道了，谢谢。啊，52路来了，凯特，快，我们走。

Dialogue 2 ● 买票和问询 Tickets and Inquiries

OK, it's my pleasure. How many tickets?

Kate, here is some money for the tickets.

爸爸给了凯特钱让她去买票，并要确定地铁路线和转乘路线，凯特能完成任务吗？

Dad gives Kate money to buy tickets and makes sure of the subway route and transfer route. Does Kate fulfill her task?

Dad: Kate, here is some money for the tickets.

Kate: OK, it would be my pleasure. How many tickets?

Dad: Two tickets for two people.

Kate: But I am only half a person and they charged both of us the same price for the tickets.

Dad: They may unless we get a half-price ticket for you.

Kate: Dad, it makes no sense.

Dad: You can ask if you can take a half-price ticket.

(A while later)

Kate: Yeah, I'll make certain of that. A half-price ticket saves us one point five Yuan.

Dad: Oh, cool. I need to check if we need to change from the Loop line to Line 1.

Kate: Yes, we'll take the Loop line and then change to Line 1 at the Jianguo Men station.

Dad: Oh, supergirl. Do we need to take buses to the Xidan bookstore after we get off the subway?

Kate: No, and first, I am superwoman. Second, we don't need to change.

Dad: OK, let's go.

爸爸：   凯特，给你些钱去买票吧。

凯特：   好的，我很乐意。要买几张票？

爸爸：   两人得两张票啊。

凯特：   但我只是个儿童啊，他们居然也收同样价格的票。

爸爸：   是啊，除非我们能买到一张半价票。

凯特：   爸爸，这讲不通哦。

爸爸：   你可以问一下你是否可以买一张半价票。

（过了一小会儿）

凯特：   好了，我买到了半价票，节省了一块五。

爸爸：   噢，酷。我要核实一下我们是否需要从环线换乘到一号线。

凯特：   要换乘，我们乘环线然后在建国门站换乘一号线。

爸爸：   噢，真酷，小超人。我们出地铁后需要再坐公交车去西单图书大厦吗？

凯特：   不，首先，我是女超人。其次我们不需要换乘。

爸爸：   好吧，我们走。

富家女艾莉·安德鲁小姐搭乘长途巴士离家出走，在巴士上偶遇落魄记者彼得·华恩。在长途汽车站，艾莉要乘的车子开走了，只有彼得在那等候她。

A rich girl Ellen Andrew escapes from home by taking the long-distance bus. On the bus she meets a sorehead journalist Peter Warne. At the bus station, Ellen's bus has gone and only Peter is waiting for her.

Ellen:	Where's the bus to New York?
Station Clerk:	Well, it left about 20 minutes ago.
Ellen:	Oh, that's ridiculous. I was on that bus. I told them to wait.
Station Clerk:	I'm sorry, Miss, but it's gone.
Peter:	Good morning. Remember me? I'm the fellow you slept on last night.
Ellen:	Seems to me, I've already thanked you for that. What time's the next bus?
Station Clerk:	8:00 tonight.
Ellen:	8:00? That's 12 hours.
Station Clerk:	Sorry, Miss.
Peter:	What's the matter? Wouldn't the old meanness wait for you?
Ellen:	Why are you so excited? You missed it, too.
Peter:	Yeah, I missed it too.
Ellen:	Don't tell me you did it on my account. I hope you haven't any idea that what happened last night is...Now, look here, young man, you needn't concern yourself about me. I can take care of myself.
Peter:	You're doing a pretty sloppy job of it. Here's your ticket.
Ellen:	My ticket?
Peter:	I found it on the seat.
Ellen:	Thank you. It must have fallen out of my purse.

艾莉：	到纽约的巴士呢？
车站职员：	哦，20分钟前就开走了。
艾莉：	噢，这太荒谬了，我也坐那辆巴士，我有叫他们等我。
车站职员：	抱歉，小姐。但是车已经开走了。
彼得：	早安，记得我吗？你昨晚睡在我身上。
艾莉：	我已经谢过你了。下一班什么时候开？
车站职员：	今晚八点钟。
艾莉：	八点钟？还有12个小时呢！
车站职员：	抱歉了，小姐。

彼得:	怎么了，坏司机没等你吗？
艾莉:	你高兴什么，你也没赶上。
彼得:	没错。
艾莉:	别告诉我，你是为了我才错过的。我希望昨晚的事不会让你有任何误解。年轻人，你不需要担心我，我会照顾自己的。
彼得:	看来你照顾得不太好，你的车票在这里。
艾莉:	我的票？
彼得:	我在位子上找到的。
艾莉:	谢谢你，车票一定是从钱包里掉出来的。

词句荟萃 Words and Sentences Gathering

take [teɪk] *vt.* 拿，取

schedule ['skedjuːl] *n.* 时间表，一览表

quick [kwɪk] *adj.* 快的，迅速的

ask [ɑːsk] *vt.* 问，要求

excuse [ɪksˈkjuːs] *vt.* 原谅

change [tʃeɪndʒ] *vt.* 改变

loop [luːp] *n.* 环线

sorehead [ˈsɔːhed] *adj.* 落魄的

meanness [ˈmiːnɪs] *n.* 卑鄙的行为

疯狂链接 Interlinkage

交通规则词汇

交通规则 traffic regulation

路标 guide post

里程碑 milestone

停车标志 mark car stop

红绿灯 traffic light

自动红绿灯 automatic traffic signal light

红灯 red light

绿灯 green light

黄灯 amber light

交通岗 traffic post

岗亭 police box

交通警 traffic police

打手势 pantomime

单行线 single line

双白线 double white lines

双程线 dual carriage-way

斑马线 zebra stripes

划路线机 traffic line marker

交通干线 artery traffic

车行道 carriage-way

辅助车道 lane auxiliary

双车道 two-way traffic

自行车通行 cyclists only

单行道 one way only

窄路 narrow road

潮湿路滑 slippery when wet

陡坡 steep hill

不平整路 rough road

弯路 curve; bend

连续弯路 winding road

之字路 double bend

之字公路 switch back road

下坡危险 dangerous down grade

道路交叉点 road junction

十字路 crossroads

左转 turn left

右转 turn right

靠左 keep left

靠右 keep right

慢驶 slow

速度 speed

超速 excessive speed

速度限制 speed limit

恢复速度 resume speed

禁止通行 no through traffic

此路不通 blocked

不准驶入 no entry

不准超越 keep in line ; no overhead

不准掉头 no turns

让车道 passing bay

回路 loop

安全岛 safety island

停车处 parking place

停私人车 private car park

只停公用车 public car only

不准停车 restricted stop

不准滞留 restricted waiting

临街停车 parking on-street

街外停车 parking off-street

街外卸车 loading off-street

Section 3

Sir, please turn right at the next corner. And stop at the taxi stand.

OK!

TAXI

■ 出租车
Taking a Taxi

疯狂表达 Expressions

乘车 Taking a Taxi

出租车!
Taxi!
去哪?
Where are you going?
举一反三
Where do you want to go?　你想去哪里?
To Shenzhen Safari Park. How long will it take?　到深圳野生动物园。到那儿要多久?
It is quite far from here. It will take about half an hour.　路挺远的。大约要半个小时。

赶时间 In a Hurry

请到肯尼迪机场。我得在7点前赶到那里。
Kennedy Airport, please. I have to be there before 7:00.
不敢保证，不过我尽力而为。
I can't promise anything, but I'll do my best.
举一反三
Don't worry! I'll get you there in time.　别担心! 我会及时把您送到那儿去的。
We'll be all right if traffic's not very heavy.　假如交通不拥挤的话，我们能赶到的。
We shouldn't have any trouble if the traffic isn't too heavy.
如果交通不太拥挤的话，我们不会有什么困难。
We should be OK if the lights are with us.　假如一路绿灯的话，我们能赶到的。

227

询问车费 Asking about Taxi Fee

要多少钱啊？

What is the rate?

我的车是1.2元钱一公里。

Mine is 1. 2 yuan a kilometer.

举一反三

Do you use the meter?　你使用计价器吗？

Let me check the meter out.　我查看一下计价器。

It's 135 Yuan on the meter.　里程表上是135元。

付钱 Paying

这里是150元钱。零钱不用找了。

Here's 150 Yuan. Keep the change.

到了。请付12美元。

OK. That'll be $12.00, please.

多谢。这是车费。

Thanks a lot. Here.

举一反三

Thank you very much. Here's $ 10.00. Give me $1.00 back, please.

太谢谢你了。这是10美元，找我1美元就行了。

Here we are. $8.50, please.　我们到了。请付8.5美元。

Thank you. Here's $10.00. Keep the change.　谢谢你。这是10美元，不用找了。

Thank you very much. Here's the fare and this is for you.　真得谢谢您。这是车费，这是给您的。

闲谈 Chatting

我的一个朋友告诉我说在北京很难打到出租车。

One of my friends told me it's very difficult to get a cab in Beijing.

这辆车是你自己的吗？

Does this car belong to you?

举一反三

Do you have good business being a taxi driver?　出租车生意好吗？

I've rented the car since last year.　我从去年就租了这辆车。

Look at those yellow minis, almost all the drivers own the car they're driving.

你看那些黄的面包车，多数司机都是开自己的车。

Slow down please so that I can enjoy the sights.　开慢点，我们好欣赏景色。

There is blue sky, beautiful trees and big buildings ahead.

晴空丽日，前面是婀娜多姿的树木和高楼大厦。

Dialogue 1　赶时间 In a Hurry

> Oh, no. We're going to be late for the meeting.

> No. We'll get a cab. It's faster than taking the bus or the subway.

张教授和李老师开会要迟到了，两人决定坐出租车，那样会快得多。

Professor Zhang and Mr. Li are going to be late for the meeting. They decide to take a taxi. That will be much faster than the bus or the subway.

Prof. Zhang:	Oh, no. We're going to be late for the meeting.
Mr. Li:	No. We'll get a cab. It's faster than taking the bus or the subway.
Prof. Zhang:	Oh, good.
Mr. Li:	How much will it cost?
Prof. Zhang:	Well, cabs are more expensive than the bus or the subway. It'll probably cost around six dollars.
Mr. Li:	Taxi!!!
Prof. Zhang:	I can't find the business card. Do you know the address?
Mr. Li:	I met with them back in March, remember?
Prof. Zhang:	Right.
Mr. Li:	Driver, 1600 Pennsylvania Ave., please.

张教授:	噢，糟糕。我们开会要迟到了。
李先生:	不会的。我们坐出租车去。那比坐公车或搭地铁快。
张教授:	哦，好啊。
李先生:	要多少钱？
张教授:	嗯，坐出租车比坐公车或地铁贵。可能大概要花6美元吧。
李先生:	出租车！！！
张教授:	我找不到名片了，你知道地址吗？
李先生:	我在三月还和他们见过面，记得吗？
张教授:	对呀。
李先生:	司机。去宾夕法尼亚大街1600号。

Dialogue 2 ● 打的 Take a Taxi

公交车迟迟没有来，眼看时间一分一秒地过去，妈妈最终决定乘坐出租车。在出租车上，妈妈和司机聊了些什么呢？

The bus isn't coming. Seeing time fly, Mother decides to take a taxi. In the taxi, what does mother talk about with the driver?

Mom:	Joy Chain elementary school, please.
Taxi driver:	Will do.
Mom:	How frustrating! The bus is still not coming.
Taxi driver:	Ma'am, take your kid to school?
Mom:	Yes. I am in a hurry. Please take a shortcut.

Taxi driver:	No problem. Don't worry. The taxi is faster than the bus.
Mom:	The traffic is terrible on Monday morning. It takes us almost 1 hour to get to school.
Taxi driver:	My son is the same. But he always gets an early start in the morning, and enjoys listening to the English program "Let's talk in English" on the way.
Mom:	That's wonderful. He is killing two birds with one stone.
Mom:	Sir, please turn right at the next corner. And stop at the taxi stand.
Taxi driver:	OK!
Mom:	What is the fare?
Taxi driver:	It's 14.5 Yuan.

(Mother gives 15 Yuan to the taxi driver.)

| Mom: | Keep the change! |
| Taxi driver: | Thanks, Ma'am. |

妈妈:	麻烦去卓成小学。
出租车司机:	好的。
妈妈:	真让人烦躁！公交车到现在都还没到。
出租车司机:	女士，您是送孩子上学吧?
妈妈:	是啊，我赶时间。请走近路吧。
出租车司机:	没问题，别担心，出租车可比公交车快多了。
妈妈:	周一早晨，交通总是很糟糕。到学校要花近一个小时的时间呢。
出租车司机:	我儿子也是这样的。但他早晨总会早些出发，在路上他喜欢听"让我们一起来学英语"这个英语节目。
妈妈:	这太好了。他还真是一箭双雕啊。
妈妈:	师傅，请在下一个路口右转。停在出租车站牌那边好了。
出租车司机:	好的!
妈妈:	多少钱?
出租车司机:	十四块五。

（妈妈给师傅15块钱。）

| 妈妈: | 不用找了! |
| 出租车司机: | 谢谢，女士。 |

维克多•纳沃斯基终于进入了美国境内，来到纽约市区，他正乘坐出租车到他想去的地方。

Viktor Navorski finally arrives in America, in New York. Now he is taking a taxi to the place where he wants to go.

Driver: Where you go?

Viktor: 161, Lexington. Please take Van Wyck Expressway to Queensboro Bridge. It's faster than BQE.

Driver: Where you from?

Viktor: Krakozhia. Viktor Navorski.

Driver: I'm Goran. Albania.

Viktor: When do you come to New York?

Driver: Thursday.

司机： 去哪儿?

维克多： 列克星敦161号，走范怀克高速到皇后大桥，比BQE高速要快。

司机： 你打哪来?

维克多： 克罗西亚。维克多•纳沃斯基。

司机： 我是格兰。阿尔巴尼亚人。

维克多： 你什么时候来纽约的?

司机： 星期四。

词句荟萃 Words and Sentences Gathering

frustrating [frʌs'treɪtɪŋ] *adj.* 令人沮丧的

kid [kɪd] *n.* 孩子

shortcut ['ʃɔːtkʌt] *n.* 近路，捷径

terrible ['terəbl] *adj.* 严重的

program ['prəʊɡræm] *n.* 节目

fare [feə] *n.* 费用

change [tʃəndʒ] *n.* 零钱

be in a hurry 赶时间

He is killing two birds with one stone. 一箭双雕；一石二鸟。

Keep the change! 不用找零了。

各种地图图标说法

城 city	报摊 newsstand
首都 capital	商品交易所 Commodity Exchange
大都市 metropolis	股票交易所 Stock Exchange
市中心 centre	市政厅 town hall
商业区 shopping centre	法院 Law court
市政当局 municipality	教堂 church
市的，市政的 municipal	大教堂 cathedral
区 district	小礼拜堂 chapel
居民区，住宅区 residential area	墓地、公墓 cemetery
市区的 urban	坟，墓 grave, tomb
近郊区 suburb	学校 school
郊区 outskirts	大学 university
贫民窟，贫民区 slum	图书馆 library
贫民区 shantytown	剧院 theatre
村 village	博物馆 museum
小村 hamlet	动物园 zoo
狭小破旧的住房 hole, dump	游乐园 fairground, fun fair
所在地 locality	运动场 stadium
唐人街 Chinese quarter	邮政总局 general post office
范围，扩展 extension	车站 station
房子 house	美术馆 art museum
楼房 building	画廊 art gallery
摩天楼 skyscraper	植物园 botanical garden
居住单元，套房 flat	纪念碑 monument
商店 shop, store	公用电话 public telephone
百货公司 department store	公共厕所 public lavatory
市场 bazaar	国道 national highway
市场，集市 market	交通灯 traffic light
旧货店 junk shop	兵营 barracks

Section 4

> The car park in this community is over-crowded, isn't it?

■ 私家车
Private Cars

> Yeah, there are more and more cars. People should try to take public transportation.

疯狂表达 Expressions

停车 Parking

你不能把车停在这儿。会罚款的。

You can't park here! You'll get a ticket!

真够受。在这个城市里停车简直是受罪！咱们还是找个停车场吧。

I've had it! Parking in this city is a nightmare! Let's look for a parking lot.

举一反三

There's one right over there, and it's only two dollars an hour.

那边有个停车场，而且一个小时只收2美元。

Hi. Here's your ticket. Back up in that space next to the blue Toyota.

这是你的停车票。请倒车停在那辆蓝色本田车旁边的位置。

Just leave the keys in the car, but remember that we're not responsible for any valuables left in your car.　把钥匙留在车里，但是我们对留在车里的贵重物品是不负责任的。

In that case, I'll take my bag with me.　如果是这样的话，我最好把我的皮包带上。

交通阻塞及抱怨 Traffic Jams and Complaints

真糟糕，公路上又堵车了。

Oh, damn. There's another traffic jam on the highway.

我想是否又出事故了。

I wonder if there was an accident.

How can there be a traffic jam on a 16-lane highway every day?
16车道的主干道上怎么可能堵车?

There are just too many people, and too many cars.　因为人太多，车太多。

Should we get out and help?　我们要出去帮帮忙吗?

It's pretty bad.　真糟糕。

Let's put on some music.　我来放点音乐。

We're going to be stuck in this for a while.　可能要困在这里一会儿。

It looks like we're in for a long drive.　看来我们驾车时间是不会短的了。

车祸 Car Crash

好像又出了严重的车祸了。

That looks like a bad accident.

是呀。我们要下车帮帮忙吗?

Yeah, should we get out and help?

不用了，后面有一辆警车。他会停的。

No, there's a police car behind us. He'll stop.

举一反三

Looks like the one guy lost control in all this rain, and the other one hit him.
好像是有人在这样的下雨天让车失控了，另一辆撞上了这辆。

Yeah. That's awful, that car looks like a coke can.
是。真是糟糕。那辆车撞得像个汽水罐一样。

These accidents always cause traffic jams on rainy days.　下雨天出车祸往往引起堵车。

Yeah, it looks like we're in for a long drive.　对。看起来我们的驾车时间不会短了。

Ah, well. Put on the news. I got up late and missed it.
哦，那么，听点新闻吧。我起得晚，没听到新闻。

All right.　好的。

污染 Pollution

瞧，日落真漂亮。我从未见过这么火红的日落。

Man, that sunset is beautiful. I've never seen one so red.

对，很漂亮。可是颜色之所以这么红是因为空气污染。

Yeah, it's pretty nice, but it's so red because of air pollution.

举一反三

Really?　真的吗?

Yeah, the smog from all these cars gets into the air and turns the sunlight red.
是的，汽车产出的烟雾进入空气中，日光便显出这种红色。

I never knew that.　我可不知道这个。

Yeah, more people need to take public transportation or carpool.
是呀，应该有更多的人搭乘公交车或拼车。

Well, we're already doing our part.　噢，我们自己已经尽力了。

Dialogue 1 ● 我为我的车子操心 *I'm Worrying about My Car*

> **Well, I've been really worried. It's my car. It's in the shop again.**

> **What's the matter? Aren't you feeling well?**

威尔森和苏珊一起去吃饭，可似乎威尔森有什么心事，什么都吃不下，到底他在担心什么呢？

Wilson and Susan go to have dinner together. It seems that Wilson is worried about something and he has no appetite. What is he worried about?

Susan: What's the matter? Aren't you feeling well?

Wilson: Well, I've been really worried. It's my car. It's in the shop again.

Susan: Really? What's wrong this time?

Wilson: I don't know exactly. Something's wrong with the brakes, I think.

Susan: Well, at least that shouldn't cost you much to fix. Parts are cheaper for all the American cars like yours. Did the mechanic say how much it would cost?

Wilson: He said he would call me with an estimate later on today.

Susan: Watch out so that he doesn't try to take advantage of you.

Wilson: What do you mean?

Susan: Well, some car mechanics, if they think that someone doesn't know much about cars, they may try to overcharge that person.

Wilson: Maybe so. But I trust this guy. He was recommended by one of my neighbors. He has done some work for me in the past and his prices seemed to be reasonable.

Susan: Oh, that's good to know. Maybe I'll call him when I need a mechanic in the future. By the way, do you need a ride home after class today?

Wilson: Oh, I'd really appreciate it. It's really tough getting around without a car when you live off-campus.

苏珊: 你怎么了？是不是不舒服？
威尔森: 我一直很担心，我的车又送去修了。
苏珊: 真的吗？这次是什么毛病？
威尔森: 我也不太清楚。我想是刹车出了问题。
苏珊: 至少修理刹车花费不会太大。美国车的零件都很便宜，像你的那辆。修车工说要花多少钱了吗？
威尔森: 他说等他看一下，今天晚些时候告诉我。
苏珊: 当心他想占你便宜。
威尔森: 这是什么意思？
苏珊: 你知道有些汽车修理工，如果看你对汽车知之甚少，他们可能多收你的钱。
威尔森: 也许有这种事。但是我相信这个人。是我的一个邻居介绍我去他那修的。他以前也给我修过，而且价格还算合理。
苏珊: 哦，这还不错。也许将来我也去找他。顺便问一下，你今天放学后要不要搭我的车？
威尔森: 哦，那真是太感激你了。住在校外如果没有车的话那可太麻烦了。

Dialogue 2   停车场的故事 Story in Car Park

停车场的故事还真不少，一个接着一个！
There are many stories in the car park. Now, it seems there is one after the other.

Mr. Li: I am sorry for damaging your car, Ma'am.

Sally: Don't worry about it. Just leave it to the insurance companies.

Mr. Li: The car park in this community is over-crowded, isn't it?

Sally: Yeah, there are more and more cars. People should try to take public transportation.

Mr. Li: There aren't enough buses in this city, are there?

Sally: No, sometimes I really feel like writing a letter to the mayor.

Mr. Li: That's a bit over the top. We just want a bigger parking space.

Sally: Have you taken this to the property management, yet?

Mr. Li: No. but I'm gonna. You know, several months ago, I backed into a red Toyota when parking.

Sally: Where? On the road?

Mr. Li: No, right here in the parking lot. It was parked right here in your space. The left rearview mirror was smashed.

Sally: Is the car owner a lady with a deafening voice?

Mr. Li: Yes! How did you know that?

Sally: That's my mom!

Mr. Li: You mean…

李先生： 真抱歉弄坏你的车，女士。

莎丽： 别担心。让保险公司来处理吧。

李先生： 我们小区的停车场太拥挤了，不是吗？

莎丽： 是啊，私家车越来越多了。人们应该试着使用公共交通。

李先生： 我们市里没有那么多公交车，不是吗？

莎丽： 是啊，有时我真想给市长写信。

李先生： 那倒不至于。我们只要有一个大点的停车场就好了。

莎丽： 你跟小区管理处反映过这事儿吗？

李先生： 没有。但我正有此打算。几个月前，我停车时，倒车倒到一辆红色丰田车上去了。

莎丽： 在哪儿？路上吗？

李先生： 不，就在这个停车场。那辆车就停在你现在的地方。我把它的左后视镜给撞碎了。

莎丽： 那辆车的车主是不是一个嗓门很大的人？

李先生： 是啊！你怎么知道的？

莎丽： 那是我妈妈。

李先生： 你是说……

一对黑人夫妇在路上出了交通事故，警察正在调查事故。

A black couple runs into a traffic accident. A policeman is investigating the accident.

Husband:	It's the sense of touch.
Wife:	What?
Husband:	Any real city, you walk, you know you brush past people. People bump into you. In L.A., nobody touches you. We're always behind this metal and glass. I think we miss that touch so much that we crash into each other just so we can feel something.
Policeman:	You guys okay?
Wife:	I think he hit his head.
Husband:	You don't think that's true?
Policeman:	Stay in your car.
Wife:	Graham, I think we got rear-ended. I think we spun around twice. And somewhere in there, one of us lost our frame of reference. And I'm gonna go look for it.
Policeman:	Calm down, ma'am.
Woman:	I am calm!
Policeman:	I need to see your registration and insurance.
Woman:	Why? It's not my fault! It's her fault! She do this!
Wife:	My fault?
Policeman:	Ma'am, you really need to wait in your vehicle.
Wife:	My fault?
Woman:	Stop in middle of street! Mexicans no know how to drive. She "brake" too fast.
Wife:	I "brake" too fast? I brake too fast! I'm sorry you no see my "brake" lights.
Policeman:	Ma'am!
Wife:	See, I stop when I see a long line of cars stopped in front of me. Maybe you see over steering wheel, you "brake" too!

丈夫:	碰触的感觉。
妻子:	什么？
丈夫:	走在任何城市，你和人们总会碰撞或擦身而过。在洛杉矶，不会有人来碰到你。我们都在玻璃和金属制成的车厢里，或许就是太怀念碰触的感觉，才会撞在一起，想找回些什么感觉吧。

警察： 你们没事吧？

妻子： 他好像撞到头了。

丈夫： 你不会认为我在胡扯吧？

警察： 待在车上。

妻子： 葛伦，好像是从后面撞上来的，而且车子打转了两圈。我们两部车一定有一部出了错。我要下去看看。

警察： 女士，冷静些。

女士： 我很冷静。

警察： 请出示行照和保险单。

女士： 为什么？又不是我的错，是她不对，她害的。

妻子： 我的错？

警察： 女士，请待在车上。

妻子： 我的错？

女士： 在马路中央停下来，墨西哥人不会开车。她突然刹车。

妻子： 我突然刹车？我突然刹车！对不起，请看我的刹车灯。

警察： 女士！

妻子： 看到前面塞车我才停下来的，你看到也会踩刹车的。

词句荟萃 Words and Sentences Gathering

highway ['haɪweɪ] *n.* 公路；干道

accident ['æksɪdənt] *n.* 事故；灾祸

sunset ['sʌnset] *n.* 日落，日落的景象

pollution [pə'luːʃən] *n.* 污染

smog [smɒg] *n.* 烟雾

carpool ['kɑːpuːl] *v.* 拼车

traffic jam 交通拥挤

rearview mirror 后视镜

get out 动身，下车（飞机）

lose control 失控

世界名车车名

梅塞德斯-奔驰 Mercedes-Benz	菲亚特 Fiat
宝马 BMW	阿尔法罗密欧 Alfa Romeo
奥迪 Audi	兰博基尼 Lamborghini
雷克萨斯 Lexus	现代 Hyundai
丰田 Toyota	大宇 Daewoo
吉普 JEEP	起亚 Kia
悍马 HUMMER	尼桑 Nissan
大众 Volkswagen	英菲尼迪 Infiniti
路虎 Land Rover	马自达 Mazda
雪佛兰 Chevrolet	本田 Honda
凯迪拉克 Cadillac	讴歌 Acura
旁蒂克 Pontiac	三菱 Mitsubishi
别克 Buick	铃木 Suzuki
福特 Ford	斯巴鲁 Subaru
克莱斯勒 Chrysler	大发 Daihatsu
林肯 Lincoln	标致 Peugeot
道奇 Dodge	雷诺 Renault
捷豹 Jaguar	雪铁龙 Citroen
欧宝 Opel	沃尔沃 Volvo
保时捷 Porsche	萨博 Saab
莱斯劳斯 Rolls-Royce	西亚特 Seat
罗孚 Rover	斯柯达 Skoda
阿斯顿马丁 Aston Martin	宾利 Bentley
法拉利 Ferrari	莲花 Lotus

Section 5

Will you tell me when we get there?

■ 火车
Taking the Train

You can listen to the announcement on the train, and it will tell you when we get there.

疯狂表达 Expressions

买票 Buying Tickets

你要坐哪一班火车？

What train are you taking?

请给我一张去A地的单程票。

Please give me a one-way ticket to A.

举一反三

Two first class tickets on the express at ten, please.　两张10点的头等快车票。

A lower bunk ticket for the night train at eight o'clock tonight.　今晚8点的夜车下铺车票一张。

I'd like to reserve a sleeper to Chicago.　我要预订去芝加哥的卧铺。

I'd like to have two soft bunk/bed tickets to Shanghai for tomorrow.
我想买两张明天到上海的软卧票。

May I have two lower beds?　我可以要两张下铺吗？

Sorry. We usually sell the upper and lower together.
对不起，我们通常上下铺搭配在一起卖。

询问售票处及车次 Asking about the Booking-office and the Train

售票窗口在哪里？

Where's the ticket window?

往下走就到了

Down there.

这是去上海的列车吗？

Is this the train to Shanghai?

举一反三

Please tell me where the ticket office is?　请你告诉我售票处在哪里好吗?

Go up the stairs to your right.　顺阶梯上去往右方就到了。

Is this the 8 a.m. fast train to Beijing?　这是8点去北京的快车吗?

Yes, it's the express No. 233 to Beijing.　是的，这是去北京的233次快车。

Do you have a train going to Washington round about nine tomorrow morning?
你们有明天早上9点左右开往华盛顿的列车吗?

Yes, we have an express at nine ten.　有的，9点10分我们有一班快车。

We have a local train just at nine.　9点整我们有一班普通车。

询问火车到、离站时间 Asking about the Time of Arrival and Departure

往A地的火车开了吗?

Has the train to A left already?

不，还没有，10分钟以后发车。

No, not yet, but it will in ten minutes.

请你告诉我去A地的下一班火车是什么时候?

Can you tell me when the next train is to A?

举一反三

When is the next express?　下一班快车是什么时候?

That's the last one.　这是最后一班。

The next express is two hours later.　两个小时后还有一班快车。

询问站台和车道 Asking about Platform and Track

这列火车从哪一个站台出发?

From which platform does the train depart?

从另一边，第4站台。

From the other side. At the fourth platform.

开往波士顿的列车将在第几道开出呢?

From which track does the train to Boston leave?

第5道。

It's from track No.5.

举一反三

From which platform does the train leave?　这列火车从哪个站台开出呢?

What platform does the train leave from?　这班车从哪个站台开出呢?

Where do I wait for the express to Edinburgh?　我到哪里等候开往爱丁堡的快车呢?

It will arrive at track No.3, so please wait there.　它将停靠在第3道，请在那里等候。

询问所需时间 Asking about the Time Needed

火车要在这里停多久?

How long will the train stop here?

要停5分钟。

It stops for five minutes.

You have five more minutes. You had better hurry.　你只有5分多钟，最好快点。

How many hours does it take to get to London by express?　搭乘快车到伦敦需要几个小时？

It takes about seven hours to cross the Strait of Dover.　横渡多佛海峡需要7个小时左右。

在站台上 On the Platform

请注意，从南昌来的2次列车就要到站了。

Attention, please, train No. 2 from Nanchang will arrive soon.

旅客们请注意，从北京来的5次列车将于13:36到站。

Attention, please, train No. 5 from Beijing is due in at 13:36.

举一反三

There, the train is coming in now, stand back please!　看，火车来了，请往后站！

Hurry up; the signal for boarding the train has been given.　快！上车信号已经给过了。

The train is about to leave now. I'm very grateful for your coming to see me off.

火车就要开了，很感谢你们来给我送行。

Not at all. Please give my best regards to your mother when you see her.

不用谢。见到你妈妈代我向她致意。

Good-bye. I hope you have a very pleasant journey.　再见。祝您旅途愉快。

在火车上 On the Train

我们在第几车厢？

Which carriage are we in?

到了，14车厢。

Here we are, Car 14.

这个座位有人坐吗？

Is this seat taken?

绿色车厢在哪里？

Where is the green car?

从后面数第5车厢。

The fifth from the back.

举一反三

Excuse me, is this seat vacant?　对不起，这个座位有人吗？

Will you please keep this seat for me while I am away?　我走开时请你帮我保留这个座位好吗？

Seats No. 20 and 21. It's nice that we've got a window seat.

20和21座。真好，我们有了靠窗的座位。

Let's put our suitcases on the rack.　我们把手提箱子放到架子上。

But I prefer the aisle seat here.　可我想要靠走道的座位。

What's the next station?　下一站是哪里？

How long does this train stop at the next station?　这列车在下一站停多久？

Where can I find the conductor?　我到哪里可以找到列车长呢？

Do you know when the train is due in at Beijing?　你知道这趟车什么时候到北京？

Dialogue 1 ● 坐火车 Take the Train

> About 20 minutes.

> Do you know how long we are going to stop here?

罗斯第一次坐火车出远门，有很多事情不知道，他向坐在邻座的乔伊询问。

Rose travels by train for the first time. She is not sure about many things. So she asks her neighbor, Jay.

Rose:　Do you know how long we are going to stop here?

Jay:　　About 20 minutes.

Rose:　When will we get to the destination?

Jay:　　In 2 hours, I suppose.

Rose:　What stop is this?

Jay:　　It is New York.

Rose:　How many stops are there from here to the destination?

Jay:　　12 stops.

Rose:　Will you tell me when we get there?

Jay:　　You can listen to the announcement on the train, and it will tell you when we get there.

罗斯：　您知道我们要在这里停留多久吗?

杰伊：　大约20分钟。

罗斯：　我们什么时候到达目的地?

杰伊：　我想大概得两小时以后吧。

罗斯：　这是哪一站?

杰伊：　是纽约。

罗斯：　从这里到目的地还有多少站?

杰伊：　还有12站。

罗斯：　当我们到站时你能提醒我一下吗?

杰伊：　您可以听车上广播。我们到站时广播公告会提醒您。

When will we get to Dorsett then?

In about two hours.

　　杰克和伊丽莎白搭火车旅行，两个人很高兴可以坐火车，这样可以欣赏风景。不过似乎她们的车票出了点问题，到底是什么呢？让我们来看看。

　　Jack and Elizabeth travel by train. They are happy to take the train because they can enjoy the scenery from the window of the train. However, there is something wrong with their tickets. What happened? Let's find out together.

Elizabeth:	I'm glad we took the train. I don't like buses.
Jack:	Yes, I agree. We can see the scenery better. In a bus, all you see are the roads.
Elizabeth:	Even in China, I always liked to take the train. It is more comfortable.
Jack:	I agree. Buses bounce too much. After two or three hours, you feel too tired.
Elizabeth:	Look at that village!
Jack:	Beautiful.
Elizabeth:	Do you think I can take a picture through this window?
Jack:	I don't know if it will turn out good. The window might cause the picture to be blurry.
Elizabeth:	I will try.
Jack:	Who is that man in the aisle?
Elizabeth:	Oh, he is coming to check tickets. We have to show him our tickets.
Man:	Tickets, please. You are on the wrong train, lady. These tickets are for the express train.
Elizabeth:	The express train?

Man:	Yes. The train you are on is the local train. The local train stops at every station.
Jack:	Oh, no! We want to get to Dorsett. Where are we going on this train?
Man:	You are going to Dorsett on this train too. But it will take longer. The express train goes straight to Dorsett without stopping. This train is the local train. It stops at every station.
Jack:	When will we get to Dorsett then?
Man:	In about two hours.
Jack:	That isn't bad. I don't mind at all. We are enjoying the view of the countryside.
Man:	It's alright this time. I won't make you buy two new tickets. But next time, please be sure you are on the right train.
Elizabeth:	We will read the signs more carefully next time. Thank you.

伊丽莎白:	我很高兴搭火车，我不喜欢搭公车。
杰克:	我也是。搭火车可以更好地欣赏风景，搭公车只看得到马路。
伊丽莎白:	甚至在中国，我也是喜欢搭火车，比较舒服。
杰克:	没错。公车颠簸得太厉害，两三个小时下来，很累的。
伊丽莎白:	你看那乡村!
杰克:	好漂亮。
伊丽莎白:	我可以隔着窗户拍照吗?
杰克:	我不知道效果好不好，窗户可能会使照片模糊。
伊丽莎白:	我试试看。
杰克:	走道上的那个人是谁?
伊丽莎白:	喔，他是来验票的，我们必须让他看车票。
验票员:	车票! 小姐，你们搭错火车了。这是快车的车票。
杰克:	快车?
验票员:	是的。你们搭的这辆是普通列车，每站都会停。
杰克:	不会吧! 我们要到多塞特，这是到哪里的火车?
验票员:	这班火车也有到多塞特，但是比较慢。快车会直达多塞特，中途不停靠站。这班火车是普通列车，每站都停。
杰克:	那么要多久才会到呢?
验票员:	大概两个小时。
杰克:	那还可以，我不介意，我们喜欢欣赏乡村风景。
验票员:	这次就算了，我不要求你们再重新买票。不过下次别搭错车喔。
伊丽莎白:	下次我们会仔细看标示的，谢谢你。

玛丽匆忙地来到火车站，要买一张去米兰的车票。

Mary hurries to the railway station and wants to buy a ticket for Milan.

Mary: Please, when does the next train leave for Milan?

Conductor: Milan? There is one in 20 minutes, at 7.

Mary: Then could you tell me what train I could take from Milan to Paris?

Conductor: Why not take the 8:30 that goes straight through the Paris?

Mary: No. No. I'll take the one at 7. Where do I buy the ticket?

Conductor: Window 5.

Mary: Thank you.

玛丽： 请问一下，下一趟去米兰的火车是几点？

售票员： 米兰吗？20分钟后有一趟，7点。

玛丽： 你能告诉我从米兰到巴黎，我应该乘哪趟车吗？

售票员： 为什么不乘8:30直达巴黎的那趟呢？

玛丽： 不，不，我还是坐7点的那趟，请问在哪买票？

售票员： 第五窗口。

玛丽： 谢谢。

词句荟萃 Words and Sentences Gathering

couchette [kuːˈʃet] *n.* 卧铺

express [ɪkˈspres] *n.* 快车

conductor [kənˈdʌktə] *n.* 售票员；列车员

platform [ˈplætfɔːm] *n.* 站台，月台

whistle [ˈwɪsl] *n.* 汽笛

valid [ˈvælɪd] *adj.* 有效的

porter [ˈpɔːtə] *n.* 搬运工

track [træk] *n.* 轨道

car [kɑː] *n.* 车厢

aisle [aɪl] *n.* 过道；走道

announcement [əˈnaʊnsmənt] *n.* 宣告；通告；广播

bounce [baʊns] *v.* 弹起；颠簸

blurry [ˈblɜːrɪ] *adj.* 模糊的；不清楚的

local train 平快车

baggage rack 行李架

火车旅行词汇

铁路 railway; railroad
轨道 track
火车 train
火车头、机车 locomotive
铁路系统 railway system, railway network
特别快车 express train
快车 fast train
直达快车 direct express
慢车 stopping train, slow train
游览列车 excursion train
市郊火车 commuter train, suburban train
轨道车 railcar
车厢 coach, carriage
卧车 sleeping car, sleeper
餐车 dining car, restaurant car, luncheon car
双层火车 double-decker train
双层卧铺车 sleeper with couchette

铺位 bunk
上行车 up train
下行车 down train
行李车 luggage van, baggage car
邮政车 mail car
车站 station, railway station
车站大厅 station hall
售票处 booking office, ticket office
收票员 ticket-collector, gateman
验票员 ticket inspector
月台，站台 platform
站台票 platform ticket
终点站 terminal
乘警 railway policeman
小卖部 buffet
候车室 waiting room
母子候车室 mother-and-child room
贵宾候车室 VIP room
天桥 platform bridge

Section 6

Yes, I'd like to make a reservation to go to Boston next week.

■ 飞机
Taking a Plane

Good morning, United Airlines. What can I do for you?

疯狂表达 Expressions

预订机票 Booking a Ticket

我想预订一张去伦敦的机票。

I am calling to book a plane ticket to London.

我大约在5月10号到12号出门，有空位吗？

I'd like to leave between May 10th and 12th; do you have seats available?

是的，大概有。你要全价票还是打折票？

Yes, sir, it's possible; do you want a full fare or a reduced one?

打折票。有早上航班吗？

A reduced fare, do you have a morning flight?

举一反三

I want a package deal including airfare and hotel.　我需要一个成套服务，包括机票和住宿。

I'd like two seats on today's Northwest flight 7 to Detroit, please.

我想订两张今天西北航空公司7班次到底特律的机票。

I'd like to sit in the front of the plane.　我要坐在飞机前部。

I'd like to change this ticket to first class.　我想把这张票换成头等舱。

I'll pick up the ticket at the airport counter.　我会在机场柜台拿机票。

询问 Inquiring

我们在这里停留多久？

How long will we stop here?

在候机室有免税店吗？

Are there any duty-free shops in the waiting area?

举一反三

How can I get to the connecting flight counter of China Airline?
我如何找到中国航空公司办理转机柜台？

Where is the boarding gate for China Air CA173?　国航CA173登机口在哪里？

Where can I check in?　在哪里办理登机手续？

What is the gate number?　在几号登机口登机？

换乘航班 Changing a Flight

你好，我是杨峥。我预订了张9月10号去日本的LJ88航班的机票。

Hello, this is Yang Zheng. I am booked on flight LJ88 for Japan on September, 10th.
请稍等……是的。您已经预订了。

Hold on please. Yes, you have booked already.

举一反三

Now I am afraid I can't get to the airport on that day. I want to change my flight to the 12th. Is that all right?
恐怕我那天不能按时去机场了，我想将我的航班换到12号，请问可以吗？

I am sorry. Flight LJ88 on that day is full. What about the 13th?
抱歉，12号LJ88航班已经预订满了，13号的票行吗？

Fine. Thank you so much.　好的，非常感谢。

退票 Returning a Ticket

我想退票。

I want a refund for my ticket.
可以在售票处退票。

Tickets may be turned in at the ticket counter.

举一反三

What is your cancellation policy?　我怎么退票？

Have you got any cancellations?　有退票吗？

Do I have a chance of getting one of the cancellations?　我能退票吗？

I would like to apply for a refund of my ticket.　我想退票。

办理登机手续 Checking In for a Flight

早上好，先生。可以为您效劳吗？

Good morning, sir. Can I help you?
好的，我要办理11点20分开往纽约的航班的登机手续。

Yes, I need to check in for the 11:20 flight to New York, please.
好的，您的票据呢？

OK. Ticket, please.

在这儿。

Here you are

举一反三

Where will you be flying today?　你今天去哪里?

Los Angeles.　洛杉矶。

May I see your ticket, passport, and visa, please?　请出示您的机票、护照和签证。

Here you go. My visa's on page six of my passport.　都在这儿了。签证在护照第六页。

Would you like a window or an aisle seat?　你要靠窗口的座位还是靠过道的座位?

Aisle, please.　请给我靠过道的座位。

I have 13A available.　我可以给你13A座。

Here's your boarding pass. The plane will board half an hour prior to departure. You'll be leaving from gate three, on your left.

这是你的登机牌。起飞前半小时开始登机。从3号门出发，就在你的左边。

Here you are. Seat 12c. Please go to gate 23 after passing through the security checkpoint.

给您的票，座位是12c。通过安全关卡后请到23号门。

飞机饮食 Food on the Plane

抱歉，请问你在飞机起飞后想喝些什么?

Excuse me. What do you want to drink after takeoff?

举一反三

What do you want for breakfast? Western food or Chinese food?　早餐吃什么? 中餐还是西餐?

Which do you like better for dinner, beef or chicken?　晚餐你喜欢牛肉还是鸡肉?

I like chicken.　我要鸡肉。

What kind of drinks do you have?　你们有什么饮料?

We have coke, orange juice and cocktails. But it costs one dollar per cocktail. Soft drinks are free.　我们有可乐、橘子汁和鸡尾酒，但是喝鸡尾酒要付1美元，不含酒精的饮料免费。

I want coke.　我要可乐。

飞机电影 Movie on the Plane

我们今天可以看电影吗?

Will we be able to watch the movies today?

晚餐后可以看。

After dinner.

举一反三

Do you want to watch one of our movies?　你要看我们的电影吗?

Yes, but what kind of movies are there to enjoy?　是的，但是我们能看什么影片?

The Last Hard Man starring Charlton Heston is an interesting Western movie.

一部由卡尔登•希斯顿主演的有趣的西部片《生死斗》。

I'll watch that.　我会看。

Two dollars for the earphones. I'll bring them to you soon.　耳机要2美元，我马上拿给你。

Dialogue 1 订机票 *Booking a Seat*

史密斯先生要订一张下周去波士顿的机票，他来到了美国联合航空公司。
Mr. Smith wants to make a reservation to Boston next week. He goes to United Airlines.

Clerk:	Good morning, United Airlines. What can I do for you?
Mr. Smith:	Yes, I'd like to make a reservation to go to Boston next week.
Clerk:	When do you want to fly?
Mr. Smith:	Monday, September 12.
Clerk:	We have Flight 802 on Monday. Just a moment, please. Let me check whether there're seats available. I'm sorry we are all booked up for Flight 802 on that day.
Mr. Smith:	Then, any alternatives?
Clerk:	The next available flight leaves at 9:30 Tuesday morning September 13th. Shall I book you a seat?
Mr. Smith:	Er... it is a direct flight, isn't it?
Clerk:	Yes, it is. You want to go first class or coach?
Mr. Smith:	I prefer first class, what about the fare?
Clerk:	One way is $176.
Mr. Smith:	OK. I will take the 9:30 flight on Tuesday.
Clerk:	A seat on Flight 807 to Boston 9:30, Tuesday morning. Is that right, sir?
Mr. Smith:	Right. Can you also put me on the waiting list for the 12th?
Clerk:	Certainly. May I have your name & telephone number?

Mr. Smith:	My name is Lorus Anderson. You can reach me at 52378651.
Clerk:	I will notify you if there is a cancellation.
Mr. Smith:	Thank you very much.
Clerk:	My pleasure.

职员:	早上好，美国联合航空公司。我能为您做些什么？
史密斯先生:	是的，我想订一张下周飞往波士顿的机票。
职员:	您想何时去？
史密斯先生:	周一，9月12日。
职员:	我们周一有802次航班。请稍等，让我查一下那天是否有座。非常抱歉，802次航班机票已订完。
史密斯先生:	那还有别的吗？
职员:	有一次航班在9月13日周二上午9:30起飞，我能为您订个座位吗？
史密斯先生:	哦……是直航对吗？
职员:	是的。您愿意订头等舱还是经济舱的机票？
史密斯先生:	我想订头等舱的机票，多少钱？
职员:	单程是176美元。
史密斯先生:	好的，我将订周二9:30的机票。
职员:	一张周二早晨9:30飞往波士顿的807次航班机票，对吗，先生？
史密斯先生:	对。你能把我放到12号等候名单中吗？
职员:	当然可以。请您告诉您的名字和联系方式？
史密斯先生:	我叫罗瑞斯·安德森，52378651，您可以用这个号码和我联系。
职员:	若取消我将通知您。
史密斯先生:	非常感谢。
职员:	不客气。

Dialogue 2 搭火车旅行 Traveling by Train

托马斯在飞机场，准备乘飞机回北京。但是他却把他的护照当成了登机牌，那么没有登机牌的托马斯能够登上飞机吗？这到底是怎么回事呢？一起往下看吧！

Thomas is at the airport getting ready to fly back to Beijing, but he mistakes his passport for his boarding pass. Without boarding pass, could Thomas board the plane? What is the matter? Let's read!

Clerk: Good morning, sir. Can I see your boarding pass, please?

Thomas: Here you are.

Clerk: Excuse me, sir. This is your passport.

Thomas: Really? Uh…Is there any difference?

Clerk: Yes. As a matter of fact, you can't board the plane without a boarding pass.

Thomas: Gee. I must have left it in my hotel room.

Clerk: I'm sorry, sir. I can't let you pass.

Thomas: But when does the plane take off?

Clerk: Ugh, in about thirty minutes, sir.

Thomas: Oh, my God! What shall I do now? Bone head, bone head, bone head.

(He smashes his head with his hand.)

Clerk: Calm down, sir. You are creating a commotion.

(The speaker in the airport says: "Mr. Thomas: we now have a boarding pass by the name of Thomas at Lost and Found.")

Thomas: Is that me?

Clerk: Could be.

Thomas: Oh, thank God. Thank you, I'll be right back.

(Thomas starts to run and then he seems to remember something and returns.)

Thomas: Ugh, excuse me, where is the Lost and Found?

Clerk: It's down in the lobby. Turn left at exit B.

Thomas: Thank you, thank you, thanks again.

服务员：　早上好，先生。能给我看一下您的登机牌吗？
托马斯：　给你。
服务员：　先生，非常抱歉，这是您的护照。
托马斯：　是吗？嗯……这有区别吗？
服务员：　是的，事实上，没有登机牌您就不能登机。
托马斯：　天啊。我一定是把它留在旅馆的房间了。
服务员：　对不起，先生，我不能让您过去。
托马斯：　飞机什么时候起飞？
服务员：　嗯，大概还有30分钟，先生。
托马斯：　噢，天哪！那我现在该怎么办呢？笨蛋，笨蛋，笨蛋。
（他用手捶着他的头。）
服务员：　先生，请镇定一点。您会制造混乱的。
（机场广播："托马斯先生，现拾到托马斯先生的登机牌，请到失物招领处认领。"）
托马斯：　那是在说我吗？
服务员：　可能吧。
托马斯：　噢，谢天谢地。谢谢你，我马上就回来。

（托马斯转身正准备跑，但是他好像想起了什么，又转过了身。）

托马斯：　嗯，打扰一下，失物招领处在哪里？

服务员：　在大厅向左的B出口。

托马斯：　谢谢，谢谢，非常感谢。

Dialogue 3 经典影像观摩 The Emulation of Classical Movies

来自东欧国家的旅客维克多·纳沃斯基来美国完成父亲的遗愿，可是在机场检查时却遇到了麻烦。他被带到机场保安办公室接受询问。

Viktor Navorski comes to the United States to fulfill his dead father's will. However, at the airport, there is something getting wrong, so he is taken to the police office to be questioned.

Policeman:　What exactly are you doing in the United States, Mr. Navorski?

Navorski:　Yellow taxicab, please. Take me to Ramada Inn, 161, Lexington.

Policeman:　Staying at the Ramada Inn?

Navorski:　Keep the change.

Policeman:　Do you know anyone in New York?

Navorski:　Yes.

Policeman:　Who?

Navorski:　Yes.

Policeman:　Who?

Navorski:　Yes.

Policeman:　No, do you know anyone in New York?

Navorski:　Yes, yes, yes.

Policeman:　Who?

Navorski:　Yes. 161, Lexington.

Policeman:　OK, Mr. Navorski, I need to see your return ticket, please. No, your return ticket. Your...

Navorski:　Oh... Yes.

Policeman:　Ah. This is just a standard procedure. I'm going to need the passport also.

Navorski:　Oh... OK.

Policeman:　No, no.

Navorski:　Thank you.

Policeman:　Mr. Navorski. That. Passport.

警察:	您到美国做什么，纳沃斯基先生？
纳沃斯基:	请帮我叫出租车，去拉玛达酒店，列克星敦街161号。
警察:	您要住在拉玛达酒店？
纳沃斯基:	不用找零了。
警察:	在纽约有熟人吗？
纳沃斯基:	是的。
警察:	谁？
纳沃斯基:	是的。
警察:	谁？
纳沃斯基:	是的。
警察:	不，你在纽约有认识的人吗？
纳沃斯基:	是的，是的，是的。
警察:	谁？
纳沃斯基:	是的，列克星敦161号。
警察:	好吧，纳沃斯基先生，请出示您的回程机票。不，您的回程机票。你的……
纳沃斯基:	哦，是的。
警察: 啊，	只是例行公事。还需要护照。
纳沃斯基:	哦，好的。
警察:	不，不是。
纳沃斯基:	谢谢。
警察:	不，纳沃斯基先生，那个，护照。

词句荟萃 Words and Sentences Gathering

commotion [kə'məʊʃən] *n.* 混乱

take off （飞机）起飞

Lost and Found 失物招领

Bone head, bone head, bone head. 笨蛋，笨蛋，笨蛋。

关于机场各个部门及乘务人员的词汇

急救站 emergency service

特别休息室 special waiting room

补票处 stand-by ticket counter

签派室 dispatch office

问询处 information office

盥洗室 lavatory

医疗中心 medical center

乘务员 flight attendant

维修区 maintenance area

领航员 navigator

飞行员 pilot

机长 captain

乘务长 chief attendant

主任乘务长 chief purser

地面服务人员 ground service staff

机场巴士 airport bus

商务中心 business center

国际、港澳台登机 international & Hong Kong-Macau-Taiwan boarding

国内登机 domestic boarding

航站楼 Terminal

长途汽车 Long distance bus

停车库 Parking lot

酒店班车 shuttle bus for hotels

汇合点 meeting point

向上自动扶梯 escalator up

向下自动扶梯 escalator down

无障碍洗手间 facilities for disabled person

行李寄存 baggage deposit

失物招领 lost and found

Section 7

■ 轮船

On a Ship

We may travel by sea.
It's cheaper.
Will you travel by
sea or by air?

疯狂表达 Expressions

买票 Buying Tickets

头等舱还有没有空位？

Are there any unreserved first-class cabins?

没有，头等舱位都满了。

No, all first-class cabins are reserved.

举一反三

There are still some second-class cabins. 二等舱还有一些舱位。

I want to reserve a second-class cabin bed. 我要预订一个二等舱的卧铺。

询问时间 Asking about Time

这艘船什么时候出发去檀香山？

When will the ship leave for Honolulu?

7月8日6点出港。

It will leave the port at six on July 8th.

举一反三

When will this ship enter the port? 这艘船什么时候进港?

What time must I get on board? 我应在什么时候上船?

How many days does it take from here to Jilong? 从这里到基隆要几天时间?

It takes about a week. 大约一星期。

询问地点 Asking about Place

这艘船会停香港港吗?

Does the ship call at the port of Hong Kong?

举一反三

Is there a daily passenger ship to Dalian? 每天都有班船开往大连吗?

How many ports do we call at on our passage to Dalian? 去大连一路上要停靠几个港口?

A sea trip is always enjoyable in fine weather like this.

遇到这样的好天气,乘船旅行总是使人惬意的。

航运服务 Shipping Service

请问我可以用船运寄东西吗?

May I ship these things?

当然可以,先生。我们有非常好的航运服务。

Of course, sir. We have a very good shipping service.

举一反三

I wonder whether you can ship the things we have bought here to the UK.

请问你们可以把我们在这儿买的东西寄到英国去吗?

Yes, we can pack and ship anything for you. 可以,我们会为您包装和运送您购买的物品。

That's very nice. 太好了!

上船 Getting on Board

船就要开了,我们上船吧。

The ship is about to leave. Let's get on board.

举一反三

Look, The ship is lifting the anchor. 瞧,船起锚了。

Maybe we'll be in port before long. 我们可能快进港了。

晕船 Getting Seasick

这艘船有点摇晃，不是吗?

The ship is rolling a little, isn't it?

我想我晕船了。

I think I'm seasick.

举一反三

I feel ill. 我觉得不舒服。

The ship is rolling and pitching now. 船摇晃起来了。

You look pale. Are you seasick? 你脸色不太好，是不是晕船?

I have some tablets for seasickness. 我有止晕药片。

The sea is very rough. 风浪很大。

I'm afraid I'm going to vomit. 恐怕我要吐了。

乘船旅游 On the Cruise

喂! 约翰，一起去乘船旅行吧!

Hey! John. Let's embark on the cruise.

乘船巡游? 票价不便宜的。

The cruise? The fare is not cheap.

举一反三

What special activities will there be on the boat? 在船上有什么特别的活动呢?

Such as buffet dinners, dance parties and you can enjoy the breeze. 有自助餐、跳舞派对，你还可以感受微风。

Yeah! But I won't waste time enjoying the breeze. Hey! We could make some new friends at the dance. 我就不会浪费时间吹风了。喂，在舞会上我们可以交上一些朋友。

Dialogue 1　乘船度假 *Take Holidays by Ship*

> We may travel by sea. It's cheaper.

> Will you travel by sea or by air?

汤姆打算假期出国旅行，可能坐船，因为那样便宜些。

Tom will go abroad by sea because it's cheaper.

Alice:　Where are you going to spend your holiday this year, Tom?

Tom:　We may go abroad, my wife wants to go to Egypt, and I'd like to go there too. We haven't made up our mind yet.

Alice:　Will you travel by sea or by air?

Tom:　We may travel by sea. It's cheaper.

Alice:　I'm sure you'll enjoy yourselves.

艾丽斯：你们今年打算去哪儿度假，汤姆?

汤姆：　我们可能出国，我太太想去埃及，我也想去。我们还没下定决心。

艾丽斯：你们打算乘飞机还是乘船旅行?

汤姆：　可能坐船，便宜些。

艾丽斯：我相信你们一定会玩得很高兴的!

鲍勃坐船旅行，可是不幸的是，他晕船了，而且很严重。

Bob is traveling by ship, but unfortunately, he gets seasick, and what's more, it's very serious.

Woman:	Where are you going?
Bob:	Qingdao.
Woman:	What's wrong with you? You look pale. Are you seasick?
Bob:	I feel ill. I think I'm seasick.
Woman:	Don't worry. I have some tablets for seasickness. Take some and you'll feel better.
Bob:	That's very kind of you. Thanks a lot.

女士:	你去哪?
鲍勃:	青岛。
女士:	你怎么了? 你看起来脸色苍白。你晕船了吗?
鲍勃:	我感觉不舒服，恐怕我晕船了。
女士:	别着急，我有一些晕船药。吃一些你会感觉好点的。
鲍勃:	你真好，谢谢。

巨轮泰坦尼克号就要起航了，人们吵闹着、欢呼着、告别着。女主人公罗斯和母亲露丝、男友卡尔正准备登船。

The giant ship Titanic is going to sail with people shouting, cheering and greeting. The heroine Rose is waiting to board with her mother Ruth and boyfriend, Cal.

Man:	Look at the boat.
Boy:	Dad, it's a ship.
Man:	You are right.
Rose:	I don't see what all the fuss is about. It doesn't look any bigger than the Mauritania.
Cal:	You can be blasé about some things, Rose, but not about Titanic. It's over a hundred feet longer than Mauritania, and far more luxurious. Your daughter is far too difficult to impress, Ruth.
Ruth:	So this is the ship they say is unsinkable.
Cal:	It is unsinkable. God himself couldn't sink this ship.
Porter:	Sir, you'll have to check your baggage through the main terminal; it's round that way, sir.
Cal:	I put my faith in you, good sir. See my ma'am.
Porter:	Yes, sir. My pleasure, sir. I can do anything at all.
Lovejoy:	Yes, right. All the trunks in that car there, 12 from here, and safe to the Palace Suite Rooms B52, 54 and 56.
Cal:	Ladies, we'd got to hurry.

男士：	看这船!
男孩：	爸爸，是大轮船。
男士：	你说得对。
罗斯：	没什么大不了的嘛！不会大过茅利塔尼亚号。
卡尔：	绝对不能小看泰坦尼克号，她比茅利塔尼亚长一百尺，而且豪华得多。你女儿真是挑剔啊，露丝。
露丝：	人家说她是不沉之船?
卡尔：	没错，绝对不会沉……
搬运工：	先生，请到另一边上行李。
卡尔：	拜托你了，我要照顾女士。
搬运工：	是的，先生，我的荣幸，请随时吩咐。
拉维耶：	是的，好的。那部车上全部的箱子，这部车有12箱，还有保险箱，送到宫殿套房B52、54和56号。
卡尔：	小姐们，快点。

amidships [ə'mɪdʃɪps] *adv.* 在船舰中部

anchor ['æŋkə] *n.* 锚

knot [nɒt] *n.* 结；海里

roll [rəul] *v.* 左右摇晃

pass up the gangway 上船

乘船旅行用语

客船 Passenger boat	船尾 stern
客货船 cargo passenger boat	船长 captain
定期航线 liner	船医 ship's doctor
船舱 cabin	码头 pier; wharf
甲板 deck	铸锚 cast(weigh) anchor
船首 bow	入基隆港 put in at Jilong

Section 8

Would you mind telling me the purpose of your visit to the U.K.?

■ 出入海关
Going through Customs

I am here to study at a university.

疯狂表达 Expressions

来访目的 Purpose of Visit

你来访的目的是什么？经商还是旅游？

What's the purpose of your visit? Business or pleasure?

旅游。

Pleasure.

举一反三

What are you going there for?　你去那边有什么事？

I'm going there for sightseeing.　我去那里只是观光而已。

I'm going there on business.　我去那里出差。

I'm going there for my degree.　我去留学。

停留时间 Staying Time

你打算在美国待多长时间？

How long will you be staying in the United States?

三个月。

Three months.

举一反三

How long do you intend to stay in England?　你想在英国停留多长时间？

About three weeks.　大约三个星期。

OK. Please proceed to customs.　好的。请去海关办理手续。

检查证件 Checking Documents

你有旅行文件吗？

Do you have your travel documents?

是的，我有护照、签证、黄皮书和机票。

Yes, I have a passport, visa, yellow card and air ticket.

举一反三

Please show me your passport and declaration card.　请把你的护照和海关申报书给我。

May I have your ticket?　让我看看你的机票好吗？

Yes, here it is.　是的，在这。

And for international departure, I need to have an I-94 which might be in your passport.
因为这是国际航线出境，我需要你护照里面的I-94表。

Transit passenger! Are you a transit passenger?　过境旅客！你是过境旅客吗？

Yes, I am.　是的，我是。

Transit card, please.　请出示过境卡。

检查物品 Examining Goods

你是否带有奶制品或肉制品？

Do you have any dairy or meat products with you?

举一反三

Any fruit or vegetables?　有没有带水果或蔬菜？

No.　没有。

OK, you're all set.　行了，你没事了。

申报物品 Declaring Things

您有什么要申报的吗?

Anything to declare?

举一反三

Anything to declare in particular?　有没有什么要特别申报的?

No, I don't.　不,我没有。

What is in this box?　这箱子里面装了什么?

There are Chinese rice crackers that I'm giving as a souvenir for a friend of mine.

Shall I open them?

这是送朋友当纪念品的中式米饼,要打开吗?

Not necessary. I'll say OK. Give this declaration card to that officer at the exit, please.

不必。好了。请把申报书拿给在出口处的官员。

缴税物品 Taxing Things

这个需要缴税。

It needs to be taxed.

举一反三

What's this? Open this box, please.　这个是什么?请打开这个盒子。

Souvenir for my wife.　给我妻子的纪念品。

Is there liquor or cigarettes here?　里面有酒和香烟吗?

One bottle of whisky and one carton of cigarettes. Is that taxable?

有一瓶威士忌和一条香烟。需要缴税吗?

No. It's OK.　不,不用了。

Dialogue 1 在过境入境处 At the Customs

Where are you going to stay?

The Hilton Hotel in Paris.

兰登先生去法国做短暂的商务旅行，正在海关接受询问。
Mr. Landon goes to France for a short business trip. Now he is being questioned at customs.

Clerk:	Your passport, please.
Mr. Landon:	Here you are.
Clerk:	How long are you going to stay here?
Mr. Landon:	Two weeks.
Clerk:	Where are you going to stay?
Mr. Landon:	The Hilton Hotel in Paris.
Clerk:	What will you do here?
Mr. Landon:	Business.
Clerk:	OK, we're through now.

工作人员：	请出示您的护照。
兰登先生：	给您。
工作人员：	您在此逗留多长时间?
兰登先生：	两个星期。
工作人员：	在此期间您在哪里落脚?
兰登先生：	巴黎的希尔顿酒店。
工作人员：	您此行的目的是什么?
兰登先生：	商务旅行。
工作人员：	好了，您可以通过了。

I am here to study at a university.

Would you mind telling me the purpose of your visit to the U.K.?

李明来到英国留学，他带了一些草药做的药丸，他能顺利通过海关检查吗？

Li Ming goes to England to study. He takes some herbal pills. Will he get through customs smoothly?

Officer: Would you mind telling me the purpose of your visit to the U.K.?

Li Ming: I am here to study at a university.

Officer: May I see your passport?

Li Ming: Of course, here you are.

Officer: Would you please open the suitcase? What are these?

Li Ming: That is Chinese medicine. Only some pills.

Officer: Are they gifts for friends?

Li Ming: Oh, no. They are for my own use.

Officer: Could you tell me the ingredients?

Li Ming: They are made of herbs.

官员： 请告诉我你到英国来的目的，好吗？

李明： 我是到大学读书的。

官员： 我可以看看你的护照吗？

李明： 当然可以，请看。

官员： 请把箱子打开。这是什么？

李明： 中药。只是一些药丸。

官员： 是给朋友的礼物吗？

李明： 不，是自己用的。

官员： 你能告诉我药丸的成分吗？

李明： 它们是草药做的。

美国国际机场，旅客们刚下飞机，正在接受海关官员的检查，以便顺利进入美国。

At the international airport, passengers just got off the plane. They are being examined by customs officials, so as to go into America smoothly.

Announcement:	United Airlines announcing the arrival of Flight 9435 from Beijing, Customer service representative, report to Gate C42. All visitors to the US should line up at booths one through 15. Please have your I-94 forms filled out.
Official A:	What's the purpose of your visit?
Official B:	What is the purpose of your visit?
Official C:	What is the purpose of your visit? Business or pleasure?
Passenger A:	Just visiting, shopping.
Passenger B:	Pleasure.
Passenger C:	Business.
Official B:	How long will you be staying in United States?
Official C:	Could I see your return ticket, please?
Official D:	What's the purpose of your visit? Business or pleasure?
Passenger D:	One month.
Official D:	Enjoy your stay.

机场通知：	联合航空公司的从北京飞来的9435号航班即将降落。客户服务代表，请到C42门报到。所有旅客排好队从15号通道到一号亭，请填写一下I-94表格。
官员A：	您此行的目的是什么？
官员B：	您此行的目的是什么？
官员C：	您此行的目的是什么？商务旅行还是观光？
旅客A：	观光，购物。
旅客B：	观光。
旅客C：	商务旅行。
官员B：	您打算逗留多久？
官员C：	能出示一下您的回程机票吗？
官员D：	您此行的目的是什么？商务旅行还是观光？
旅客D：	一个月。
官员D：	祝您旅行愉快！

customs ['kʌstəmz] *n.* 海关

sightseeing ['saɪtsi:ɪŋ] *n.* 观光；旅游

document ['dɒkjʊmənt] *n.* 文件

passport ['pɑːspɔːt] *n.* 护照

visa ['viːzə] *n.* 签证

transit ['trænsit] *n.* 经过；横越

souvenir [suːvəˈnɪə] *n.* 纪念品

taxable ['tæksəbl] *adj.* 应付税的

ingredient [ɪnˈgriːdjənt] *n.* 成分

herb [hɜːb] *n.* 草药

yellow card 黄皮书

declaration card 海关申报书

Would you mind telling me…? 你介意告诉我……?

Here are … 这是……

…are/is made of 由……制成

出入境相关词汇

机场指示牌 airport signs

机场费 airport fee

国际机场 international airport

国内机场 domestic airport

国际候机楼 international terminal

国际航班出港 international departure

国内航班出站 domestic departure

入口 entrance

出口 exit; out; way out

进站（进港、到达） arrivals

不需报关 nothing to declare

海关 customs

登机口 gate; departure gate

候机室 departure lounge

航班号 FLT No. (flight number)

来自 arriving from

预计时间 scheduled time (SCHED)

实际时间 actual time

已降落 landed

前往 departure to

起飞时间 departure time

延误 delayed

登机 boarding

由此乘电梯前往登机 stairs and lifts to departures

迎宾处 greeting arriving

由此上楼 up; upstairs

由此下楼 down; downstairs